WJEC GCSE GEOGRAPHY

Study & Revision Guide

MADE FOR WALES

Rachel Crutcher
Steph Robinson

Published in 2025 by Extend Education Ltd., Sunningend Business Centre, Unit 22 Lansdown Industrial Estate, Cheltenham, UK, GL51 8PL

www.extendeducation.com

The moral rights of Rachel Crutcher and Stephanie Robinson to be identified as the authors of this work have been asserted by them in accordance with the Copyright, Designs and Patents Act 1988.

All rights reserved. No part of this publication may be reproduced, stored in a retrieval system or transmitted in any form or by any means, electronic, mechanical, photocopying, recording or otherwise, without permission in writing from the copyright owner, except in accordance with the provisions of the Copyright, Designs and Patents Act 1988 or under the terms of a licence from the Copyright Licensing Agency Limited. Further details of such licences (for reprographic reproduction) may be obtained from the Copyright Licensing Agency Limited, Barnard's Inn, 86 Fetter Lane, London EC4A 1EN (www.cla.co.uk). Applications for the copyright owner's written permission should be addressed to the publisher.

British Library Cataloguing in Publication Data

A catalogue record for this book is available from the British Library.

ISBN 978-1-917481-30-4

Printed in the UK by Cambrian Printers Ltd

Design and layout by EMC Design

Every effort has been made to identify and acknowledge sources, seek appropriate permissions, and ensure that all copyrighted material used in this book has either been included with formal consent from rights holders or used in accordance with the provisions for fair dealing under UK copyright law. For example, such material has been used sparingly, solely for the purposes of education, criticism, or review, and has been properly acknowledged. If any unintentional omissions or errors have occurred, the publisher will be pleased to make corrections at the earliest possible opportunity.

Acknowledgments

The publishers gratefully acknowledge permission to reproduce the following copyright material.

Cover © Maskot/DigitalVision via Getty Images

stock.adobe.com ©

p12 trevormayes; p16 leighton collins; p20 Jackie Davies; p25 postywood1; p26 acceleratorhams; p27 www.januszkurek.com; p27 zen_light; p28 terry; p28 Remus Moise; p28 Paul; p42 whitcomberd; p47 Emma - stock.adobe.com; p48 deep; p69 ibreakstock; p72 tish11; p80 AnnaStills; p99 icemanphotos; p113 JasonScott; p130 Ross; p130 Ricochet64; p133 ananaline; p143 philipbird123

iStock.com ©

p5 SDI Productions; p6 pawopa3336; p17 SteveAllenPhoto; p20 TonyBaggett; p40 serts; p40 holgs; p46 Bim; p52 WhitcombeRD; p53 ijeab; p67 Tenedos; p67 VichienPetchmai; p76 izusek; p84 cinoby; p84 AaronAmat; p84 LittleCityLifestylePhotography; p85 Prostock-Studio; p86 VictorHuang; p87 VictorHuang; p118 Brasil2; p122 josemoraes; p126 Fourleaflover; p137 Sladic

Shutterstock.com ©

p4 steve bridge; p4 Drazen Zigic; p4 Thomas La Mela / Shutterstock.com; p5 Shakirov Albert; p7 nnattalli; p7 Nicku; p14 zen_light; p15 goran_safarek; p16 Sian Elin Davies; p19 Richard Whitcombe; p27 Kirstudiofilms; p29 Desintegrator; p29 Michael G McKinne; p30 Janossy Gergely / Shutterstock.com; p31 Ruslan Lytvyn / Shutterstock.com; p31 Alessia Pierdomenico / Shutterstock.com; p32 Trent Inness / Shutterstock.com; p33 Monkey Business Images; p34 Featureflash Photo Agency / Shutterstock.com; p35 Daniel Samray / Shutterstock.com; p36 Ruben2533 / Shutterstock.com; p36 Grindstone Media Group / Shutterstock.com; p37 Nicolas Economou / Shutterstock.com; p37 Maxim Elramsisy / Shutterstock.com; p38 Tinseltown / Shutterstock.com; p42 Leighton Collins / Shutterstock.com; p42 Leighton Collins / Shutterstock.com; p42 Leighton Collins; p42 SJ-3009 / Shutterstock.com; p42 Vicky Jirayu / Shutterstock.com; p42 David Pimborough / Shutterstock.com; p43 Diane J Payne / Shutterstock.com; p45 wasiolka; p47 Dzm1try; p47 ESB Professional / Shutterstock.com; p47 Richie Chan; p48 Everson Bueno; p49 Pandora Pictures; p52 Prostock-studio; p53 Dean Drobot; p54 attilio pregnolato; p54 Samib123; p55 David Pimborough / Shutterstock.com; p60 DFree / Shutterstock.com; p62 Samib123; p71 Gorodenkoff; p78 Andrey_Popov; p85 Ground Picture; p87 Richard Juilliart / Shutterstock.com; p92 Sean Aiden Calderbank / Shutterstock.com; p93 Axel Bueckert; p93 MichaelJayBerlin; p93 Dusan Petkovic; p94 Boxed Lunch Productions; p97 arindambanerjee / Shutterstock.com; p98 Aitor Serra Martin / Shutterstock.com; p100 Paulo Figueiredo Junior; p100 Henrykc; p102 Viacheslav Lopatin; p103 pingebat; p103 Peter Hermes Furian; p105 Matt Gibson; p106 Designua; p106 noraismail; p107 Andramin; p108 Rendix Alextian; p108 BEST-BACKGROUNDS; p108 Marcin Woch; p110 Robert Adrian Hillman; p111 Leighton Collins / Shutterstock.com; p112 EOSMan; p113 FashionStock.com / Shutterstock.com; p116 FotoKina; p117 Arrush Chopra / Shutterstock.com; p118 pingebat; p119 Claudio Caridi; p119 Mumemories; p121 Nandalal Sarkar; p121 Caz Harris Photography; p123 Danae Abreu; p123 Manfred Ruckszio; p124 Petr Klabal; p127 icemanphotos; p127 Alwayswin; p128 Euroscript AB; p129 Mwivanda Gloria / Shutterstock.com; p130 John Gomez / Shutterstock.com; p131 Joseph Creamer; p131 Liv Oeian / Shutterstock.com; p131 Matthew Conboy / Shutterstock.com; p133 TAUFIK ART / Shutterstock.com; p136 steved_np3; p136 Prostock-studio; p136 William Barton / Shutterstock.com; p137 Kateryna Onyshchuk; p138 Ceri Breeze / Shutterstock.com; p143 Cliff Day / Shutterstock.com; p144 Ceri Breeze / Shutterstock.com; p144 Ceri Breeze / Shutterstock.com; p144 eldo; p146 Ceri Breeze / Shutterstock.com; p148 chrisdorney / Shutterstock.com; p153 Simon Mayer

Open Government Licence

p77 Office for National Statistics © Crown copyright 2013 (OGL v3.0); p90 Office for National Statistics © Crown copyright 2023 (OGL v3.0); p91 © Llywodraeth Cymru Welsh Government, 2025 (OGL v3.0); p134 © Llywodraeth Cymru Welsh Government, 2025 (OGL v3.0); p138 © Foreign and Commonwealth Office (OGL v1.0); p140 © Llywodraeth Cymru Welsh Government, 2025 (OGL v3.0); p142 © Llywodraeth Cymru Welsh Government, 2025 (OGL v3.0); p155 © Llywodraeth Cymru Welsh Government, 2025 (OGL v3.0); p156 © Llywodraeth Cymru Welsh Government, 2025 (OGL v3.0)

Ordnance Survey

pp16, 26, 57, 144, 153, 154 © Crown copyright and database right Ordnance Survey licence number AC0000869678

Other

p18 © Gareth James/Wikimedia Commons (CC BY-SA 2.0); p21 British Geological Survey image P707131 © UKRI 1993 (source: BGS GeoScenic); p26 © Photo: Courtesy of the University of Miami; p31 Woods et al. (2021), *A Rural Vision for Wales: The Evidence Report*; p34 Adapted from World Intellectual Property Organization (2013), *Committee on Development and Intellectual Property (CDIP), Twelfth Session, Geneva, November 18 to 21, 2013* (CC BY 4.0); p35 © Yusuf Hussein Ismail; p38 © Statista; p39 © Daily Express; p39 © Independent Digital News & Media Ltd; p40 © Anwar saadat; p44 Adapted from The World's Cities in 2018 Data Booklet, by United Nations, ©2018 United Nations. Used with the permission of the United Nations. p45 © Oxford Economics; p47 Adapted from Willard (2010), *Three Sustainability Models*. Sustainability Advantage; p52 © Nikeush/Wikimedia Commons (CC BY-SA 4.0); p55 © Jeremy Krause; p58 © Spudguy67/Wikimedia Commons (CC BY-SA 4.0); p58 Maptitude Logo © Caliper, HERE. Maptitude® mapping software; p62 Adapted from Geographical Association; p65 © pbctoday; p66 © The Island Geographer; p68 © Field Studies Council. Urban Geography; p68 © Our Place [www.placestandard.scot]; p69 © Project for Public Spaces; p71 © Fiona Sherrif; p77 © Spencer Chainey; p78 © Cmichel67/Wikimedia Commons (CC BY-SA 4.0); p88 © Danny Dorling, photographed by Stacy Hewitt; p92 © United Nations [https://www.un.org/sustainabledevelopment]. The content of this publication has not been approved by the United Nations and does not reflect the views of the United Nations or its officials or Member States; p92 © Hitachi Rail/Wikimedia Commons (CC BY 3.0); p92 © HS2 Ltd; p93 © Coffey Architects; p96 © World Bank Group. All rights reserved [https://blogs.worldbank.org/en opendata/world-bank-country-classifications-by-income-level-for-2024-2025]; p98 © FAIRTRADE Mark used with permission. The FAIRTRADE Mark is a registered certification label of Fairtrade International; p100 Adapted from ClimateData [https://en.climate-data.org]; p101 © GlamorganStar; p113 © Mapbox, Ian Villeda; p114 © Model Integrated Risk Management. Federal Office for Civil Protection. 2019; p117 Adapted from Willard (2010), *Three Sustainability Models*. Sustainability Advantage; p118 Adapted from Maslin, Mark. (2016). *In Retrospect: Forty years of linking orbits to ice ages*. Nature. 540. 208-210. 10.1038/540208a; p120 © Autopilot/Wikimedia Commons (CC BY-SA 3.0); p123 © NASA; p124 Adapted from Sémhur/Wikimedia Commons (CC BY-SA 3.0); p133 © Cleaner Oceans Foundation Ltd (COFL); p133 © The Ocean Cleanup™; p138 © Department of Foreign Affairs and Trade [www.dfat.gov.au] (CC BY 4.0); p139 Adapted from Willard (2010), *Three Sustainability Models*. Sustainability Advantage; p140 © United Nations [https://www.un.org/sustainabledevelopment]. The content of this publication has not been approved by the United Nations and does not reflect the views of the United Nations or its officials or Member States; p141 From Key Features and Principles of the 2030 Agenda, by Carol Pollack/Department of Economic and Social Affairs, © 2022 United Nations [https://sdgs.un.org/sites/default/files/2022-04/4.Ms_.%20Carol.Pollack-Key%20features-and-principles-of-the-2030-Agenda_CP%2027%20March%20Version.pdf]. Reprinted with the permission of the United Nations; p141 © Emmanuel Ola-Olowoyo; p150 Adapted from Willard (2010), *Three Sustainability Models*. Sustainability Advantage; p151 © United Nations [https://www.un.org/sustainabledevelopment]. The content of this publication has not been approved by the United Nations and does not reflect the views of the United Nations or its officials or Member States

Contents

How to use this book 2

Unit 1: Our Physical and Human World

- Chapter 1.1: Drainage basin and rivers 6
- Chapter 1.2: Changing coastlines 20
- Chapter 1.3: Migration 30
- Chapter 1.4: Settlement change 40

Unit 2: Developing Fieldwork Skills

- Chapter 2.1: Planning an enquiry 54
- Chapter 2.2: Collecting evidence 62
- Chapter 2.3: Processing and presenting evidence ... 72
- Chapter 2.4: Analysing and applying evidence ... 76
- Chapter 2.5: Drawing conclusions 78
- Chapter 2.6: Evaluating techniques 80

Unit 3: Our Dynamic and Diverse World

- Chapter 3.1: The geography of inequality 86
- Chapter 3.2: The highs and lows of our weather ... 100
- Chapter 3.3: Wild weather 112
- Chapter 3.4: Continual climate change 118
- Chapter 3.5: Managing global challenges 130

Unit 4: Sustainable Solutions

- Chapter 4.1: The concept of sustainability 138
- Chapter 4.2: Making sustainable decisions 144

Exam Preparation and Practice 152

Index 157

How to use this book

Throughout this book, **spotlight** boxes shine a light on real-world examples of Geography in action. These in-context case studies and extra information help you see how the concepts and skills you're learning apply beyond the classroom – in communities, environments, and events in Wales and around the world.

Ace your revision boxes help you focus on key points and strategies to boost your exam preparation. These handy tips and revision reminders provide practical advice, summarise essential content, and offer exam-focused techniques that will guide you through your study sessions.

Brain break boxes provide quick exercises, games or ideas to refresh your mind and body.

These **profiles** introduce you to influential figures who relate to the locations you are studying or show people who have made significant contributions to the field of Geography. They help you understand the real people behind the concepts you're studying.

Key terms

- **Biological weathering:** the breakdown of rocks by animals or plants.
- **Erosion:** the wearing away of the landscape by the river.
- **Load:** the rocks, soil or silt that is being carried in the river water.
- **Mechanical/physical weathering:** weathering that is caused by physical factors such as wind, rain, etc.
- **Weathering:** the process that breaks down rocks in situ by the weather or biological organisms.

Spotlight

Knowing how and where a river is likely to erode will help town planners decide the safest locations on which to build.

Ace your revision

Learn the terminology for the types of river erosion and river transportation. Don't mix them up!

Brain break

Jump up and do:
20 × jumping jacks
20 × heel kicks
20 second sprint on the spot!

William Morris Davis

Born in 1850 in the USA, William developed the theory of cycle erosion seen in natural landforms. He is often called the 'father of American geography'.

1.1.3 Drainage basin characteristics

The processes operating within a drainage basin

Not only does the volume of water in different parts of the drainage basin continually change, but so does the landscape itself. The river channel and the surrounding land, together with the landforms that the river creates, are all continually changed by the following processes.

Weathering

- **Freeze-thaw weathering** is a type of **mechanical/physical weathering**. It happens when water enters a crack. At night, when the temperature drops below 0 °C, the water freezes and turns to ice. The ice has a larger volume than water and exerts pressure on the rock, widening the crack. The following day, when temperatures increase, the ice thaws, releasing the pressure on the rock which makes it contract and crack. This process repeats, with the crack gradually getting wider until the rock falls apart.

▼ Freeze-thaw action

| Water | Pressure widens the gap | Ice thaws and more water can enter the crack | Eventually rock falls apart due to repeated temperature changes |

- **Biological weathering** occurs when plants and animals break up rocks in the drainage basin. For example, the roots of plants growing into cracks in rocks which then force the crack to widen.
- **Chemical weathering** happens when rainwater lands on rocks. Rainwater is slightly acidic, and this can react with some rocks in a drainage basin causing them to slowly wear away.

Erosion

There are different erosional processes that erode the river channel.

- **Hydraulic action** – the erosion of the channel due to the sheer force of the water hitting the bed and banks of the river. This compresses air pockets in the rock or soil, which causes them to break away from the channel.
- **Abrasion/corrasion** – when the **load** of the river crashes into the bed or banks of the channel and causes parts to break off and wash away.
- **Solution/corrosion** – chemicals in the water react with chemicals in the river channel rocks/soil, dissolving them and allowing the water to wash them away.

The amount of erosion that takes place will vary constantly and is influenced by the quantity of water in the channel, the speed at which the water is moving and the material that the river channel is made from.

Erosional processes also erode the load that the water is carrying:

- **attrition** – the erosion of the river's load by particles (e.g. stones) crashing into each other as they are moved by the water
- **abrasion/corrasion** – when the load of the river hits the river channel, it not only erodes the bed and banks of the river, but also the bed load itself.

The effect of this erosion leads to the bed load becoming smoother and rounder as you move downstream.

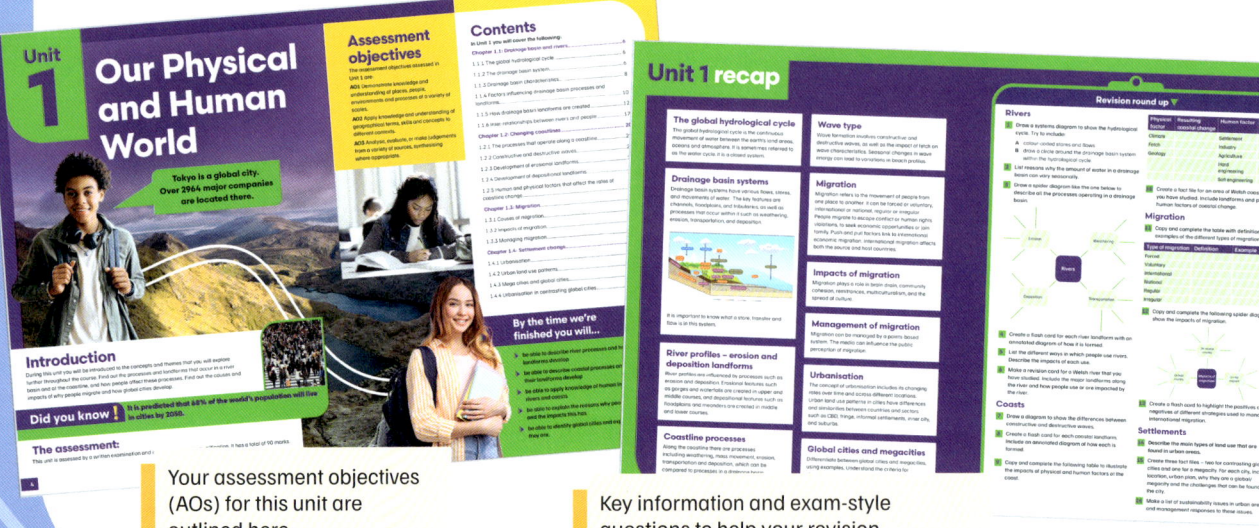

Your assessment objectives (AOs) for this unit are outlined here.

Key information and exam-style questions to help your revision.

Transportation

Rivers transport or move their load downstream. This can happen in several ways.

▼ *Methods of river transportation*

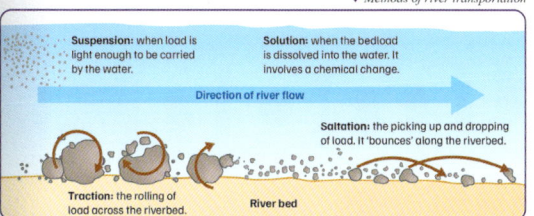

The method of transportation will depend on a number of factors including the speed of water flow and the weight of the bedload.

Deposition

A river will deposit (drop) its load when the water is moving too slowly to carry it. This may happen for the following reasons.

- There are low levels of water in the river channel due to lack of rainfall or high evaporation rates.
- The river is near its mouth and therefore entering the sea. This causes a disruption to flow and deposition to occur.
- The channel is changing direction, and a meander is created. Deposition occurs on the inside of a meander.

The features of a drainage basin

All drainage basins have common features. They are shown on the following diagram.

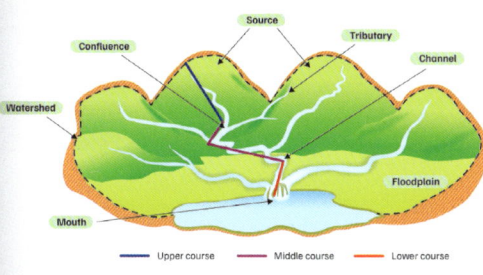

Key terms

- **Channel:** *where the river flows – a narrow body of water between two land areas.*
- **Confluence:** *the point where two river channels meet.*
- **Deposition:** *the laying down of material when the force of the water is too weak to carry it.*
- **Floodplain:** *the flat area either side of a river channel that is covered in water during a flood event.*
- **Mouth:** *the point where the river enters a larger body of water such as the sea or large lake.*
- **Source:** *the starting point of a river in a drainage basin.*
- **Transportation:** *the movement of material in the river from one place to another.*
- **Tributary:** *a smaller river which flows into a larger river channel.*
- **Watershed:** *the outside edge of the land that drains into a particular river basin.*

Put into practice

Learn all the definitions in this chapter.

Fun fact

The longest river in the world is thought to be the River Nile at 6,650 km long.

Now try this ▼

1. Describe where in a drainage basin weathering may happen.
2. Draw detailed annotated diagrams to show the impact of freeze-thaw on the environment.
3. Explain why attrition is a unique type of river erosion.
4. Name two occasions when a river may deposit material.

The **key terms** you need to learn and understand are highlighted in the main text and are added into these boxes with their definitions.

Put into practice activities are a great way to test your understanding, build confidence, undertake extra research, and prepare for exam-style questions. These might be short tasks or more in-depth investigations.

Fun fact boxes are packed with interesting and surprising information that add something extra to your Geography GCSE.

Now try this questions are designed to test your understanding of what you have learned so far in the chapter.

Exam-style questions to prepare you for your exam.

You will find an index at the end of the book.

Answers

You can download answers here: extendeducation.co.uk/answers

Unit 1

Our Physical and Human World

> Tokyo is a global city. Over 2964 major companies are located there.

Introduction

During this unit you will be introduced to the concepts and themes that you will explore further throughout the course. Find out the processes and landforms that occur in a river basin and at the coastline, and how people affect these processes. Find out the causes and impacts of why people migrate and how global cities develop.

Did you know ! It is predicted that 68% of the world's population will live in cities by 2050.

The assessment:

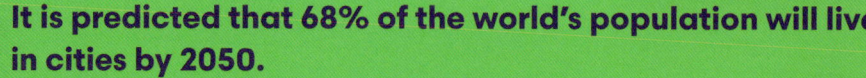

This unit is assessed by a written examination and is worth 30% of the qualification. It has a total of 90 marks.

Assessment objectives

The assessment objectives assessed in Unit 1 are:

AO1 Demonstrate knowledge and understanding of places, people, environments and processes at a variety of scales.

AO2 Apply knowledge and understanding of geographical terms, skills and concepts to different contexts.

AO3 Analyse, evaluate, or make judgements from a variety of sources, synthesising where appropriate.

Contents

In Unit 1 you will cover the following:

Chapter 1.1: Drainage basin and rivers 6
1.1.1 The global hydrological cycle 6
1.1.2 The drainage basin system 6
1.1.3 Drainage basin characteristics 8
1.1.4 Factors influencing drainage basin processes and landforms 10
1.1.5 How drainage basin landforms are created 12
1.1.6 Inter-relationships between rivers and people ... 17

Chapter 1.2: Changing coastlines 20
1.2.1 The processes that operate along a coastline ... 20
1.2.2 Constructive and destructive waves 23
1.2.3 Development of erosional landforms 24
1.2.4 Development of depositional landforms 27
1.2.5 Human and physical factors that affect the rates of coastline change 28

Chapter 1.3: Migration 30
1.3.1 Causes of migration 30
1.3.2 Impacts of migration 34
1.3.3 Managing migration 37

Chapter 1.4: Settlement change 40
1.4.1 Urbanisation 40
1.4.2 Urban land use patterns 41
1.4.3 Mega cities and global cities 44
1.4.4 Urbanisation in contrasting global cities 46

By the time we're finished you will...

▸ be able to describe river processes and how their landforms develop

▸ be able to describe coastal processes and how their landforms develop

▸ be able to apply knowledge of human impacts on rivers and coasts

▸ be able to explain the reasons why people migrate and the impacts this has

▸ be able to identify global cities and explain what they are.

Chapter 1.1 Drainage basin and rivers

AO1 AO2 AO3

🔑 Key terms

- **Closed system:** a system where material moves between areas and nothing is added or taken away.
- **Drainage basin:** an area of land that is drained by a river.
- **Flows:** how water moves from one place to another.
- **Hydrological:** a term used to describe water.
- **Inputs:** how water enters the drainage basin system.
- **Open system:** a system where material can cross into and out of the system.
- **Outputs:** how water leaves the drainage basin system.
- **Seasonally:** at a particular time of the year.
- **Stores:** a place where water stays in one place.
- **Transfers:** how water is moved through the drainage basin system.

Ace your revision

You need to be able to add examples of stores and flows to a diagram.

Spotlight

Knowing the stores and flows of water in an area helps Natural Resources Wales to plan the management of water supply in Wales.

1.1.1 The global hydrological cycle

The global **hydrological** cycle is the continuous movement of water between the earth's land areas, oceans and atmosphere. It is sometimes referred to as the water cycle. It is a **closed system** which means no water leaves or is added to the system.

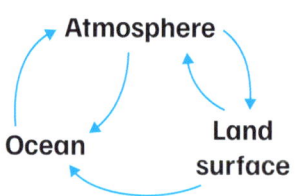

Water moves between areas of the system through a series of **flows** and remains in some areas in **stores**. The diagram below illustrates the major stores and flows in the hydrological system.

▼ *Stores and flows in the hydrological system – a closed system*

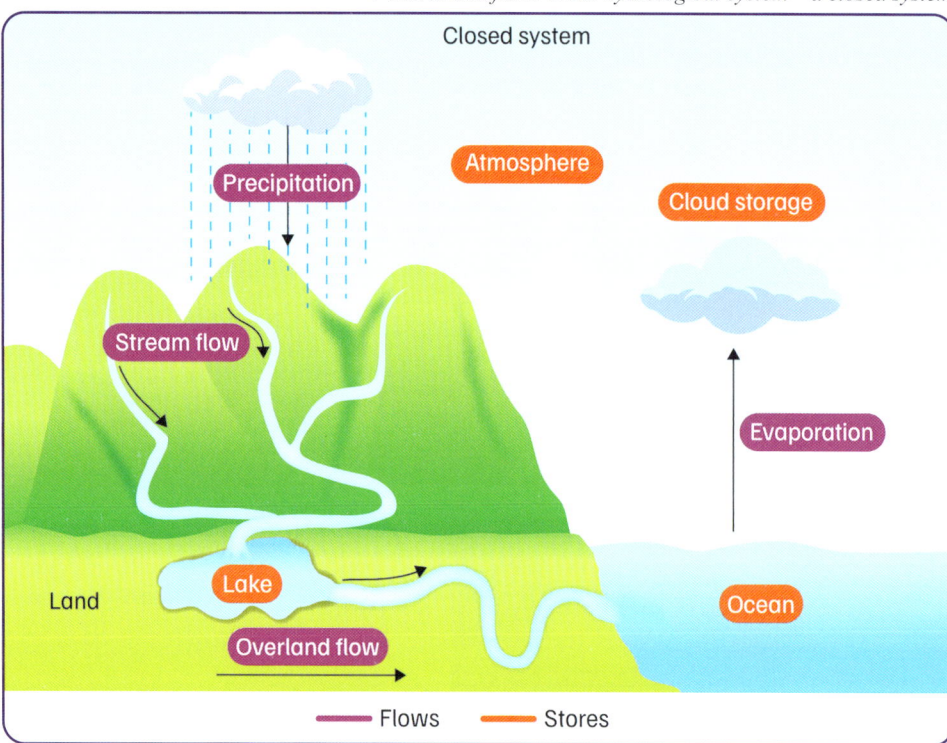

1.1.2 The drainage basin system

A drainage basin is all the land that drains into a river channel. Most of the water moves across the land surface or through the ground to get into the river channel, which ultimately ends when it meets the sea or ocean. The drainage basin system is an example of an **open system** where water both enters and leaves the system.

Inputs into the **drainage basin** system include all types of precipitation – rain, hail, sleet and snow. **Outputs** from the drainage basin system include evaporation, transpiration and run off into the sea. Within the drainage basin system there are many places where water flows from one area to the next (**transfers**) while in other areas the water remains still (stores).

Put into practice

1. Describe what a closed system is.
2. Identify the key processes that move water from:
   - atmosphere to the land surface
   - land surface to the ocean
   - ocean to the atmosphere.

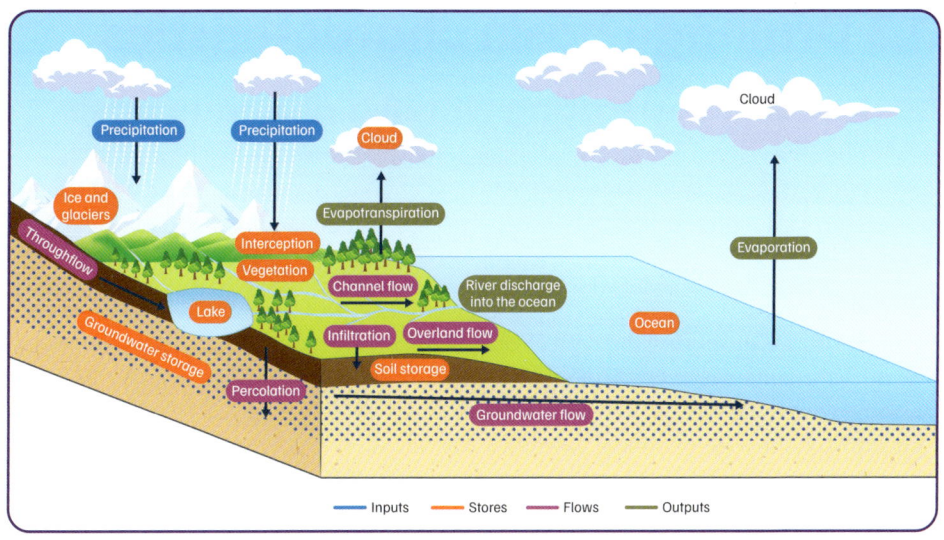

◄ *The drainage basin system – an open system*

Fun fact
The Atlantic Ocean holds around 310,410,900 km³ of water. If we convert the units to litres this is 3×10^{20} litres!

Movement of water
After water enters the drainage basin through precipitation, it may be intercepted by the vegetation it lands on. Water will run down the stem or trunk of the plant to reach the ground. It may then travel across the surface as overland flow until it reaches the river channel or it may infiltrate (sink) into the soil where it moves between soil particles until it reaches the river. Some water will travel further down (percolate) into the rock layer and move through gaps in the rock until it reaches the river channel. At any point in the drainage basin, water may stay still and be temporarily stored within the system.

Outputs from the drainage basin
Although most water leaves the drainage basin when the river channel enters the ocean, there are several other ways it could leave the system. The water may evaporate if it is on the land surface, in a lake or in a river channel. Evapotranspiration may also take place. This involves the water leaving a plant in two ways. First, by evaporating if it is on the surface of the plant. Second, if water has been taken up by the plant's roots, then it is released as a gas through the plant's leaves.

Why does the amount of water vary?
The amount of water in a drainage basin varies **seasonally**. In the UK, there is a higher amount of rainfall (more inputs) in the autumn and winter and this adds more water to the system. In the summer months, there is often less water within drainage basins due to lower rainfall and higher evaporation rates, which removes water from the system (fewer inputs and more outputs).

▼ *Interception*

Put into practice

Match the following drainage basin terms with the correct definitions:

- Infiltration — The movement of water in the river channel.
- Interception — The movement of water from the soil into the rocks below.
- Groundwater flow — The movement of water from above ground into the soil.
- Channel flow — The movement of water across the surface of the ground.
- Overland flow — Water changing from a liquid to a gas.
- Percolation — The combined movement of water into the atmosphere from the surface and within vegetation.
- Evaporation — The movement of water through rocks.
- Evapotranspiration — When water is prevented from reaching the ground by plants or buildings.

Carl Ritter
Born in 1779, Carl Ritter was one of the co-founders of modern geographical science. He compared the world to the human body, with features such as rivers, mountains and glaciers being like organs. Each feature has its own function.

1.1.3 Drainage basin characteristics

The processes operating within a drainage basin

Not only does the volume of water in different parts of the drainage basin continually change, but so does the landscape itself. The river channel and the surrounding land, together with the landforms that the river creates, are all continually changed by the following processes.

Weathering

- **Freeze-thaw weathering** is a type of **mechanical/physical weathering**. It happens when water enters a crack. At night, when the temperature drops below 0 °C, the water freezes and turns to ice. The ice has a larger volume than water and exerts pressure on the rock, widening the crack. The following day, when temperatures increase, the ice thaws, releasing the pressure on the rock which makes it contract and crack. This process repeats, with the crack gradually getting wider until the rock falls apart.

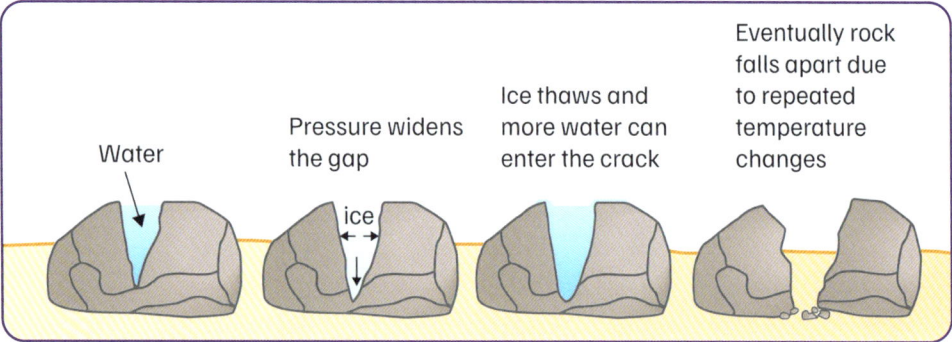

▼ *Freeze-thaw action*

- **Biological weathering** occurs when plants and animals break up rocks in the drainage basin. For example, the roots of plants growing into cracks in rocks which then force the crack to widen.
- **Chemical weathering** happens when rainwater lands on rocks. Rainwater is slightly acidic, and this can react with some rocks in a drainage basin causing them to slowly wear away.

Erosion

There are different erosional processes that erode the river channel.

- **Hydraulic action** – the erosion of the channel due to the sheer force of the water hitting the bed and banks of the river. This compresses air pockets in the rock or soil, which causes them to break away from the channel.
- **Abrasion/corrasion** – when the **load** of the river crashes into the bed or banks of the channel and causes parts to break off and wash away.
- **Solution/corrosion** – chemicals in the water react with chemicals in the river channel rocks/soil, dissolving them and allowing the water to wash them away.

The amount of erosion that takes place will vary constantly and is influenced by the quantity of water in the channel, the speed at which the water is moving and the material that the river channel is made from.

Erosional processes also erode the load that the water is carrying:

- **attrition** – the erosion of the river's load by particles (e.g. stones) crashing into each other as they are moved by the water
- **abrasion/corrasion** – when the load of the river hits the river channel, it not only erodes the bed and banks of the river, but also the bed load itself.

The effect of this erosion leads to the bed load becoming smoother and rounder as you move downstream.

Key terms

- **Biological weathering:** *the breakdown of rocks by animals or plants.*
- **Erosion:** *the wearing away of the landscape by the river.*
- **Load:** *the rocks, soil or silt that is being carried in the river water.*
- **Mechanical/physical weathering:** *weathering that is caused by physical factors such as wind, rain, etc.*
- **Weathering:** *the process that breaks down rocks in situ by the weather or biological organisms.*

Spotlight

Knowing how and where a river is likely to erode will help town planners decide the safest locations on which to build.

Ace your revision

Learn the terminology for the types of river erosion and river transportation. Don't mix them up!

Brain break

Jump up and do:
20 × jumping jacks
20 × heel kicks
20 second sprint on the spot!

William Morris Davis

Born in 1850 in the USA, William developed the theory of cycle erosion seen in natural landforms. He is often called the 'father of American geography'.

Transportation

Rivers transport or move their load downstream. This can happen in several ways.

▼ *Methods of river transportation*

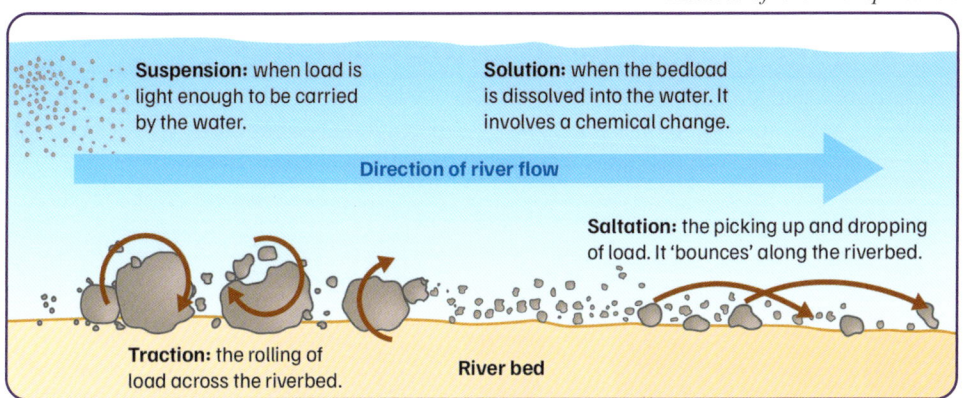

The method of transportation will depend on a number of factors including the speed of water flow and the weight of the bedload.

Deposition

A river will deposit (drop) its load when the water is moving too slowly to carry it. This may happen for the following reasons.

- There are low levels of water in the river channel due to lack of rainfall or high evaporation rates.
- The river is near its mouth and therefore entering the sea. This causes a disruption to flow and deposition to occur.
- The channel is changing direction, and a meander is created. Deposition occurs on the inside of a meander.

The features of a drainage basin

All drainage basins have common features. They are shown on the following diagram.

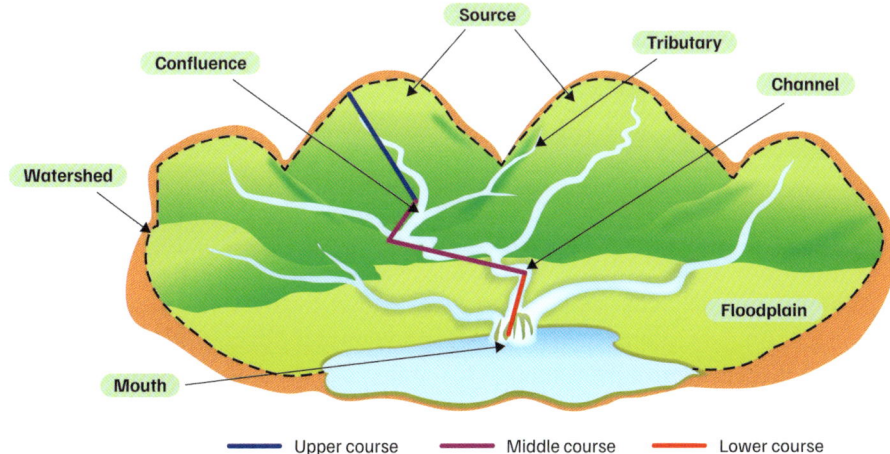

Key terms

- **Channel:** where the river flows – a narrow body of water between two land areas.
- **Confluence:** the point where two river channels meet.
- **Deposition:** the laying down of material when the force of the water is too weak to carry it.
- **Floodplain:** the flat area either side of a river channel that is covered in water during a flood event.
- **Mouth:** the point where the river enters a larger body of water such as the sea or large lake.
- **Source:** the starting point of a river in a drainage basin.
- **Transportation:** the movement of material in the river from one place to another.
- **Tributary:** a smaller river which flows into a larger river channel.
- **Watershed:** the outside edge of the land that drains into a particular river basin.

Put into practice

Learn all the definitions in this chapter.

Fun fact

The longest river in the world is thought to be the River Nile at 6,650 km long.

Now try this ▼

1. Describe where in a drainage basin weathering may happen.
2. Draw detailed annotated diagrams to show the impact of freeze-thaw on the environment.
3. Explain why attrition is a unique type of river erosion.
4. Name two occasions when a river may deposit material.

Key terms

- **Geology:** *the type and structure of rocks.*
- **Lower course:** *the final section of a river before its mouth.*
- **Longitudinal profile:** *the angle of slope of the river's channel along its course.*
- **Middle course:** *the section which is between the upper and lower course of a river, where the river valley gradient is not as steep as the upper course.*
- **River discharge:** *the volume of water flowing in a river at any point.*
- **Upper course:** *section of a river's course that is closest to the source.*

Brain break

Look out of the window for one minute. Write down three things you noticed towards the end of the minute that you didn't see at first glance.

Fun fact

A hydrologist is a person who studies rivers and other water systems, in order to manage them effectively.

Spotlight

Knowing the factors that naturally influence rates of erosion enables hydrologists to predict what areas are naturally vulnerable to erosion and therefore where best to spend money on preventing erosion.

1.1.4 Factors influencing drainage basin processes and landforms

Changing river channel characteristics

The features of a drainage basin are constantly changing, and this includes the long profile of a river. The long profile shows how the elevation changes along a river's course. This can be split into three sections – the upper, middle and lower course.

▼ *The long profile of a river*

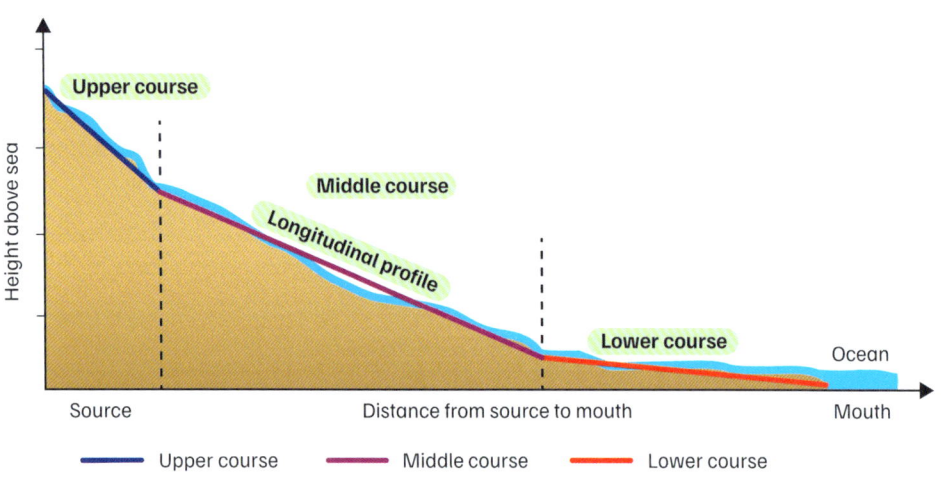

As you can see from the diagram above, the steepness of the land changes from the source of a river to the mouth, with a steep slope being a key feature of the upper course. The land is less steep in the middle and gently sloping or flat in the lower course. This also has an impact on the river channel shape, which we can see in the following cross profiles.

▼ *Cross profiles of a river*

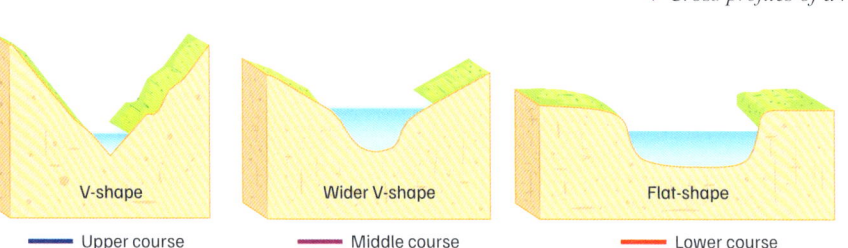

The cross profiles show that the shape of the river channel and the valley sides change as a river moves from the source to the mouth. In addition to the change in the volume of water present, there are also subtle changes to the shape of the cross profiles.

Rates of erosion and deposition

We have already looked at how river erosion and deposition take place in the river, but the rate (how fast or slow it happens) of river erosion or deposition depends on several factors.

- **River discharge** – the larger the discharge, the more energy a river will have to erode the channel by hydraulic action. A larger discharge means there will be more water that does not come into contact with the channel and it is able to move faster. Larger load particles are transported, which will create more opportunities for abrasion, making the channel deeper and wider. When discharge is lower, the river has less energy to transport load particles and a greater amount of deposition occurs.
- **Geology** – the type and structure of the rock that the river is flowing over may vary

across the drainage basin. This will have an impact on the rates of erosion and deposition.

- Where the river flows over hard rocks (e.g. granite) there will be lower rates of erosion because the rocks are more resistant. The river may also carry less sediment due to the low rate of erosion and deposition is less likely. If the underlying rocks are soft (e.g. chalk) then erosion occurs far more easily. There will also be more sediment being carried by the water, which leads to higher deposition rates.
- The joints within a rock also have an impact on the rate of river erosion. Some rocks (e.g. limestone) have lots of joints and cracks. As the river flows, water gets into these joints and erodes the rock by solution. This enlarges the joint allowing more water to enter. This can happen to such an extent that the river ends up flowing underground. This decreases the erosion in the river channel due to lack of flow. Deposition rates decrease due to lack of movement of material in the channel.

> **Key terms**
> - **Gradient:** *how steep or gentle the slope of the land is.*
> - **River velocity:** *the speed that the water is flowing in the river channel.*

▼ *The effect of rock structure on river processes*

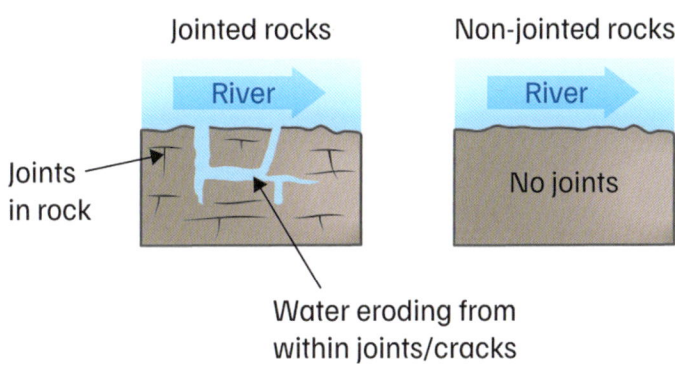

- **Gradient** – the steeper the land the water is flowing over, the faster the flow of water will be due to gravity pulling it downslope, which leads to more erosion. Faster water increases hydraulic action rates as the speed of water hitting the channel is greater. It also increases abrasion as faster water carries more load. If the gradient is gentler then the water will flow at a slower speed, and deposition will occur.
- **River velocity** – the faster the water flows, the greater the chance of more and larger particles being transported, which provides more opportunities for abrasion and hydraulic action. If the velocity decreases, the river will no longer be able to transport larger pieces of load and these will be deposited, leading to increased deposition.

> **Ace your revision**
> Know how to draw a long profile and a cross profile of a river.

Put into practice

Complete the following tables by placing a few words in each box summarising the influence the factor has.

	Upper course	Middle course	Lower course
Gradient			
Volume of water			
Shape of river channel			
Shape of valley sides			

	Rate of erosion	Rate of deposition
River discharge		
Geology – rock type		
Geology – rock structure		
Gradient		
Velocity		

Key terms

- **Plunge pool:** *a deep pool of water found at the base of a waterfall.*
- **Vertical erosion:** *the process of a river eroding downwards and eroding the bed of the river.*
- **V-shaped valley:** *a valley in the upper course of a river shaped by river erosion and weathering.*
- **Waterfall:** *water falling over a steep drop to a river channel below.*

1.1.5 How drainage basin landforms are created

Erosional landforms in the upper and middle courses of a river

There are many landforms that are created by river erosion that are commonly found in the upper and middle courses of rivers. These include:

V-shaped valleys

A 'V' shape is often used to describe the shape of a valley in its upper course. The gradient of the land is usually steep and the river small.

▼ *A V-shaped valley on the upper reaches of the River Towy*

Labels: Weathering; V-shaped valley; Steep valley sides; Narrow river – causing **vertical erosion**

Ace your revision

Rather than simply referring to 'erosion', giving the detail of what type of erosion (e.g. abrasion) shows the examiner a greater level of understanding and is worth more marks.

Waterfalls and plunge pools

Waterfalls are a common feature in the upper course of many rivers and are created in one of two ways.

- Some waterfalls are created due to glaciation. The power of the main glacier is much stronger than the tributary glaciers, which results in the main valley being at a lower level to the tributary valleys. Once the ice has melted, any water that drains into the tributary valleys will form a waterfall to flow into the main lower valley.
- Some waterfalls are created due to a difference in geology. The river may run over rocks that are hard or more resistant to erosion, these might overlie a band of soft rock, which is more easily eroded (sometimes referred to as differential erosion). As a result, the floor of the channel will be at different levels and a waterfall is created.

▼ *Waterfall formation by* *differential erosion*

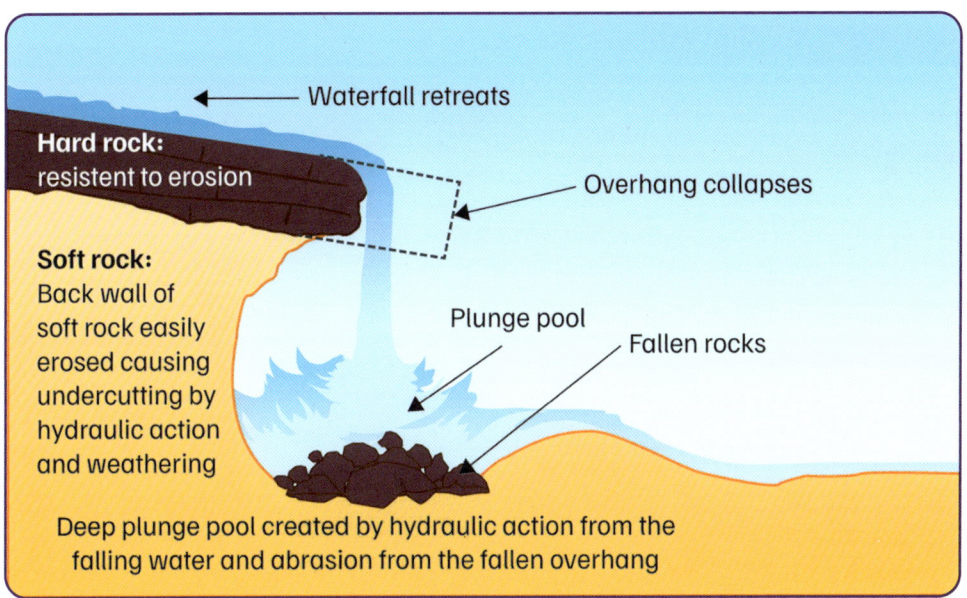

Key terms

- **Differential erosion:** when rocks erode at a different rate e.g. soft rock erodes faster than hard rock.
- **Gorge:** a steep-sided, narrow valley usually found below a waterfall.

Fun fact

Pistyll Rhaeadr waterfall, located in the Berwyn Mountains in Powys, is the tallest waterfall in Wales at 90 metres high.

Gorges

Gorges are also linked to waterfall formation. A **gorge** is a very steep sided valley with a river flowing along the valley floor. It is formed when a waterfall retreats.

▼ *Formation of a gorge*

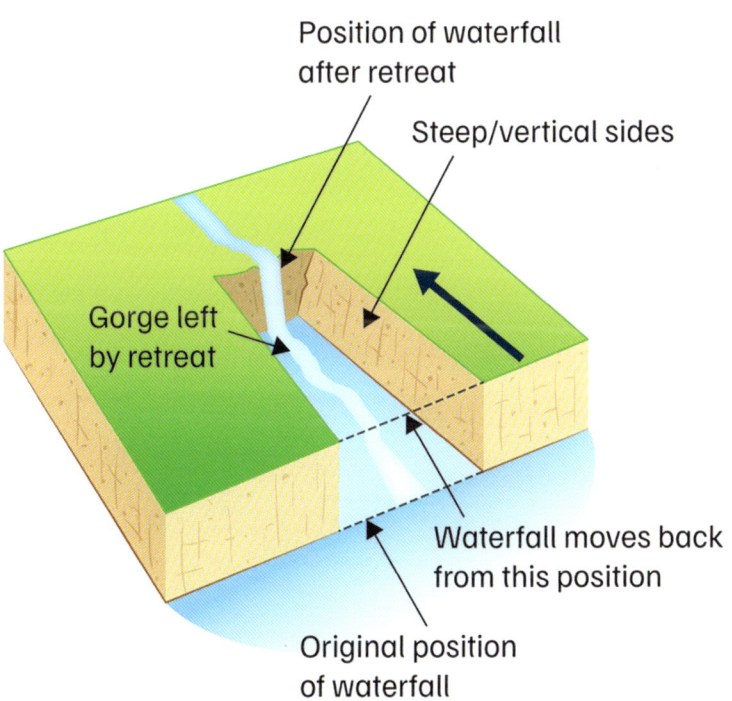

Brain break

Hold your left ear with your right hand and hold your nose with your left hand. Slowly at first, change these around so that you are then holding your right ear with your left hand and your nose with your right hand. Increase the speed trying to maintain your coordination.

Ed Stafford

Born in 1975, Ed is an English explorer and survivalist. He holds the Guinness World Record for being the first human to walk the full length of the Amazon River.

Now try this ▼

1. Describe how weathering helps to create a V-shaped valley in a river's upper course.
2. Explain how a waterfall can cause the formation of a gorge.
3. Describe the weathering and erosional processes that are involved in the creation of an overhang on a waterfall.
4. What is a plunge pool and how is it formed?

Key terms

- **Alluvium:** *a term used to describe the clay, silt, sand and gravel that is deposited when a river floods.*
- **Floodplain:** *flat land either side of the river channel that is covered in water when the river floods.*
- **Meander:** *a curve or bend in the river's course.*

Depositional landforms in the middle and lower courses of a river

In the middle and lower courses of a river basin, there are several landforms that are formed by deposition of the river's load. These include:

Floodplains

A floodplain is an area of flat land either side of a river. It forms as the valley sides widen in the middle and lower courses of the river and there is more land on the valley floor rather than just the river channel seen in the upper course.

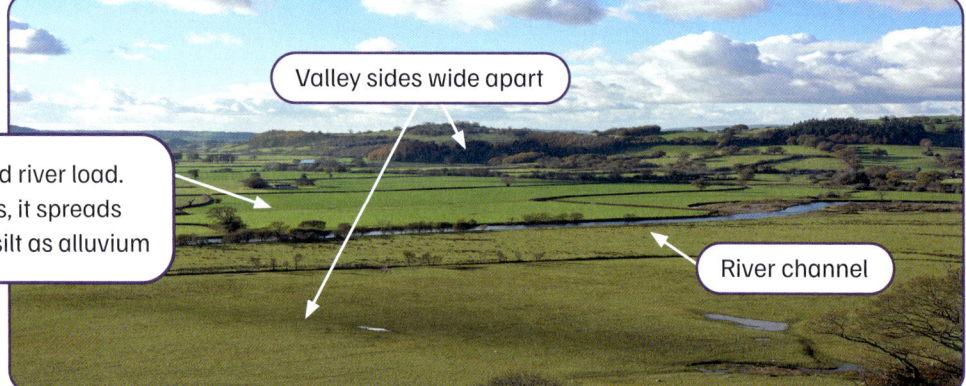

▼ *Floodplain on the River Towy*

Wide floodplain made of deposited river load. When the river overflows its banks, it spreads across the flat land and deposits silt as alluvium

Valley sides wide apart

River channel

A floodplain forms:

- when there is a flood event, which causes the channel to overflow and water spreads across the flat land either side of the river
- as the water spreads across the land, it can no longer 'hold' its load due to the shallower depth and slower speed
- **alluvium** containing silt is deposited across the flat land.

Meanders

As the valley floor is wider in the middle and lower course of a river, the river channel often twists and turns across the valley floor rather than flowing in a straight line. These bends are known as meanders.

▼ *The formation and key features of a meander*

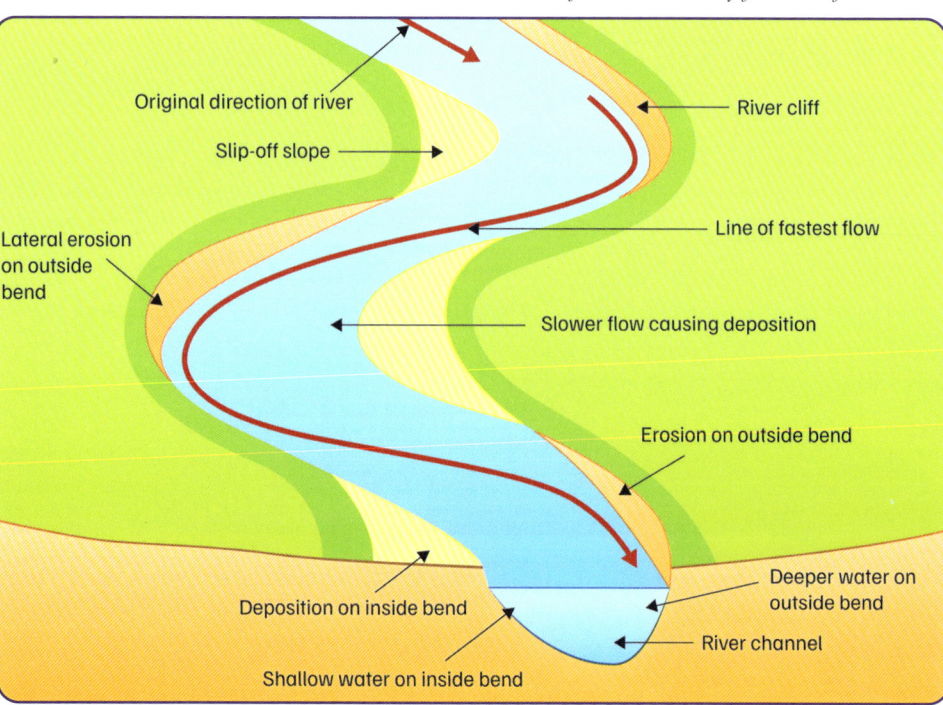

Spotlight

Farmers use floodplains to grow crops as the alluvium deposited by the floodwater makes the land more fertile.

A meander forms when:
- a river is in the middle or lower course and the wider valley floor and river channel allows the river to move around obstacles in the river bed. This leads to different speeds of river flow across the river channel.
- the river changes course to erode any softer rock in the banks of the river nearby – **lateral erosion**. As a result, a bend is formed.
- the bend is enlarged by the deeper, faster flow on the outside of the bend causing more erosion on this side of the channel. A **river cliff** is often formed as a result.
- on the opposite side of the channel (inside bend) the river is shallower and flows more slowly, leading to deposition and the development of a **slip-off slope**.
- over time, the meander migrates across the valley floor as the channel moves sideways.

Oxbow lakes

Oxbow lakes are crescent-shaped lakes that are cut off from the main river. They used to be meanders, but the river has cut through the neck of the meander and now runs straight across.

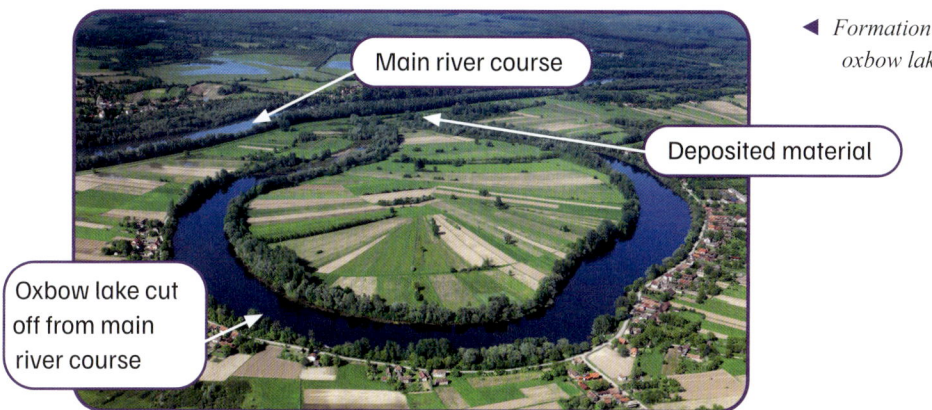

◀ *Formation of oxbow lakes*

Key terms

- **Lateral erosion:** *the process of a river eroding sideways and eroding the banks of the river.*
- **Oxbow lake:** *the loop of an old meander that is no longer connected to the river channel by flowing water.*
- **River cliff:** *a steep bank which forms on the outside of a meander bend due to erosion.*
- **Slip-off slope:** *the gentle slope on a river beach that is formed by deposition of sediment on the inside bend of a meander.*

Put into practice

Create a flash card for each landform created by rivers. Include a diagram of how it is formed and the processes involved.

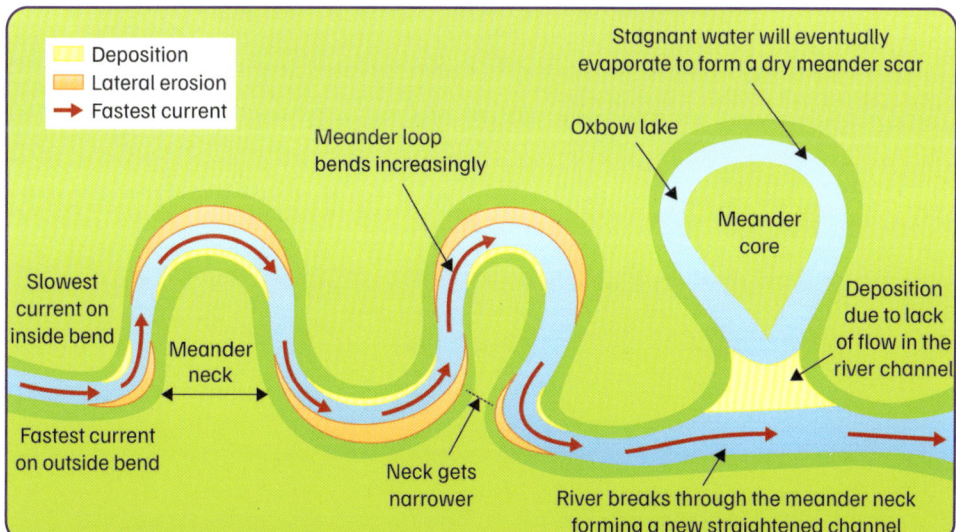

Now try this ▼

1. What is the difference between a meander and an oxbow lake?
2. Explain why erosion and depositional processes are required for the formation of a meander.
3. Describe how the river channel 'moves' due to meanders.
4. Why do floodplains not occur in the upper course of a river?

Key terms

- **Biodiversity:** *the variety of species that are found in a habitat.*
- **Greenfield land:** *land that has not been built on before.*
- **Monoculture:** *a farm which grows a single type of crop.*
- **Unsustainable:** *when resources are used that do not maintain an ecological balance and compromise future generations from meeting their own needs.*

An example of a Welsh river valley

The River Neath is in South Wales. It has its source in the Bannau Brycheiniog National Park and its mouth reaches the sea at Baglan Bay. The river has a number of tributaries, one of which is the River Hepste where the Sgwd Gwladys waterfall is located.

Sgwd Gwladys ▶

Put into practice

On a map of a river near you, mark down examples of any river landforms you can see.

▼ *The River Neath, South Wales*

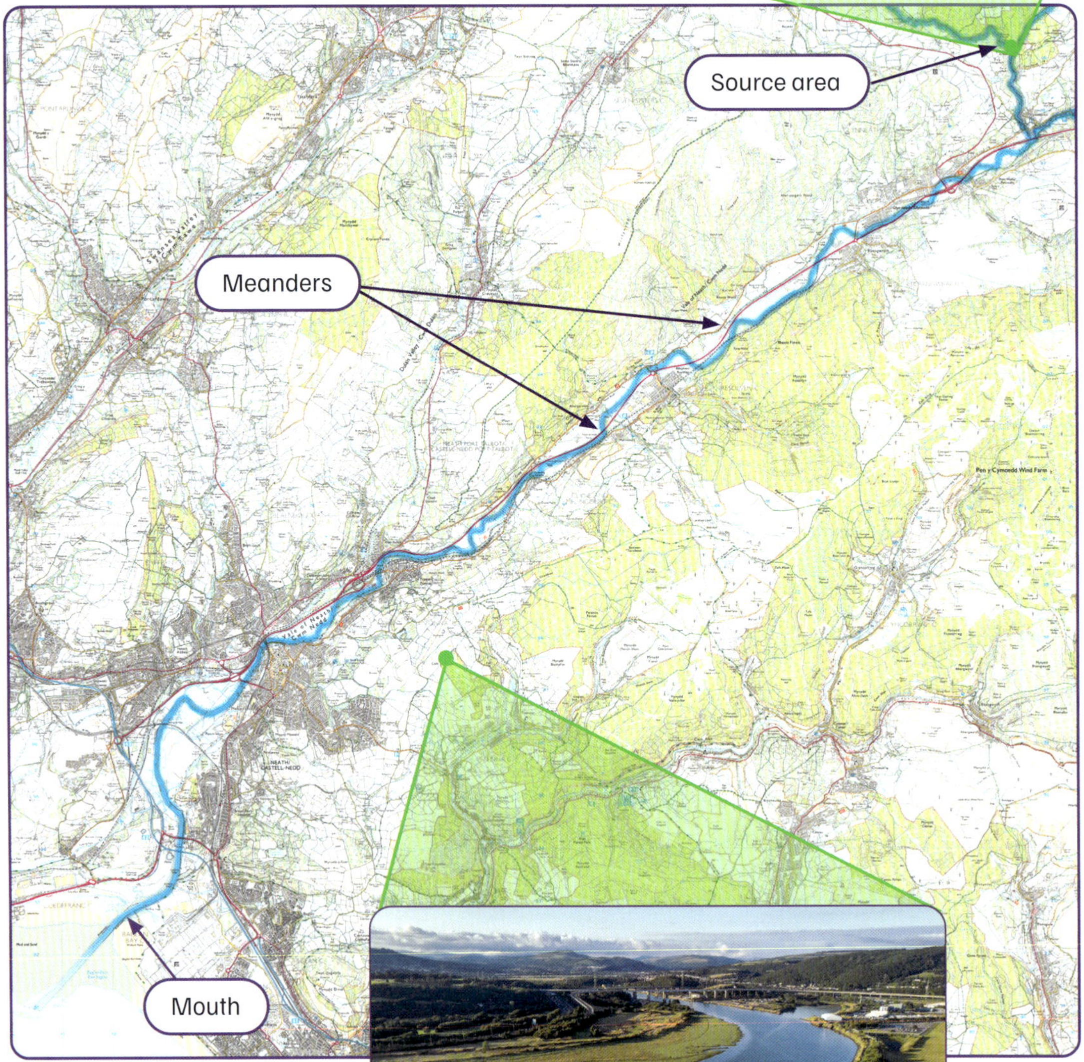

Floodplain ▶

1.1.6 Inter-relationships between rivers and people

How people use rivers and their landforms in sustainable and unsustainable ways

Rivers and their landforms have always been used by people in a number of ways. Some of these practices are more sustainable than others.

Floodplains for farming

The floodplains that are found in the middle and lower courses of a river have always been popular with farmers to grow crops or graze animals. The silt and alluvium that the river deposits on the floodplain when the land is covered by floodwater naturally increases the fertility of the soil, which enhances crop growth.

Put into practice

Create a table to show how farming on floodplains can be sustainable and **unsustainable**.

Advantages of farming on floodplains	Disadvantages of farming on floodplains
The soil is naturally fertile, so less money is spent on artificial fertilisers	The land is likely to flood so crops could be ruined in a flood event
The land is flat, so it is easier to use large machinery when harvesting crops	Farmers need to take out flood insurance which can be expensive
Floodplains provide naturally high-quality pastureland for grazing animals	Livestock will need to be moved to higher ground if there is a flood risk
The land may be cheaper to purchase due to less demand for building in flood risk areas	Farming on floodplains may lead to habitat loss for some species and reduce biodiversity
Water from the river can be used to irrigate crops	Some farming methods may lead to soil degradation, making the soil less able to store water and increasing surface run off and floods

House building on a floodplain

With the increased demand for housing and the government's plan to 'end the housing crisis', there is real pressure on developers to build more homes. When the Labour government came to power in 2024, they set a target of 1.5 million new homes to be built in five years. As a result, developers are increasingly building on **greenfield land**, much of which are floodplains. Traditionally floodplains have been used as 'buffer' zones between the river and important infrastructure, but floodplains have now become attractive to house builders due to the greater ease of construction on flat land. The land is often cheaper for developers to purchase, even though they often need to provide a commitment to improve flood defences to reduce the risk of flooding to the houses.

▲ *Newly built houses next to the flooded River Derwent in North Yorkshire*

The communities that live in these houses may well experience problems, which include:

- flooding – if a river bursts its banks, then the houses will be the first thing the flood waters run into
- difficulty getting insurance – some people who have purchased new build houses on floodplains have been refused house insurance or have been charged an increased amount due to the high flood risk.

The construction of buildings on a floodplain may also have an impact on the environment:

- hedgerows and natural habitats may be destroyed leading to an impact on **biodiversity**
- the soil may become compacted due to building work and heavy machinery, which will reduce the soil's capacity to hold water, in turn leading to more surface run off.

Fun fact

According to Natural Resources Wales, there are currently 272,817 properties in Wales that are at risk of flooding.

Now try this ▼

1. Explain why the construction of houses on a floodplain is often unsustainable.
2. Evaluate different methods of ensuring the building on floodplains is sustainable.

Key terms

- **Hydro-electric power (HEP):** *a form of renewable energy which generates electricity from moving water.*
- **Sustainable:** *using resources to meet the needs of today without compromising future generations from meeting their own needs.*
- **Tourism:** *the movement of people from one place to another for leisure purposes.*

Spotlight

The Radyr Weir Hydro Scheme, on the River Taff in Cardiff, is a small scale project that generates hydro-electric power. It creates enough electricity to power 500 homes. The Radyr Weir was built to create a 3.5 m height difference. The water flows over this drop allowing green energy to be harnessed.

Put into practice

List the advantages and disadvantages of waterfall **tourism** to the local community.

▼ *Sgwd yr Eira waterfall*

Rivers used for hydro-electric power

Hydro-electric power (HEP) is the generation of electricity by the power of moving water. It is an example of renewable energy and represents around 2% of all UK energy generation. Most of this generation is in the winter.

HEP involves water moving from a high position to a low position, and the kinetic energy of the falling water turns a turbine to create electricity. HEP stations are often located on rivers where water is naturally flowing downhill. They may also be located where there is a higher altitude river followed by a natural drop.

Put into practice

Suggest reasons why Radyr Weir Hydro Scheme is a **sustainable** form of energy production.

Waterfalls for tourism

Rivers naturally attract visitors who are looking for some relaxation time near water. Waterfalls are often a popular tourist attraction due to their dynamic nature and sizeable form.

Sgwd yr Eira is a very popular waterfall in the Bannau Brycheiniog National Park. It is part of the 'Four Waterfalls Walk', which starts to the south of Ystradfellte. At the weekend and in school holidays the car parks fill up quickly, so visitors park on grass verges at the side of the road. This not only leads to obstruction for other road vehicles but also damages the grass verge habitats. Lots of visitors take the 4.5-mile route to visit all four waterfalls, which can lead to congestion and erosion of the footpaths. Visitors can walk behind the water at Sgwd yr Eira and long queues of people are often seen waiting on the slippery rocks for their turn.

The impact of rivers and landforms on people

Rivers impact people in many ways, both positively and negatively.

Impacts of flooding

With the impact of climate change leading to a warmer and wetter UK, the impacts of flooding are being felt more frequently across the whole country. More frequent and intense low pressure weather systems bring a greater quantity of rain in a shorter time. This leads to greater surface run off due to:

- soil water and ground water stores being saturated
- rain coming down so fast that the process of infiltration does not have time to happen.

The impacts of a flood event on a community and environment can be devastating.

Common impacts of flooding

Social	Economic	Environmental
Loss of homes – residents are made homeless	Insurance premiums may increase	Farmers may lose their grazing land
Communities are fractured due to living in temporary accommodation	Cost of repair and replacement to housing and possessions	After the floodwater has receded, the land maybe more fertile
Communities may be cut off from other areas if there is damage to road and railway links	Businesses may close due to the damage that has been caused and cost of repair	Threat to some habitats as they will be underwater
Psychological trauma of the threat to life from the flood	High cost to the local government to pay for the emergency response	Greater erosion of riverbanks

The impact of erosion, transportation and deposition on people

As rivers are constantly changing, people need to respond to the changes that they make to the landscape. Riverbank erosion can lead to riverbank collapse, which can reduce available farmland, make footpaths dangerous or damage support for roads and buildings.

▼ *Riverbank erosion on the River Usk*

The processes of transportation and deposition can cause the channel to get shallower, increasing the risk of flooding.

Hard and soft river engineering/management

As a result of these processes there is a need to manage sections of the river to limit their impacts on people. The management can involve hard and soft engineering strategies.

Hard engineering	Advantages	Disadvantages
Building a dam to create a reservoir	Enables the control of the flow downriver of the dam which reduces flooding	Very expensive. Habitats are destroyed during construction and when the land is flooded
Channel straightening	Water moves through the river faster. Increases the capacity of the river channel	The river may need to be dredged on a regular basis. Can lead to flooding further downstream as water is moving faster
Embankments	Raise the banks of the river so that more water can be held in the channel	Reduces the accessibility of the river. Can look unnatural

Soft engineering	Advantages	Disadvantages
Floodplain zoning	Buildings are built on areas of low risk. High risk areas are used for grazing	Can restrict land use causing conflict
Afforestation	Increases interception and absorption rates	Restricts what the land can be used for in the future
Flood warnings and preparation	People can take precautions, which lessens the impact	Does not reduce the volume of flood water

Put into practice

Research a flood event in your local area and create a table like the one on the previous page detailing the impacts of the flood.

Brain break

Would you rather live in a house on stilts or next to a large floodwall?

Ace your revision

For a local or Welsh river, research and create a case file. You must include:
- the name and location of the river
- the dates and impacts of any flood events
- what hard and soft engineering management strategies are being used along the rivers course.

Now try this ▼

1. Explain why farming on floodplains is sometimes not sustainable.
2. Evaluate the effectiveness of river management strategies that have been used on a river you have studied.

Chapter 1.2 Changing coastlines

AO1 AO2 AO3

- **Chemical weathering:** rainwater that is slightly acidic dissolves sedimentary rock.

Ace your revision
Make sure you know the difference between the three types of weathering.

1.2.1 The processes that operate along a coastline

Weathering at the coast
Weathering is the process of rocks being broken down in situ (in place) due to the weather or living organisms. There are three main types of weathering on the coastline.

▼ *Features of coastal erosion at Dunraven Bay on the Glamorgan Heritage Coast*

▼ *Freeze-thaw weathering*

▼ *Biological weathering*

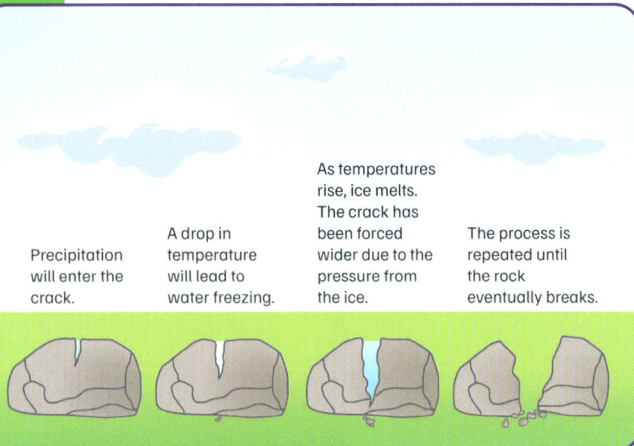

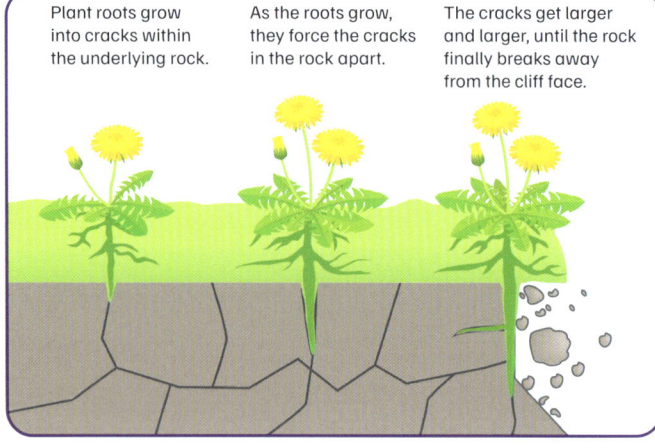

1 **Freeze-thaw (or mechanical weathering)**
When air temperatures drop below freezing and then rise again, water that had entered the crack or rock will freeze, putting pressure on the land, and then melt, releasing the pressure. It is the primary way the coastline is affected.

2 **Chemical weathering**
When minerals in the rock interact with chemicals in the atmosphere or environment, changing the composition of the rock and breaking it down. An example of chemical weathering is the action of acid rain.

3 **Biological weathering**
Seeds fall into cracks and grow roots, which causes the cracks to widen, eventually breaking down the rock. Sometimes birds will drop seeds into the cracks or use them for nesting, which might cause the cracks to widen further.

▼ *Mass movement* – *four ways sediment can move down a slope*

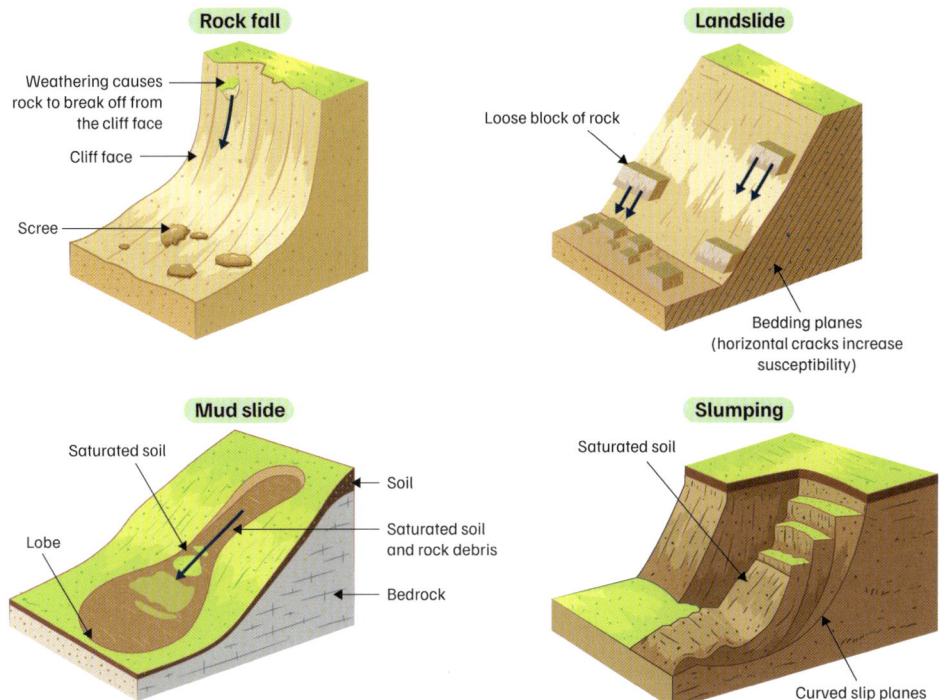

Transportation at the coast – longshore drift

Longshore drift is the geological process that moves eroded sediment along a coastline. Waves approach the beach at an angle due to the direction of the prevailing wind, which creates a zigzag motion helping to move sediment up and down the beach. This process can create a large amount of erosion by removing sediment from some areas, leaving the remaining coastline exposed to wave action.

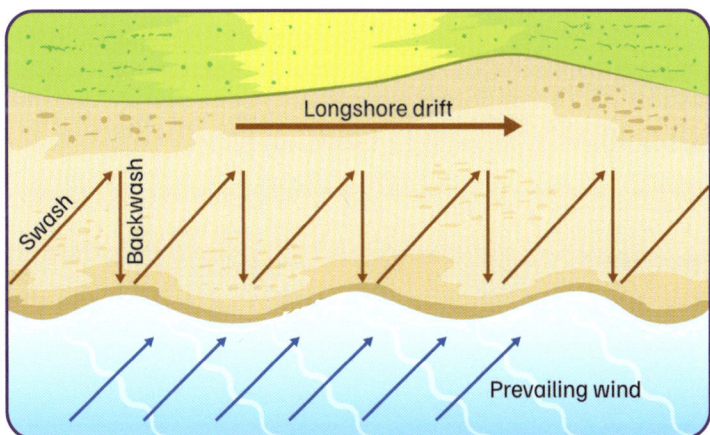

Spotlight

Landslide at Holbeck Hall, Scarborough, 1993

Likely causes of landslide:
- rainfall up to 140 mm in the two months prior to the event
- drainage was poor on the slopes, so they became saturated with water
- geology (sand, clay, gravel) easily eroded.

Key terms

- **Landslide:** *occurs in a block when material within the cliff is lubricated due to heavy rain. This leaves a pile of rocks at the foot of the cliff.*
- **Longshore drift:** *zigzag movement of sediment along a beach.*
- **Mass movement:** *when sediment (rock, soil, mud) moves downwards due to gravity and an unstable cliff.*
- **Mud slide:** *wet, fast-moving soil heavily saturated with rainwater.*
- **Rock fall:** *occurs when rocks break away, often on steep gradient cliffs, because of weathering such as freeze-thaw or heavy rainfall. Scree slopes form at the base of the cliff.*
- **Slumping:** *occurs when material slips down the cliff face but rotates back into the cliff face in a concave motion (sometimes called rotational slumping).*

Now try this ▼

1. Which feature is not formed by erosion?
   - A Cliff
   - B Bar
   - C Stack

2. What do you call the process of breaking down rocks in situ?
   - A Carbonation
   - B Weathering

3. Explain how longshore drift transports sediment at the coast.

Key terms

- **Constructive waves:** low energy, stronger swash than backwash.
- **Solution:** when minerals are dissolved in the water.
- **Saltation:** bouncing pebbles along the seabed.
- **Suspension:** fine particles carried along by waves.
- **Traction:** large boulders roll along the seabed.

Transportation at the coast – wind and wave action

Material including sediment is moved along the coast by four main types of transport, **solution**, **suspension**, **traction** and **saltation**. The larger the particles, the more energy from the waves is required to transport them. The longer material remains in the sea, the greater the dissolvement of particles.

▼ *The four main types of transportation at the coast*

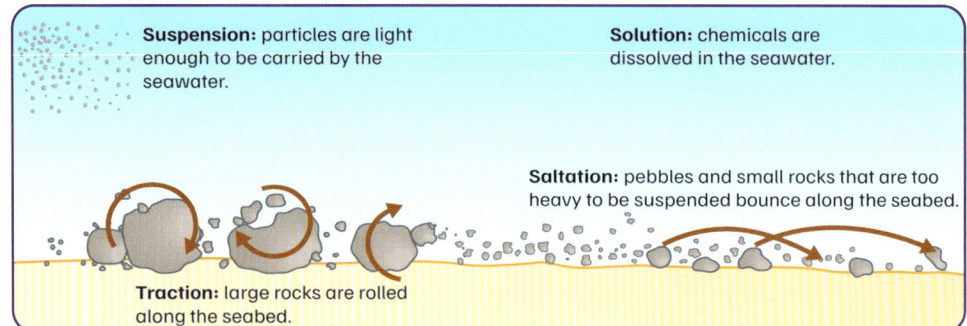

Deposition at the coast

Deposition is the process of dropping sediment such as sand, silt and pebbles onto the coast. When waves lose energy because they are carrying large amounts of sediment or have low energy to begin with, deposition is increased. This action involves **constructive waves** dropping material as sediment as the velocity of the waves slows down.

Rivers and coasts share similar processes in terms of erosion and transport, but there are some key differences you need to know.

Similarities and differences between a drainage basin and the coast

Process	River	Coastal
Weathering	Freeze-thaw (mechanical) Biological Chemical	Freeze-thaw (mechanical) Biological Chemical
Erosion	Corrasion (abrasion) Corrosion (solution) Hydraulic action Attrition	Corrasion (abrasion) Corrosion (solution) Hydraulic action Attrition
Deposition	Low energy (inside bend of river)	Low energy coastline
Transportation	Traction Suspension Saltation Solution	Longshore drift (zigzag motion) Traction Suspension Saltation Solution
Transportation (wind)		Wind is involved in the transportation of sediment due to its influence on waves. Waves then create a zigzag motion which drives longshore drift
Mass movement	Movement of weathered material down the valley sides due to gravity (upper course)	Downslope movement of rock/soil under the influence of gravity, triggered by erosion/weathering

Ace your revision

Constructive waves help to build beaches as their backwash is weaker than their swash. This means they don't drag as much material back down the beach.

Now try this ▼

1. What angle do waves move towards the beach during longshore drift?
   - A 90 degrees
   - B 45 degrees

1.2.2 Constructive and destructive waves

The type of wave is determined by the energy of the swash and backwash, for example, constructive waves are gentler, and destructive waves are more powerful.

▼ Types of wave

Key terms

- **Destructive waves:** *high energy, very high, very frequent.*
- **Fetch:** *distance over the sea that wind blows in one direction.*

Destructive waves	Constructive waves
Strong backwash	Weak backwash
High height	Low height
Short wavelength	Long wavelength
Frequent (10–14 per minute)	Low frequency (8–10 per minute)
Created in stormy conditions	Created in calm weather
High energy	Low energy

Wave formation

There are three main factors that affect the formation of waves:

1. wind speed
2. wind duration (how long it blows for)
3. fetch.

The role of fetch

- Fetch is the distance over which wind blows across an open body of water.
- The longer the fetch, the greater the wind speed.

▼ Illustration to show fetch of waves

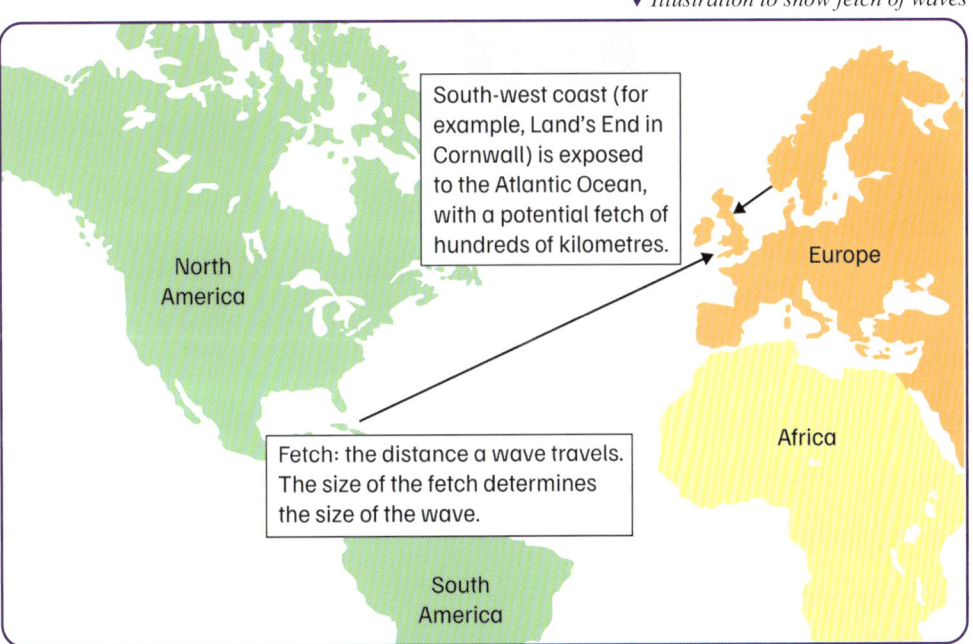

Fun fact

Waves are highest in height in the UK during the period of October to March.

Ace your revision

What could you be asked in the exam around this topic?

- Use an OS map to locate erosional or depositional features of a coastal location.
- Explain the formation of an erosional feature.
- Label an image or diagram of an erosional landform.

Seasonal changes in waves

During the winter, UK beaches will be affected by destructive waves and in the summer, there will be constructive waves.

▼ Characteristics of waves

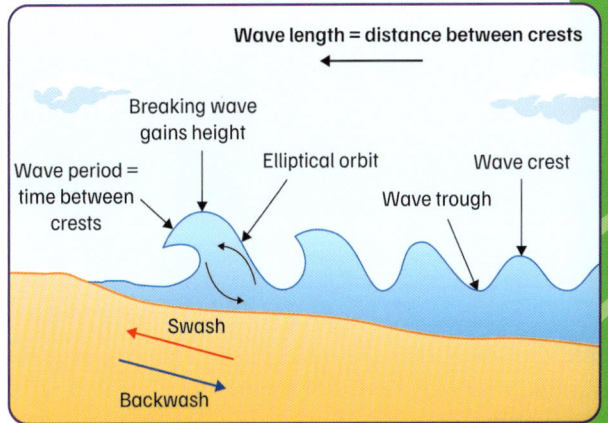

	Winter waves	Summer waves
Energy	High	Low
Height	Tall	Short
Destructive or constructive	Destructive	Constructive
Beach profile	Lower beach profile	Higher beach profile

Key terms

- **Arch:** *a natural opening in a cliff or headland where the sea can flow through.*
- **Cave:** *an enlarged indentation in the cliff or headland, created by coastal erosion.*
- **Concordant:** *some types of rock run parallel to the coast.*
- **Discordant:** *bands of hard and soft rock run perpendicular to the coast.*
- **Gravity:** *downward force.*
- **Stack:** *columns of rock that stand isolated away from the main headland.*
- **Stump:** *final stage of eroded stack which was part of the headland.*
- **Wave cut platform:** *gently sloping rock ledge from the base of a cliff.*

1.2.3 Development of erosional landforms

Human and physical factors can affect the rate of coastline change.

Caves, arches, stacks and stumps – erosional landforms

Caves, arches and stacks are formed on cliffs or headlands where the weather and the sea below the cliff wear away the faults in the rocks to form new landforms. This process happens over time until the most susceptible parts of the headland are worn away.

The geology of the headland plays a key role in the wearing away of the rock, for example soft rock is more easily eroded than hard rock, meaning caves, stacks and eventually stumps form. Hard rocks play a role as well. The harder the rock, the more it will help reflect the wave's energy back out to sea and onto another part of the headland. Eventually, the hard rock will be left jutting out into the sea while the softer more vulnerable rock is worn away.

▼ *Cave to stump sequence*

1. Hydraulic action causes cracks in the rock to appear.
2. Continuous abrasion causes cracks to grow and eventually form caves.
3. Caves grow larger.
4. A natural arch is formed as the cave stretches through the headland.
5. Weathering continues and the roof of the arch collapses.
6. This forms a stack.
7. Over time, the stack is eroded to form a stump.

Weathering processes weaken the top of arch

Direction of cliff retreat

▼ *A* **wave-cut platform** *is a flat, gently sloping surface that forms at the base of a cliff when waves erode the cliff*

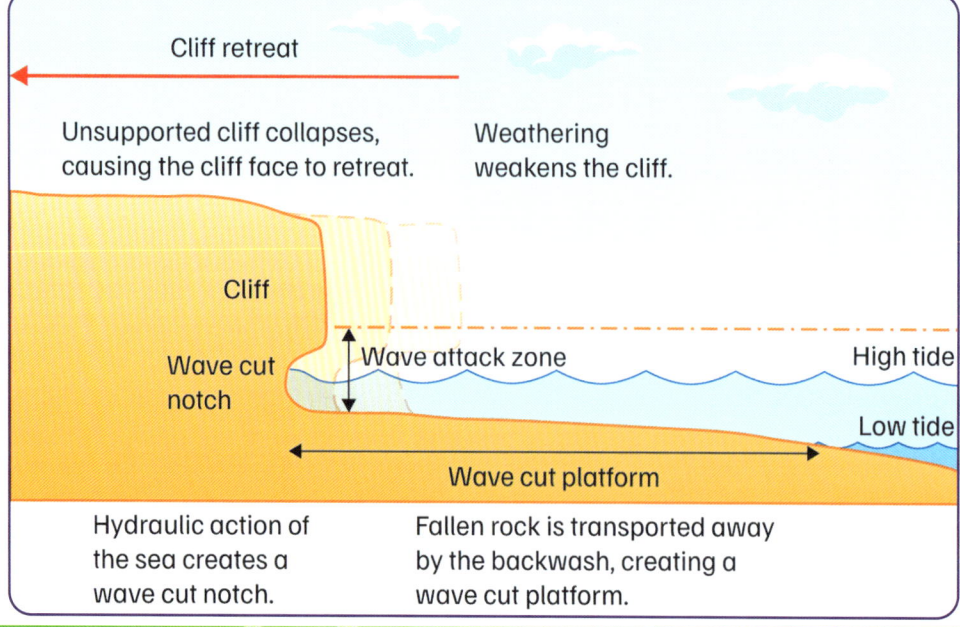

Cliff retreat

Unsupported cliff collapses, causing the cliff face to retreat.

Weathering weakens the cliff.

Cliff

Wave cut notch

Wave attack zone

High tide

Low tide

Wave cut platform

Hydraulic action of the sea creates a wave cut notch.

Fallen rock is transported away by the backwash, creating a wave cut platform.

▲ An example of a cave, arch and stack in Wales is the famous Green Bridge in Pembrokeshire

The seven steps to the formation of erosional landforms shown in the diagram:
- involve weathering processes
- involve erosional processes
- happen over time.

Gravity causes the unsupported roof of the old archway to collapse into the sea below.

◄ A model of the coastline of the Gower Peninsula

In **discordant** coastlines rock layers run perpendicular to the coast. This means that different layers erode at different rates creating a range of different landforms such as headlands and bays.

In **concordant** coastlines rock layers run parallel to the coast. This means that erosion happens along the coastline at the same rate, creating similar features along the coastline. Examples include coves.

Formation of a beach

A beach forms by a combination of constructive waves and longshore drift.

For a beach to form there needs to be:
- loose sediment material available
- low energy waves (constructive) that slow down and deposit material
- strong swash and weak backwash
- deposition process
- longshore drift to extend the beach
- low lying coastline.

Key terms

- **Aeolian:** *wind driven.*
- **Spit:** *narrow stretch of beach material formed by longshore drift.*
- **Sediment:** *material deposited by the waves.*
- **Velocity:** *speed.*

▲ *The Gower Peninsula*

Dr Harold Wanless

Harold Wanless is a professor at the University of Miami with a PhD in Geology. He specialises in hurricane effects on coastal environments and in shallow marine environments.

'We know we're going to have sea rise. This is literally a one-way street now. The only thing we're discussing now is how fast, it's not whether anymore, and then eventually how much'.

How do human and physical factors affect the coastline?

▼ *OS map of Pembrokeshire coastline*

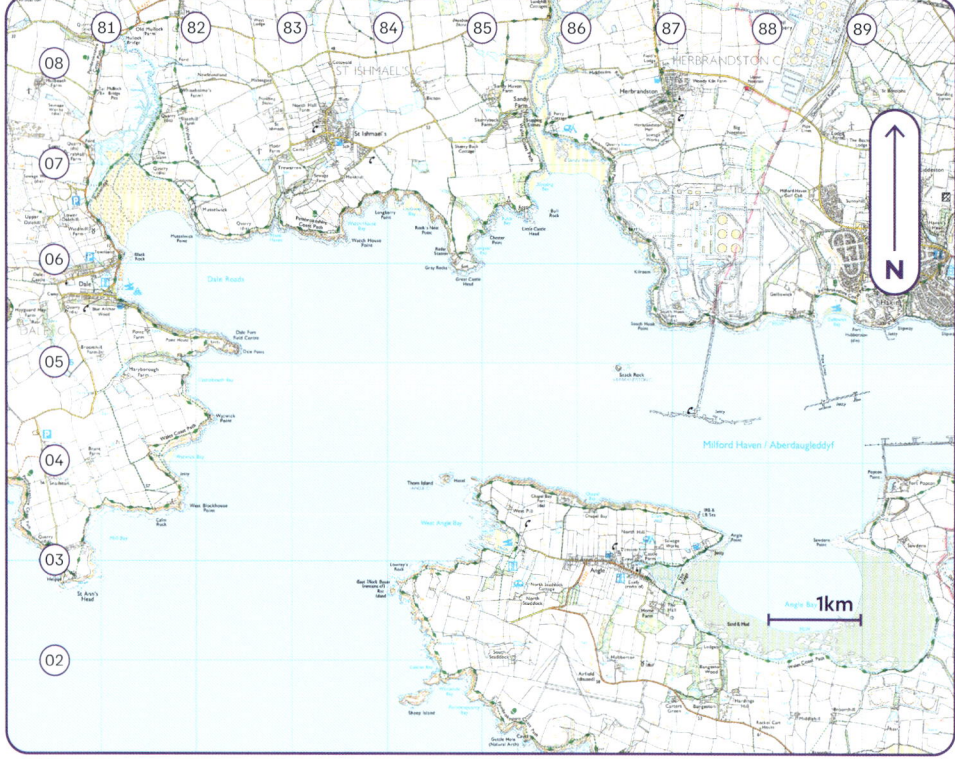

Agriculture: can affect the coast and present challenges. For example, farmers use the coastline at Freshwater East, Pembrokeshire for grazing cattle in the summer. Inappropriate cultivation can weaken soil structure, leading to increased surface run off.

Industry: can affect the coast. For example, a £60 million government initiative was announced in August 2024, which will see Pembroke Dock becoming a global hub for wind, wave and tidal power. Welsh coastal industries drive the economy forward and provide much needed energy and economic investment. Over 60% of the Welsh population live or work at the coast.

Coastal management: can have both positive and negative impacts on the coastline. Some hard engineering such as sea walls can reflect wave energy further down the coast as in Mappleton, on the Holderness Coast in the northeast of England. The village contains around 50 houses, over 300 people, one B-road and one main road. The main road is dangerously close to the edge of the coastline due to intense erosion and is only 50m away from disappearing completely. Mappleton is a good example of how natural physical factors like coastal erosion by the sea have a huge impact on the area.

Now try this ▼

1. Name and give the 4-figure grid reference for a depositional landform.

2. Name and give the 4-figure grid reference for an erosional landform.

3. Using the OS map, describe how it shows a steep gradient in grid square 8106.

4. Using the OS map, suggest why there are so many headlands and bays along this coastline.

5. In grid square 8205, describe what will happen to this landform over time.

1.2.4 Development of depositional landforms

Spit formation

Spits are formed at the coast when longshore drift deposits sediment in the sea after the coastline changes direction or at the mouth of an estuary. Spit formation continues until water becomes too deep or the sediment being deposited is removed much faster than it is being dropped.

> **Brain break**
> Spend 5 minutes outside, listening to the trees and wind and breathing in and out deeply.

▲ *Fairbourne Spit along the Welsh Coastal Path*

▲ *Example of how humans have used a natural spit to develop a tourist area in Costa Blanca, Spain*

Sand dunes

Sand dunes are formed due to aeolian (wind) processes and are an accumulation of sand grains. There are several factors that help to create sand dunes.

- Wind carries sand up the beach and deposits it around an obstacle such as driftwood, vegetation or dead animals. This begins the process of sand dune formation. When plants begin to grow the dunes are stabilised by their roots.
- Wind velocity needs to be fast enough to move particles of sand (fluid threshold velocity).
- Wet sand is more difficult to move because the particles clump together.
- Sand particles are deposited through surface creep (sand rolling along the ground), suspension or particles in the air, or by saltation.
- Kinetic energy helps to move sand grains when they strike other sand grains and cause them to move.
- A drop in wind velocity leads to deposition of sand grains.
- An abundance of sediment is needed.
- Sand grains need to be small enough to be carried by aeolian processes.
- Beaches with large tidal ranges allow time for sand grains to dry out and be transported.
- Beaches with an extensive backshore area allow for the development of sand dunes.

> **Ace your revision**
> Using acronyms such as PEEL will help you structure your longer responses to exam questions.
> **PEEL (point, evidence, explain, link back to question)**

> **Fun fact**
> Large sand particles require higher wind velocity to be moved.

▲ *Sand dunes at Nicholaston at Tor Bay, the Gower*

Ace your revision

Look at this great example answer.

Explain the formation of a coastal depositional feature. You may use an annotated diagram in your answer. [6]

A spit is a depositional coastal landform that is caused by longshore drift. Constructive waves help to drive swash up the beach at a 45° angle, with weaker backwash coming back down the beach at a 90° angle due to the force of gravity. This process happens over and over again until the headland or coastline ends. If there is no river present, a bar can form joining the old headland to the next headland and the sediment continues to grow from longshore drift. However, if a river is present and flows into the sea via the estuary, the sediment from longshore drift will be washed into the sea. If there is a sudden change in wind direction, the sediment being moved from left to right by longshore drift will blow back on itself forming a hook or recurved lateral. Behind this hook, saltmarsh will begin to form due to deposition.

1.2.5 Human and physical factors that affect the rates of coastline change

Human factors

Humans have affected the UK coastline either directly or indirectly. For example, when we decide not to protect the coast, no sea defences are put in place which can lead to faster rates of erosion.

Fairbourne is an example of soft engineering in Gwynedd. At this stretch of coastline, no sea defences are in place. Why could this be? Sometimes, if there is a limited number of properties or land worth protecting, it is cheaper to let the land flood or erode naturally than to protect it. Historically however, human activity around the coastline has involved hard engineering, which has brought sustainability to some areas, but this can cause erosion through wave refraction further down the coast.

▲ *Fairbourne*

Hard engineering also plays a role in trying to protect the coastline as you can see in the images showing tetrapods and sea walls.

▲ *Aberavon sea front showing recurved sea wall*

▲ *Tetrapods on the North Wales Coastal Path*

▲ *Seabed dredging is a soft engineering option*

▲ *Soft engineering includes the creation of salt marsh*

Physical factors

There are several physical factors that affect coastal change. For example, climate change can speed up rates of erosion and increase habitat loss. Sea levels can rise from ocean water warming and expanding (thermal expansion). Additionally, increased global temperatures can lead to glaciers melting and more water being added to the global oceans. Climate change can also lead to increased frequency of storms making coastal areas more susceptible to erosion.

Fetch plays a significant role in determining rates of coastal change because it affects the size, energy, and impact of waves reaching the shoreline. Fetch refers to the distance over which wind blows across open water, which in turn influences the size and strength of the waves that are generated. The longer the fetch, the larger the waves, which can lead to more intensive erosion.

Geology affects rates of coastal erosion in a huge way. Hard, more resistant rock (such as granite or basalt) erodes much more slowly compared to softer rock (such as sandstone or limestone). Additionally, rock structure can have an impact on rates of erosion. Rocks have joints, faults and bedding planes that allow faster dissolving or quicker erosion if water can penetrate those weaker points.

Human factors affecting the coastline	Physical factors affecting the rate of coastal change
Draining wetland areas for farming	Rock type Soft rock is more easily eroded
Building on the headlands	Discordant and concordant structures Discordant – more bays and headlands Concordant – fewer bays and headlands
Deforestation	Erosion and deposition processes
Building (or not building) sea defences	Sea level changes
Tourism	Eustatic and isostatic changes Eustatic – the amount of water in the oceans Isostatic – growth of mountains, ice sheets melting, tectonic activity
Building marinas	Weathering – breakdown of rocks in situ
Dredging seabed	Natural sea defences e.g. saltmarsh
Disposing of waste	Fetch – distance over water that wind blows in one direction

Ace your revision

The sliding scale of opinion is important for questions that ask you to *evaluate*, *assess* or say *to what extent*.

Use the three phrases below to help you get the marks for using your opinion.

- I completely agree that...
- I somewhat agree that...
- I disagree that...

Remember to explain your thinking.

Ace your revision

For 6- and 8-mark questions, it is useful to know some named places and case studies.

Now try this

1. Evaluate the causes of changes to the coastline.

Tip: When you are asked to assess, evaluate or justify, always use a sliding scale of opinion.

Chapter 1.3 Migration

AO1 AO2 AO3

🔑 Key terms

- **Asylum seeker:** a person looking for protection because they fear persecution, or they have experienced violence or human rights violations.
- **Forced migration:** the movement of people who have no option but to move to another place.
- **International migration:** the movement of people from one country to another.
- **Irregular migration:** the movement of people into a country who do not have permission to enter that country.
- **Migration:** the movement of people from one place to another.
- **National migration:** the movement of people from one location in a country to another location within the same country.
- **Permanent migration:** people who move to another location permanently.
- **Refugee:** a person who has asked for protection and has been given refugee status.
- **Regular migration:** the movement of people into a country where they have permission to enter that country.
- **Temporary migration:** people who move for a short period of time.
- **Voluntary migration:** people who have made the choice to move to another place.

1.3.1 Causes of migration

What is migration?

Migration involves the movement of people from one place to another. Sometimes people move for a short period of time (**temporary migration**) whereas others move permanently (**permanent migration**). There are a number of other ways that migration can be classified.

- **Forced migration** or **voluntary migration** – some people are forced to leave their homes and move to other areas. This could be due to natural hazards such as drought, floods, etc., or due to human hazards such as war zones. Other people may choose to leave where they live and move to another area for economic prosperity or to be close to family.
- **International migration** or **national migration** – the distance that people travel also varies greatly. Some may move across international boundaries into another country. Currently around 3.6% of the world's population live outside their country of birth. Other people move elsewhere within their own country.
- **Regular migration** or **irregular migration** – some people enter other countries in a regular way through border checkpoints, while others enter countries irregularly without documentation that allows them to do so.

The reasons for migration

Learn about the varied reasons why people migrate below.

Forced migration

As we have seen, forced migration involves people moving as they have no choice to stay. There is some threat to their lives that forces them to leave their homes.

- **Escaping conflict** – lives are endangered when there is war between countries (international) or civil unrest within a country (e.g. different groups competing for power). This forces people to leave the area they live.
- **Human rights violations** – human rights are the basic freedoms that belong to every person in the world and are regardless of age, gender, religion, nationality or ethnicity. When these rights are taken away from an individual, they may feel under threat and therefore migrate for their own safety. These **refugees** are often called **asylum seekers** as they are seeking protection from another country. For example, the Taliban, who currently rule Afghanistan, discriminate against women and girls. The Taliban have removed many women's rights such as going to work, going to school, showing their skin in public and leaving the house without a male chaperone.

Ace your revision

Although the terms *asylum seekers* and *refugees* are often used together, there is a subtle difference between them. These terms are often used interchangeably by the media and this creates a negative and incorrect image.

Voluntary migration

For many people, migration is a choice – they choose to move for a perceived benefit.

- **Economic migration** – people move for economic gain and a better quality of life. The move could be within the same country e.g. moving from an area of less economic activity (rural) to one where there is more economic activity (city) and therefore the expectation of higher paid jobs. Alternatively, some people move internationally as an economic migrant. They move from the **source country**, which might have a lower level of economic development, to the **host country** which has a higher level of economic development, and therefore a perceived higher quality of life.

The reason for international economic migration could be due to physical or human factors.

- **Physical factors** may include a natural resource that is available in a certain area that an industry uses, e.g. geologists are often employed in the oil industry and may migrate to oil rich countries such as Saudi Arabia or Qatar. Alternatively, some people migrate to study physical features in the location where they occur, e.g. volcanologists study and monitor volcanoes and therefore need to live near plate boundaries.
- **Human factors** may include any need created by society that requires a workforce, e.g. in war-torn regions, humanitarian aid workers help to get emergency aid provisions such as food and medical supplies to citizens that are unable to leave. The British Red Cross and Medical Aid for Palestinians are examples of organisations distributing humanitarian aid in the Gaza Strip.
  - **Joining family** – this type of migration involves people moving to be with other family members who live in a different country, or a different region within the same country. This could be the family of an economic migrant who is coming to join the worker once they have gained employment, or parents of adult children who are moving to be close to where their children live and work.

Spotlight

Full scale war broke out between Russia and Ukraine in February 2022, when Russian troops crossed into Ukraine. As a result, 6.8 million people (up to November 2024) have been displaced from Ukraine to other countries to escape the fighting, missiles and drone attacks. Just under 1 million of these people moved to neighbouring Poland. By June 2024, 217,000 Ukrainian people had moved to the UK under the Ukraine Family and Sponsorship Scheme.

▼ *Ukrainian refugees waiting for a train to escape to Europe*

Spotlight

A survey of young people in rural Wales in 2019, found that two in every five young people in rural areas thought they would move outside Wales in the next five years. Therefore, rural youth in Wales are a key group of the population for maintaining communities in rural areas, and for the population development of Wales as a whole.

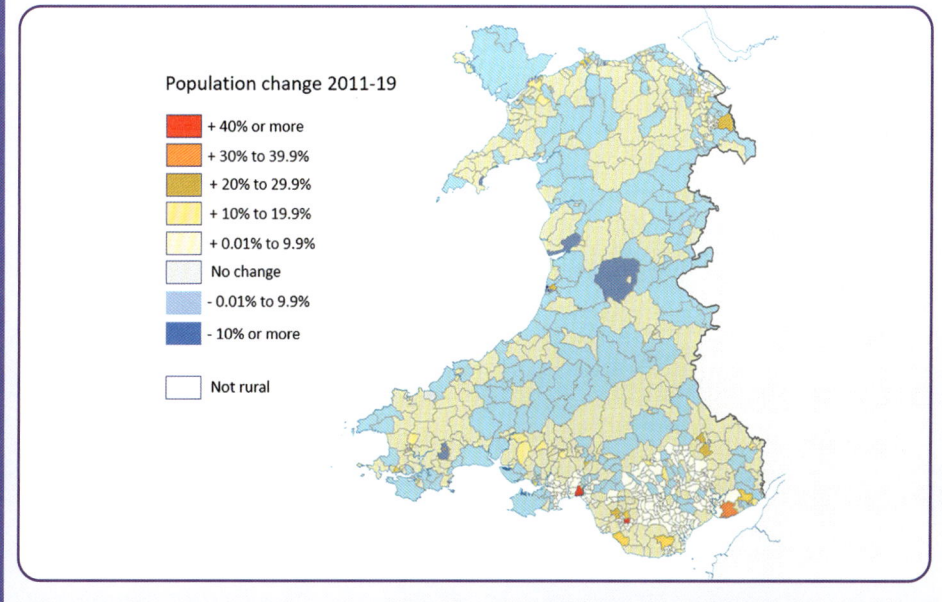

Ace your revision

Make a list of three occupations that cause economic migration for physical factors and three occupations that cause economic migration for human factors. Give located examples.

Nelson Mandela

Born in 1918 in South Africa, Nelson Mandela was a civil rights activist and campaigned for equal rights for black people. He was imprisoned for 27 years. After his release, he went on to become the first black President of South Africa.

Key terms

- **Conflict:** *a strong disagreement between two parties which may lead to physical aggression.*
- **Economic factor:** *anything that influences the economy of a person, business or place.*
- **Environmental factor:** *the physical and biological elements of an area which influence a process or place.*
- **Host country:** *where migrants move to.*
- **Human factors:** *any factor that is related to people which influences a process or place.*
- **Human rights:** *common principles/values that apply to all people.*
- **Physical factors:** *the non-living elements of the world that influence a process or place.*
- **Political factor:** *the political situation within an area which influences a process or place.*
- **Push factor:** *a factor that makes someone want to leave a location.*
- **Social factor:** *the characteristics of groups or individuals that affect a process or place.*
- **Source country:** *where migrants come from.*

Push factors causing migration

There are many reasons why people may want to leave a location. These push factors can be grouped into social, economic, environmental and political factors.

Examples of push factors

Social factors	Economic factors	Environmental factors	Political factors
Poor medical care	Lack of job opportunities	High risk of environmental disasters	Fear of persecution
Lack of/poor quality education	Poorly paid jobs	High risk of negative impacts from climate change	Government's strict birth control policy
Inaccessibility of medical care	High cost of living	Food insecurity due to drought	Lack of free speech/ freedoms
Lack of social mobility	High level of government taxes	Lack of natural resources in source country/area	Armed conflict

Spotlight

Source country: Afghanistan

Social factors – human rights violations, including loss of rights and freedoms for women, exploitation of children (e.g. into military recruitment from a young age or sexual exploitation), insecurity, a poor education system and limited health and social care provision.

Economic factors – extreme poverty (39% of the population are unable to meet their basic needs), limited employment opportunities, no formal government support for families that are struggling financially.

Environmental factors – increase in number and length of droughts due to uneven rainfall throughout the year and high temperatures. When the rain does fall it can be intense and lead to floods, increased desertification due to overgrazing and poor management of the land.

Political factors – fear of persecution for anyone that speaks against the ruling Taliban, terrorism and war, withdrawal of support for government from USA.

▲ *Afghan security forces leaving Kabul City as the Taliban take over, 2021*

Put into practice

You need to know a named country case study illustrating the push factors from that country. Extend the spotlight case study by researching what other push factors became prominent after the Taliban came back to power in Afghanistan in 2021.

Key terms

- **Pull factor:** *a factor that makes someone want to move to a location.*

Pull factors causing migration

Like push factors, there are also many reasons why people may want to migrate to a location. These factors can also be grouped into social, economic, environmental and political factors.

Examples of pull factors

Social factors	Economic factors	Environmental factors	Political factors
Freedoms, e.g. acceptance of all religions in a country, freedom of speech	Higher standard of living, which leads to a better quality of life	Away from plate boundaries, reducing the risk from tectonic hazards	Stable government/political system
Good quality education, which is accessible to all	Stable financial system and currency within the country	Natural beauty of the desired location	Fair elections
Good quality and good accessibility to health care	More employment opportunities	Climate is as desired	No fear of persecution
Near family	Higher paying jobs	Lower risk of severe impacts from climate change	Strong protection of human rights

Spotlight

Host country : UK

Social factors – healthcare system freely available to all citizens, free education system for all children, people move to be near family who have already settled in the UK, highly regarded universities.

Economic factors – contains one of the world's major global cities (London), which attracts industry and finance, well paid jobs in many sectors and high standard of living.

Environmental factors – less extreme weather events than the source country, stable food and water supply, more stable temperature.

Political factors – stable democratic government, free and fair elections, freedom of movement within the EU before Brexit.

Ace your revision

When talking about push and pull factors in your exam, make sure you 'qualify' the factors. For example, if asked for a social push factor you will get no marks for saying 'education', you need to say, 'lack of accessibility to education'.

Ace your revision

You need to know a named country case study illustrating the pull factors towards that country. Extend the Spotlight case study example by researching whether the UK became more or less attractive as a host country to people after the UK left the EU (Brexit).

▲ *Free education is available for all children in the UK (pull factor)*

1.3.2 Impacts of migration

Impacts of international migration for source and host countries

When a person migrates from one country to another it has many impacts on them, their family, the source country and the host country. When a high number of people migrate, these impacts are important to acknowledge and track. The impacts of migration can be positive and negative, and it is vital to know how these impacts will change society in both countries.

Impacts on the source country:

- **Brain drain** – this happens when a lot of highly educated or qualified people leave a source country in search of better pay elsewhere (e.g. doctors trained in the UK leave the country for better pay/working conditions elsewhere in the world). As a result, the source country has a lack of suitably qualified people for these roles leading to high vacancy rates. When this happens in industry/commerce this can have a negative impact on the country's economic development.

▼ *Brain drain from Africa – where inventors migrated to 2001–2010*

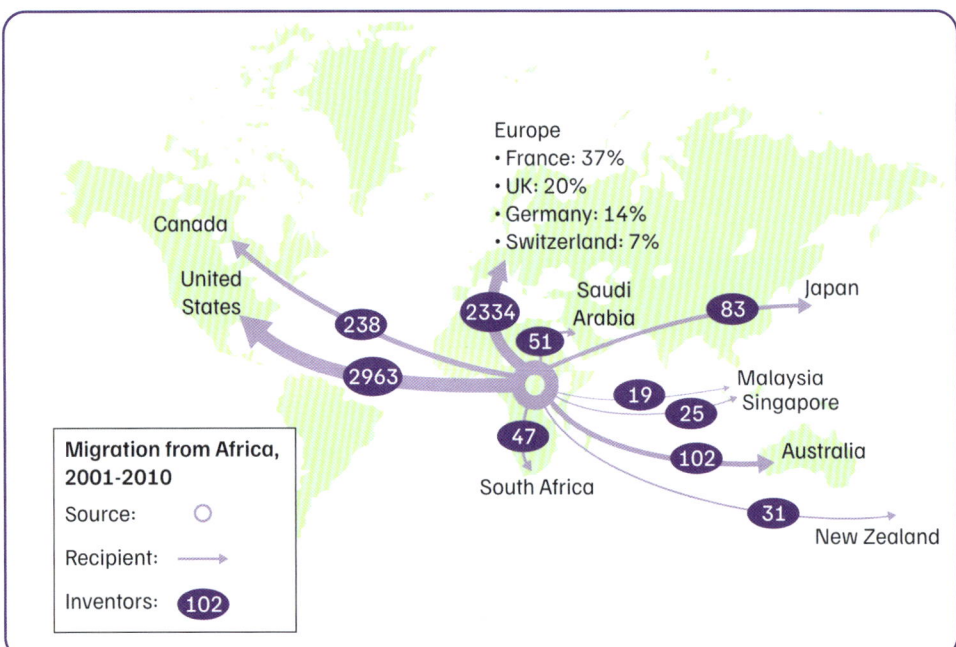

- **Remittances** – one benefit to the source country will be remittances sent by the migrants back to their families who are still in the source country. Economic migrants may travel on their own to gain a higher paying job in the host country than they were able to get in the source country. They will then send regular payments back home to support their families who are unable to join them. This will therefore increase the quality of life for those family members who have not migrated.

Impacts on the host country:

- **Community cohesion** – when migrants move to host countries, they often seek to live near other people from the same source country so that they have familiar language, religions, food types and cultural habits. Cultural cohesion refers to how well these groups of migrants work with the host country's existing communities to achieve common goals. For example, Cardiff has one of the largest Somali communities in the UK (around 10,000 people according to the 2021 census). Events such as the Cardiff Community Cohesion Cup football tournament are regularly held to promote **integration** of different communities in the city.

Key terms

- **Brain drain:** when highly qualified or educated people leave a country.
- **Community cohesion:** the ability of a community to work together positively and collaboratively to function effectively.
- **Integration:** migrants and their family become part of society in the host country.
- **Remittances:** when migrants send money or goods back to their family in the source country.

Put into practice

Create a fact file of impacts on a source country from migration. You could use the source country example in the previous section (Afghanistan) or one of your own.

Levi Roots

Born in 1958, Levi Roots is a Jamaican British businessman and celebrity chef. He is the inventor of Reggae Reggae Sauce, which brings the flavours of his Caribbean roots to the UK.

▼ *There is a thriving Somali community in Cardiff*

Key terms

- **Multiculturalism:** *when migrants and the host society integrate, share and embrace each other's cultures, traditions, food, etc.*
- **Spread of culture:** *when the culture of migrants is accepted amongst the host country's population.*
- **Segregation:** *when migrants are spatially separated from the society they move into.*

- **Integration** – when the migrants become accepted and part of the society that they have settled in within the host country. To become fully integrated, migrants will have learnt to communicate in the host country's language, engage in social activities in the host country and share their culture with the host population.
- **Multiculturalism** and the **spread of culture** – this involves the sharing of the migrants and the host countries culture/religions. Migrants' food and traditions become part of the host areas society. For example, Notting Hill Carnival in London has its roots in Caribbean culture brought to the UK with immigrants from the Caribbean in the 1950s.

▼ *Notting Hill Carnival, London*

Put into practice

Create a fact file of the impacts of migration on a host country. You can use the UK or another country of your choice.

- **Segregation** – sometimes when migrants settle in a new country, they remain separated/isolated from the host society. This is often due to barriers of language, religion or culture. This can lead to tensions in the community as the two groups of people do not understand each other.
- **Workforce** – migrants often provide a valuable source of labour to the host country for job vacancies that they might otherwise have struggled to fill. In the UK, the National Health Service (NHS) and the entertainment industry rely on migrant workers to function.

Put into practice

Write out a list of contributions that migrant workers have made to the UK. This could be to society, culture, the workforce or people in the business world.

Ace your revision

Ensure you know a case study for the impacts of migration on a host country and a source country. The impacts must give specific details about that country.

Impacts of migration on migrants

In addition to impacts on the source and host countries, it is also important to recognise that there will be significant impacts on the migrants themselves. The hope behind a migrant's motivation to move is that it results in a better life for them and their family. For many this is the case, however this is not always guaranteed. Some migrants may become segregated in their new countries and fear and isolation may become the norm for them. Two types of migrants need to be considered when looking at impacts on migrants.

- **Asylum seekers** – asylum seekers migrate due to risk of harm or persecution. They often leave quickly without their possessions. When they arrive at the host country, their application to stay will need to be processed, which can take a long time. Until then, their future is uncertain, and they are at risk of deportation. This can have multiple impacts on the asylum seeker:
  - trauma from a hurried move from their home country and possibly a difficult journey to their desired host country
  - a feeling of loss about what they have had to leave behind – family, job, friends, home, etc.
  - mental health issues, ranging from post-traumatic stress disorder (PTSD) from things they might have witnessed, to anxiety and stress from having no control over their future
  - poverty due to the small amount of financial support they are given when they arrive at the host country, while their application is being processed.

- **Refugees** – refugees experience many similar experiences to asylum seekers (but the reason for their migration differs). Refugees may also be grieving for people that they might have lost in a natural disaster or war and are more likely to arrive at the host country with very few possessions due to the nature of the hazard that forced them to leave.

▼ *Asylum seekers waiting to be processed at the El Paso/USA border*

▼ *Mexico/USA fence border*

1.3.3 Managing migration

Strategies used to manage international migration

To try to control **immigration** numbers, many countries now use a variety of strategies to manage international migration.

- **Managing irregular migration** – is a key policy for many governments around the world so that they have control over their borders and know who is coming into the country. There have been a variety of strategies from different countries, for example:
  - When president Donald Trump came to power in 2016, he vowed to build a wall along the land border between the USA and Mexico to stop the flow of irregular migrants into the USA. Only a small part of the wall was built, but he hoped the threat would deter future immigrants. When he was re-elected in 2024, one of his election promises was to remove all irregular immigrants from the USA. In the months that followed his re-election, Trump deported thousands of migrants living in the USA.
  - The UK has seen a number of policies aimed at preventing irregular immigration. The Illegal Migration Bill in 2023 stated that if you enter the UK illegally, you will be detained and removed back to your home country or, if seeking asylum, to a safe country while your case is being considered. The safe country proposed was Rwanda. In 2024, after a change of government, the focus changed from a deterrent to dealing with the people smugglers and trying to break up their network of people and small boats travelling across the English channel.

Key terms

- **Immigration:** *the process of moving into a host country.*

Put into practice

Consider two possible strategies to stop irregular migration into either the UK or the USA and list the positives and negatives for each.

▼ *Migrants on boats to the UK organised by smuggling gangs*

▼ *President Trump launching his anti immigration policies*

Spotlight

The UK introduced a point-based system for regular migration after Brexit ended the free movement of people from other EU countries. It is designed to help ensure immigrants to the UK have the skills that the country needs to fill job vacancies that the UK population cannot fill. It has defined categories such as 'skilled' and 'highly skilled' and has specialised routes for innovators, students, etc.

- **Points based migration** – to manage regular immigration, many countries use a point-based system to assess the 'contribution' that the person may be able to make to the host country.
- **Visa free travel** – a visa is a document that enables people to visit a country and stay for a set period of time. The time will vary depending on the purpose of the travel. Some countries reach agreements with other countries so that their citizens can travel between these countries without the need to apply for a visa. They would just need their passport. The UK currently has agreements with 190 countries for visa free travel for British citizens.

Rita Ora

Rita Ora is a singer, song writer and television personality. She was born in 1990 in Kosovo to Albanian parents. In 1991, her family had to emigrate due to the persecution of Albanians. They relocated to the UK.

Put into practice

Draw a spider diagram to show a range of ethical considerations when creating policies to control immigration.

UK government's point-based system for working in UK

A total of 70 points is needed to be able to apply to work in the UK.

Characteristics	Mandatory/Tradeable	Points
Offer of job by approved sponsor	Mandatory	20
Job at appropriate skill level	Mandatory	20
Speaks English at required level	Mandatory	10
Salary of £20,480 to £23,039 or at least 80% of the going rate for the profession (whichever is higher)	Tradeable	0
Salary of £23,040 to £25,599 or at least 90% of the going rate for the profession (whichever is higher)	Tradeable	10
Salary of £25,600 or above or at least the going rate for the profession (whichever is higher)	Tradeable	20
Job in a shortage occupation as designated by the Migration Advisory Committee	Tradeable	20
Education qualification: PhD in a subject relevant to the job	Tradeable	10
Education qualification: PhD in a STEM subject relevant to the job	Tradeable	20

Fun fact

In 2025, the UK introduced an Electronic Travel Authorization (ETA), which allows people from selected countries to enter the UK without a visa.

Put into practice

1. What does the table tell you about the criteria people need to meet to enter the Uk through the point-based system?
2. Describe the types of countries whose citizens can enter the UK through the ETA system.

Who needs a Visa or ETA to visit the UK in 2024?

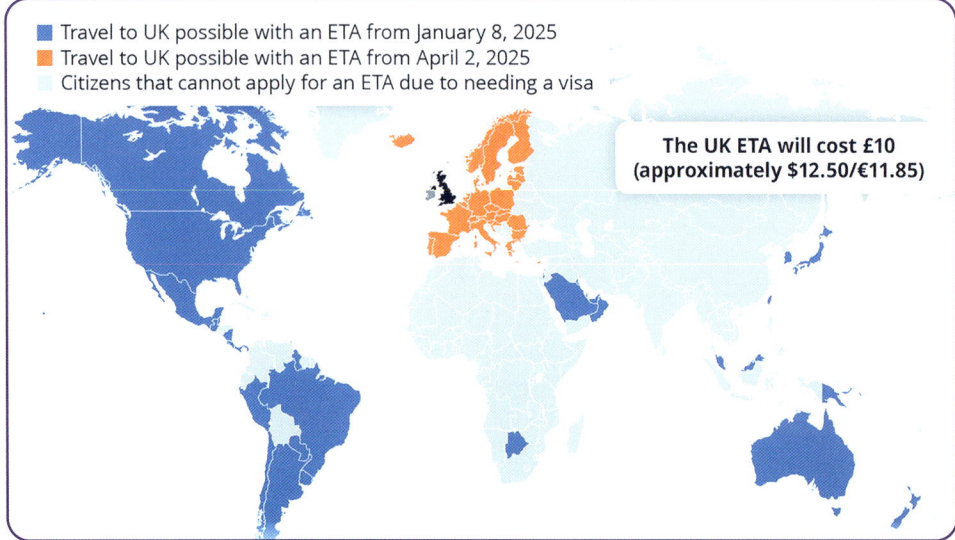

- Travel to UK possible with an ETA from January 8, 2025
- Travel to UK possible with an ETA from April 2, 2025
- Citizens that cannot apply for an ETA due to needing a visa

The UK ETA will cost £10 (approximately $12.50/€11.85)

Ethical considerations of migration (including human rights)

When determining a country's policies on immigration, the government must ensure that the policies are ethical. Considerations should include:

- human rights, especially when dealing with vulnerable people such as refugees and asylum seekers – should the host country provide food, shelter and safety to people that have entered the country illegally?
- whether the policies should comply with national and international law
- avoiding causing harm to individuals
- decisions being fair and transparent
- the length of time it takes for a decision to be made should be appropriate; leaving immigrants for extended periods of time not knowing whether they will be able to stay in the country will add to their mental distress.

Public perception and the role of the media in influencing public perception on migration

Every member of the public will have their own views of migration – what the positives and negatives are and what action they would like to see their government take. These views are often influenced by personal experiences. However, these experiences are often not from the migrants themselves, but from listening to public figures or people on social media using inflammatory language. Some examples of negative language used to describe immigrants are given below.

- In 2022, Suella Braverman, the then UK home secretary, stated that, 'Southern England was facing an "invasion" of illegal migrants.'
- In 2024, Donald Trump (during a debate while campaigning for the presidential election) stated that, 'In Springfield, they [migrants from Haiti] are eating the dogs. The people that came in, they are eating the cats. They're eating – they are eating the pets of the people that live there.'

Comments like these are remembered by people because of their extreme nature but they are often not an accurate picture of the truth. The 24-hour media will keep replaying and commenting on such statements, which perpetuates a story that is inaccurate, but many people come to believe it. Hence people gain a negative view about migration.

▼ *Newspaper articles showing different views on migrants in the UK*

Very often AO2 questions require you to draw inference from a resource. What do the two newspaper articles on migrants suggest?

Now try this ▼

1. Describe the difference between regular and irregular migration.
2. For a source country that you have studied, evaluate whether political, environmental or economic push factors were the most important.
3. Explain why the impacts of migration may be felt more in the host country than the source country. You may refer to examples that you have studied.

Chapter 1.4 Settlement change

AO1 AO2 AO3

🔑 Key terms

- **Characteristics:** *traits or key features.*
- **Global:** *from around the world.*
- **Global city:** *densely populated, home to trade and finance.*
- **HIC:** *high income country.*
- **LIC:** *low income country.*
- **Urbanisation:** *Urbanisation is when the percentage of the population live in towns and cities increases.*

Ace your revision

Try to include facts and figures in your answer – it improves your knowledge and understanding marks.

Ace your revision

You might get asked how you could improve maps like this.

1.4.1 Urbanisation

How have rates of global urbanisation changed over time?

The United Nations (UN) predicts that by 2050, two thirds of the world's population will be living in urban areas, and that urban growth is higher in low income countries (**LIC**s) than high income countries (**HIC**s). Rapid urbanisation has its own set of challenges, as we will find out.

▼ *London is a **global city***

▼ *Global cities map*

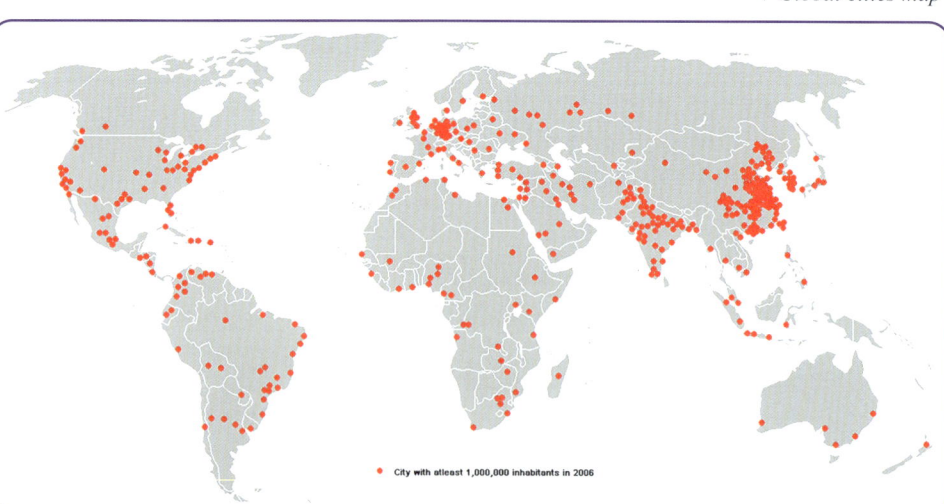

• City with atleast 1,000,000 inhabitants in 2006

From this map, we can see the **global** cities with at least 1 million people in them.

1.4.2 Urban land use patterns

▼ *What are the characteristics of urban areas?*

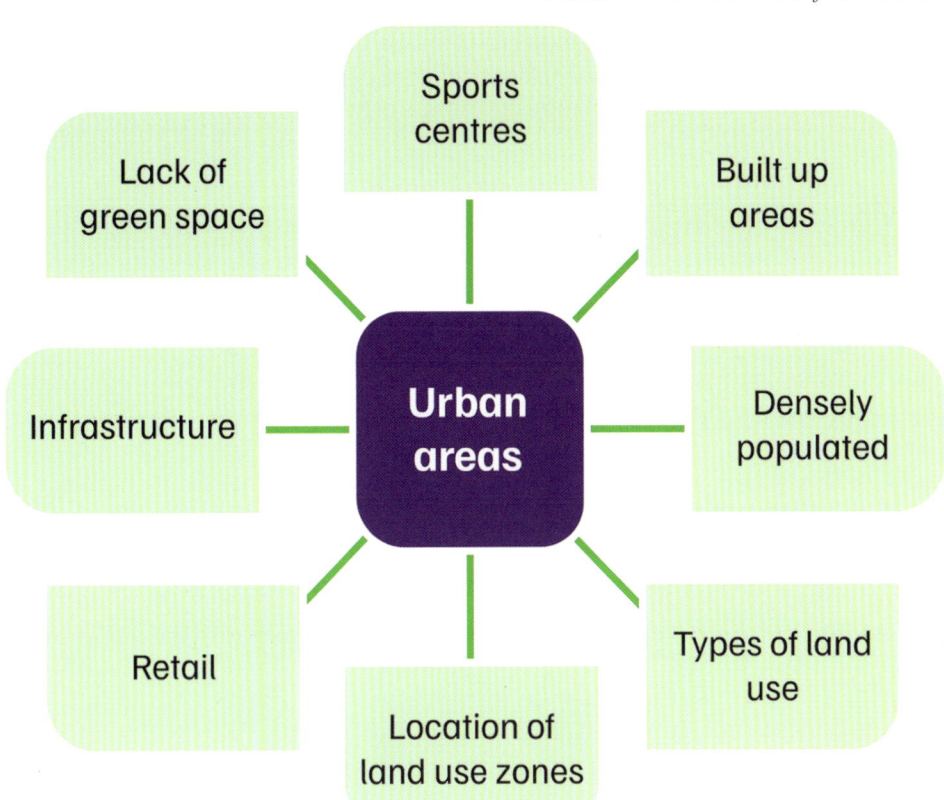

Fun fact

More than half the global population live in urban areas. By 2050, this is expected to increase to around 70%.

How do the physical and human **characteristics** of urban places change between countries?

		Low income country	High income country
Physical		Limited open space	Greater amounts of open space including public parks
		Rivers often polluted	Rivers are cleaner and better monitored
		Limited green space	Greater amounts of green space e.g. parks
Human		Quality of life is often poorer	Better quality of life (access to schools, hospitals, clean water)
		Poor infrastructure e.g. houses, hospitals	Infrastructure well built
		Land ownership – can be illegal (informal)	Legal ownership, more space
		Houses can be cramped and densely packed	Houses with more space/well developed amenities
		Railways are often overpopulated with poorer safety records	Railways – high speed, publicly funded, higher safety records
		Faster growth of urban areas	Slower rates of urban growth
		Wealth is lower	Wealth is higher
		Smaller urban populations	Larger urban populations

Put into practice

Look at the RICEPOTS survey on page 68. Can you identify different types of urban land use, with examples, in your own locality (cynefin) or nearest urban area?

Key terms

- **Fringe settlement:** *a built-up area which meets the countryside.*

Land use zones have special functions in urban areas which range from housing to industry. Commercial land use zones house businesses and are often found along major roads or at the edge of an urban areas. Industrial zones contain manufacturing and factories. 80% of urban land use is made up of residential spaces. These are the areas where people live and the types of dwellings can vary depending on each city.

Put into practice

Describe the characteristics of two different urban land use zones in a typical city. Use examples to support your answer.

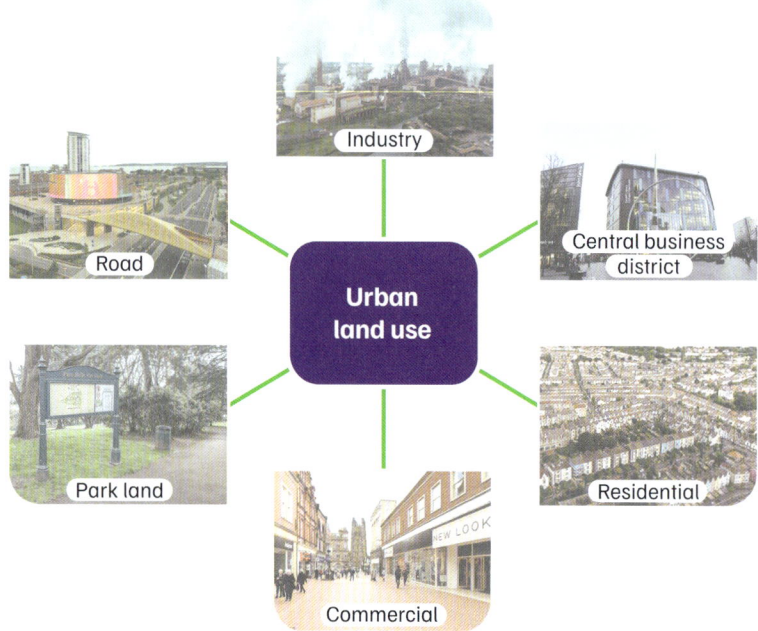

Fun fact

The word *suburb* is made up of the Latin word *sub* – meaning below or near, and the Latin word *urbs* meaning city.

Did you know

In 2023, the total amount of UK land taken up by urban areas was approximately 8% – that's around 2 million hectares!

What is the central business district?

The central business district (CBD) includes features such as tall buildings, lots of provision of services such as banks and many buildings all packed together. The centre of the city is the most expensive land, with land values getting cheaper the further out you go (in theory). Public transport links in the CBD are often well developed with good train stations and buses, and a variety of shops and social features such as pubs and bars.

What are fringe settlements?

A  is where a small settlement grows between the countryside and a town or city. It is sometimes known as a suburban fringe or settlement. Typical characteristics are mixed use land such as farming, housing and commercial (business) and is more formalised in HICs. An example of this is in Ebbw Vale.

▼ *Ebbw Vale*

What are informal settlements?

In LICs, informal settlements are sometimes called illegal settlements because they are not supported by the government. Residents have no formal rights and living conditions are very challenging with high rates of illness and poor sanitation. Informal housing can grow for many reasons, including a government's inability to build more affordable housing and the population's drive to move to areas with higher income, employment and better prospects. In 2020, nearly 1.1 billion people were living in informal settlements.

Key terms

- **Agglomeration:** *growth of multiple settlements into one larger settlement.*

▼ *Informal settlement in Nairobi, Kenya*

What are inner city areas?

This is the central part of an urban area, which often faces high levels of decay and decline, and is densely populated.

What are the suburbs?

These areas are residential and located on the outskirts of towns and cities. Suburbanisation is when cities grow outwardly, often covering surrounding villages and smaller towns into a larger collection of housing called an agglomeration.

Their characteristics are:

- lower density of population
- lower density of housing
- semi-detached housing.

1.4.3 Mega cities and global cities

Mega cities have populations of 10 million or more people. 62.9% of the world's megacities are located in Asia, with most of them in China and India. Africa has the fewest mega cities. The rate of growth of mega cities globally is seen in these maps.

A **global city** (sometimes called a **world city**) is a city that plays a significant role in global economic, political, and cultural activities. These cities are often major hubs for finance, business, media, technology, and diplomacy, and they have a large influence on global affairs.

Ace your revision

A global city provides:

A significant influence on the global economic, cultural, and political landscape

B significant influence on religion, politics and crime.

▼ Distribution of mega cities

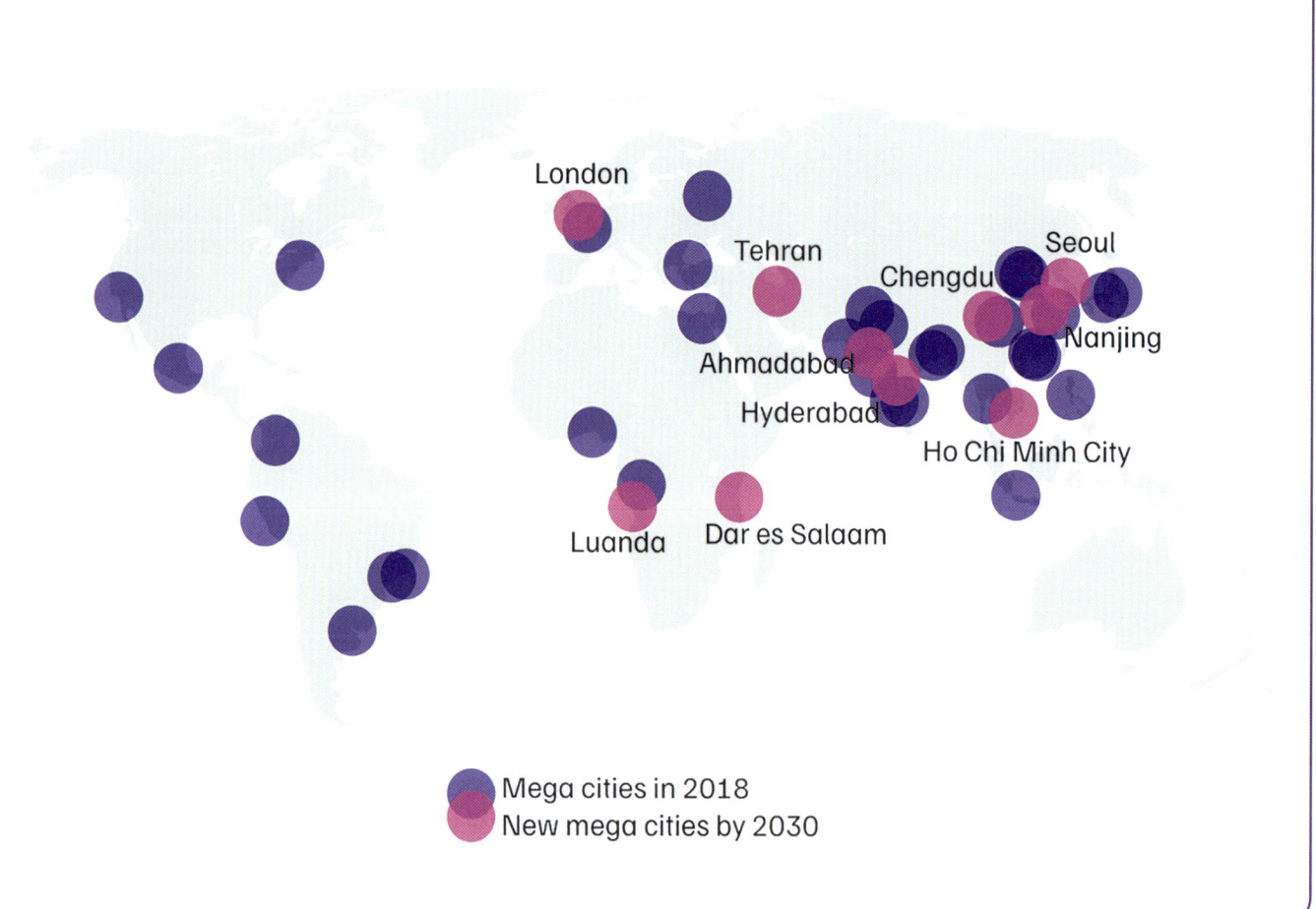

Put into practice

Describe the predicted change in areas with mega cities from 2018 to 2030.

Ace your revision

Learn about two global cities and two mega cities in different parts of the world so that you can compare them.

Global cities

These are sometimes called power cities and are the centre point for any global economic work that goes on in that country. Look at the map of global cities in 2024. HICs and LICs all have a share of global cities.

▼ *Map of global cities in 2024*

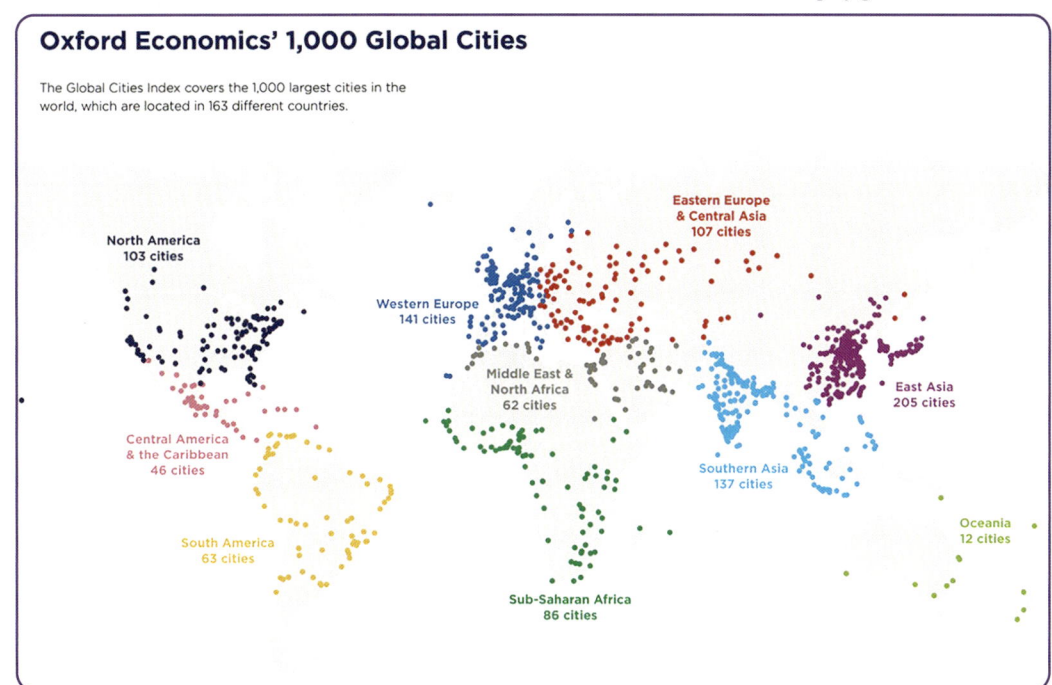

Why do some people say a global city is not a global city?

For a city to be truly global it should have access to wealth, infrastructure and economic stability, which should not be restricted to certain people or parts of that city.

When a global city does not share these factors across every person or part of that city, it is hard to think of it as truly global. Also, when a global city faces significant challenges, even if it has a large and stable economy, it will struggle to really call itself a global city. An example is Sydney in Australia. Some people might think Sydney is not yet a global city because its current infrastructure is unable to meet the business needs of the city. It also has a small population, and it lacks innovation in high-tech industries.

Fun fact

Technology has created connections between countries, which has rapidly driven globalisation.

▼ *Sydney, Australia*

Key terms

- **Economy:** *production of goods and services within a country.*
- **Infrastructure:** *physical structures that support the environment such as buildings and transport.*
- **Sustainable:** *using natural resources responsibly to support the current and future generations.*

1.4.4 Urbanisation in contrasting global cities

What causes global urbanisation?

Urbanisation is caused by migration, often from countryside (rural) to towns and cities. Urbanisation is expected to continue.

Cities become globally urbanised as a result of migration. This is a key driver where people move from rural to urban areas, often to cities that are more 'switched on'. These areas then become globally urbanised due to the influx of people in search of improved quality of life.

▼ *Causes of globalisation*

Fun fact

According to the World Bank (2024), global growth is expected to hold steady at 2.5% in 2025 and 2026.

How do cities deal with global urbanisation?

More than half the world now lives in urban areas that are dense in their structure and population. This poses serious challenges.

- **Planning** – designing open spaces, managing urban settlements so they do not sprawl out of control.
- **Infrastructure** – making sure money is invested into infrastructure, e.g. schools, roads.
- **Community** – local people keeping areas clean of litter, setting up neighbourhood watch schemes, having an input into decision making.
- **Developing the economy** – making sure there is investment into new industries.

Now try this ▼

 1 What is the minimum number of people needed to form a mega city?

  A 10 million **B** 5 million

How can global cities become more sustainable?

Making a city more sustainable involves several key factors:

- renewable energy
- green public spaces
- liveable urban centres
- sustainable transport systems
- strong city governance
- green building standards
- water conservation
- energy conservation
- waste management.

The 'stool of sustainability' is a metaphor used to describe the three core pillars of sustainability: **economic, social,** and **environmental**. These three elements are like the legs of a stool – if one leg is weaker or missing, the stool (and sustainability as a whole) becomes unstable or collapses.

A definition of a sustainable global city is:

'Improving the quality of life in a city, including ecological, cultural, political, institutional, social and economic components without leaving a burden on the future generations. A burden which is the result of a reduced natural capital and an excessive local debt.'

When global cities try to grow rapidly, there are consequences. For example, planners and developers need to consider how they manage the amount of transport on the roads and highways that can otherwise lead to congestion.

What specific cultural identities come from global urbanisation?

When an area becomes urbanised, it is not just the demographics (age, gender) of the population that are affected, but the cultural fabric too. For example, in London cultural identity has been developed in areas such as Brick Lane. A large variety of restaurants and fashion shops in this area have been influenced by immigration. Migration into and within global cities creates new urban identities, including monuments and buildings. Tokyo has been influenced by artists and creators who pride themselves on innovation and change, showing the modern-day culture of Tokyo. This, together with the need to build modern earthquake proof buildings has created a unique cultural centre.

▼ *The stool of sustainability*

▼ *Tokyo is famous for its cutting edge technology and skyscrapers*

Spotlight

An example of a sustainable global city is Melbourne.

- Melbourne is home to four million people
- Melbourne uses an urban forest strategy to plant more trees and provide habitat protection
- Currently 22% of Melbourne is covered in urban forests
- Older buildings are being retrofitted to improve their insulation.

▼ *Melbourne*

▼ *Brick Lane is famous for its colourful street art, culinary culture and vintage fashion*

Fun fact
The 85 richest people in the world have as much wealth as the 3.5 billion poorest.

Examples of two contrasting global cities
Global cities such as New York and Mumbai have very different challenges and successes, including the strength of their economies, levels of tourism and quality of life.

▼ *New York*

Spotlight
- New York's population is 50.7% smaller than Mumbai's.
- The unemployment rate in New York is 3.5% lower than in Mumbai.
- New York has $970 billion higher GDP than Mumbai.

▼ *Mumbai*

Now try this ▼

1. Assess the similarities and differences between two contrasting global cities you have studied.

	New York	Mumbai
Social challenge	Poverty and hardship are widespread. There is persistent racial inequality	Overcrowding and large squatter settlements of over 1 million people, e.g. Dharavi
Social success	Many different cultures and communities	High literacy rates and most people have access to water
Economic challenge	Between 2015 and 2019, nearly 60% of Black and Latino adults in New York City lived in poverty for at least one year	Lack of jobs in formal economy
Economic success	Large tourist hot spot. Largest metropolitan economy in the world	One of the top 10 trading centres in the world. 6% of the Indian GDP comes from Mumbai and 25% of all industrial production comes from Mumbai
Environmental challenge	High levels of pollution	Pollution, slums, disease, poor sanitation. 4,000 cases a day of diphtheria and typhoid
Environmental success	New York city has a streets master plan that focuses on sustainable transportation. Many offices have green energy efficient buildings	A 30-year road map to environmental sustainability

Political influence – **Westminster**

Economic hub and wealth creator – **London Stock Exchange**

▼ London

Communication infrastructure and connectivity – **Silicon Roundabout**

Strong transportation network – **London Underground**

Now try this ▼

1. To what extent is London a truly sustainable global city? Use the information provided and your own research in your answer.

Unit 1 recap

The global hydrological cycle
The global hydrological cycle is the continuous movement of water between the earth's land areas, oceans and atmosphere. It is sometimes referred to as the water cycle. It is a closed system.

Drainage basin systems
Drainage basin systems have various flows, stores, and movements of water. The key features are channels, floodplains, and tributaries, as well as processes that occur within it such as weathering, erosion, transportation, and deposition.

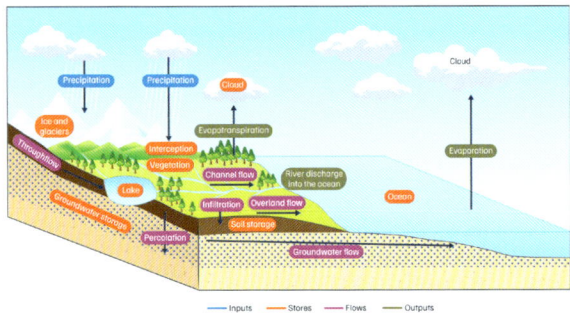

It is important to know what a store, transfer and flow is in this system.

River profiles – erosion and deposition landforms
River profiles are influenced by processes such as erosion and deposition. Erosional features such as gorges and waterfalls are created in upper and middle courses, and depositional features such as floodplains and meanders are created in middle and lower courses.

Coastline processes
Along the coastline there are processes including weathering, mass movement, erosion, transportation and deposition, which can be compared to processes in a drainage basin.

Wave type
Wave formation involves constructive and destructive waves, as well as the impact of fetch on wave characteristics. Seasonal changes in wave energy can lead to variations in beach profiles.

Migration
Migration refers to the movement of people from one place to another. It can be forced or voluntary, international or national, regular or irregular. People migrate to escape conflict or human rights violations, to seek economic opportunities or join family. Push and pull factors link to international economic migration. International migration affects both the source and host countries.

Impacts of migration
Migration plays a role in brain drain, community cohesion, remittances, multiculturalism, and the spread of culture.

Management of migration
Migration can be managed by a points-based system. The media can influence the public perception of migration.

Urbanisation
The concept of urbanisation includes its changing rates over time and across different locations. Urban land use patterns in cities have differences and similarities between countries and sectors such as CBD, fringe, informal settlements, inner city, and suburbs.

Global cities and megacities
Differentiate between global cities and megacities, using examples. Understand the criteria for classifying a city as global.

Revision round up

Rivers

1. Draw a systems diagram to show the hydrological cycle. Try to include:
   A colour-coded stores and flows
   B draw a circle around the drainage basin system within the hydrological cycle.
2. List reasons why the amount of water in a drainage basin can vary seasonally.
3. Draw a spider diagram like the one below to describe all the processes operating in a drainage basin.

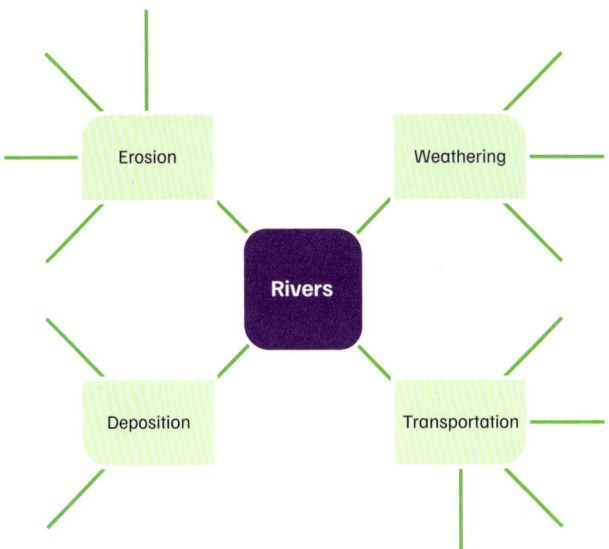

4. Create a flash card for each river landform with an annotated diagram of how it is formed.
5. List the different ways in which people use rivers. Describe the impacts of each use.
6. Make a revision card for a Welsh river that you have studied. Include the major landforms along the river and how people use or are impacted by the river.

Coasts

7. Draw a diagram to show the differences between constructive and destructive waves.
8. Create a flash card for each coastal landform. Include an annotated diagram of how each is formed.
9. Copy and complete the following table to illustrate the impacts of physical and human factors at the coast.

Physical factor	Resulting coastal change	Human factor	Resulting coastal change
Climate		Settlement	
Fetch		Industry	
Geology		Agriculture	
		Hard engineering	
		Soft engineering	

10. Create a fact file for an area of Welsh coastline that you have studied. Include landforms and physical/human factors of coastal change.

Migration

11. Copy and complete the table with definitions and examples of the different types of migration.

Type of migration	Definition	Example
Forced		
Voluntary		
International		
National		
Regular		
Irregular		

12. Copy and complete the following spider diagram to show the impacts of migration.

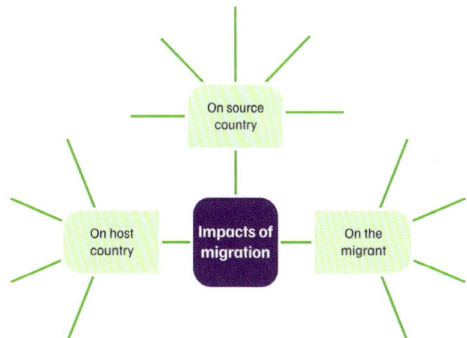

13. Create a flash card to highlight the positives and negatives of different strategies used to manage international migration.

Settlements

14. Describe the main types of land use that are found in urban areas.
15. Create three fact files – two for contrasting global cities and one for a megacity. For each city, include location, urban plan, why they are a global/megacity and the challenges that can be found in the city.
16. Make a list of sustainability issues in urban areas and management responses to these issues.

Unit 2
Developing Fieldwork Skills

Fieldwork allows researchers to study things that can't be replicated in a lab or classroom.

Introduction

During this unit you will learn the skills to carry out a fieldwork investigation in your local area. You will use the six-stage enquiry process model to plan an investigation, collect and analyse data, present evidence, draw conclusions and evaluate your outcomes.

Did you know! There is a huge list of careers you can choose from when you study Geography, from an urban planner to a climatologist... or even a basketball player! Michael Jordan has a degree in Geography!

The assessment:

This unit is a non-examined assessment and is worth 25% of the qualification. It has a total of 90 marks.

Assessment objectives

The assessment objectives assessed in Unit 2 are:

AO2 Apply knowledge and understanding of geographical terms, skills and concepts to different contexts.

AO3 Analyse, evaluate, or make judgements from a variety of sources, synthesising where appropriate.

AO4 Select, use and apply skills and techniques in practice used by geographers to support geographical enquiry.

Contents

In Unit 2 you will cover the following:

Chapter 2.1: Planning an enquiry..54
2.1.1 The six-stage enquiry process..54
2.1.2 Posing enquiry questions..56
2.1.3 Using maps to locate and plan the enquiry....................57
2.1.4 Risk and constraint considerations..................................59

Chapter 2.2: Collecting evidence..62
2.2.1 Selecting locations and sampling....................................62
2.2.2 Methods of collecting primary data................................66
2.2.3 Methods of collecting secondary data............................70

Chapter 2.3: Processing and presenting evidence..................72
2.3.1 Selecting and using appropriate quantitative and qualitative techniques..72
2.3.2 Selecting and using appropriate presentation methods for quantitative and qualitative data..................................73
2.3.3 Referencing secondary data sources..............................75

Chapter 2.4: Analysing and applying evidence.......................76
2.4.1 Selecting relevant data to answer the enquiry question......76
2.4.2 Identifying, analysing and interpreting trends and patterns 77

Chapter 2.5: Drawing conclusions..78
2.5.1 Drawing conclusions from fieldwork enquiries..............78

Chapter 2.6: Evaluating techniques..80
2.6.1 Evaluating each stage of the enquiry process................80
2.6.2 Identifying further areas of investigation/questions that could now be asked..81

By the time we're finished you will...

▶ be able to plan a fieldwork investigation

▶ be able to collect primary and secondary data

▶ be able to present and analyse data

▶ be able to draw conclusions and evaluate your investigation.

Chapter 2.1 Planning an enquiry

AO2 AO3 AO4

🔑 Key terms

- **Enquiry process:** an organised way of posing questions, gathering and processing data in order to find an answer.
- **Data:** information collected to help answer an investigation question.
- **Fieldwork investigation:** a process of collecting data about the environment, people or culture.

2.1.1 The six-stage enquiry process

During Unit 2 you will carry out fieldwork to look at 'real life' geography in your local area. You will be expected to answer questions/write up your findings on this **fieldwork investigation**.

When investigating the world around them, geographers use the six-stage **enquiry process** to structure their research and findings. It enables them to become actively engaged with the environment around them, and understand place and processes in more detail. It is important for you to understand the purpose of each stage, and how each supports future stages.

How are the enquiry stages connected?

The enquiry process requires you to make decisions at each stage. These decisions can have impacts on future enquiry stages. It is important to think about the implications of your decisions as these might influence the success or accuracy of the investigation.

- **Decisions made in planning:** these will impact every other stage of the enquiry process. Sampling method, sample size and enquiry question are all things that will greatly influence the outcomes of the investigation.
- **Collecting evidence:** if this is done incorrectly, it could lead to errors in **data** and results that do not reflect the reality of what was observed. Ensuring you know how to collect appropriate data, have a variety of data sources and are able to access secondary data are all important considerations. The data collected will form the basis for the remaining stages of the enquiry and it is vital that it is accurate.
- **Processing and presenting data:** after collecting the data, it needs to be processed and presented in a way that helps the reader understand patterns or trends. The type of statistical technique applied, or the graph/map chosen to display the data can influence the ease of seeing a pattern or alter the pattern itself.

```
Planning an enquiry
      ↓
Collecting evidence
      ↓
Processing and
presenting evidence
      ↓
Analysing and
applying evidence
      ↓
Drawing conclusions
      ↓
Evaluating techniques
      ↑_____|
```

◀ *Fieldwork investigating ecosystems*

✏️ Put into practice

Explain why your choice of sample size might have an influence on the outcomes of the enquiry process.

Evaluating techniques is at the end of the enquiry process, but it can have an influence on future investigations. Explain why.

How to select a topic for enquiry

Each year, the Welsh Joint Education Committee (WJEC) will provide two **geographical topics** (from: geographical flows, sustainability, change over time, mitigating risk, place and space, inequality, settlement and use of transects) within which fieldwork enquiries will need to be based.

Your centre will choose one topic for the academic year in which you will be assessed. However, within this topic you will be able to decide on your area of focus. All geographical enquiries should be individual and therefore they should be different (even if only slightly) from other learners in your class (you may work in small groups to design an enquiry and collect data, but after that all work must be individual). Try to choose an area of focus that you are interested in, something that you have always been curious about in your local environment. The possibilities are endless – the only restriction is the topic that your school has chosen. You can see some examples below:

Topic	Examples of enquiry focus
Use of transects	How discharge changes from source to mouth
	How land use changes across a city
	How vegetation changes across a sand dune system
Change over time	How a meander has changed over time
	Population change in a place
	Changing beach profile

▼ *Wrexham town centre*

Key terms

- **Geographical topic:** a theme through which geographers explore processes and place, etc.

Margaret Roberts

Margaret Roberts was a former president of the Geographical Association. She helped to adapt the six-stage enquiry process for use in geographical investigations.

Ace your revision

AO4: Select, use and apply skills and techniques in practice used by geographers to support geographical enquiry.

Most of your marks for Unit 2 will be based on AO4. Keep this in mind throughout your geographical enquiry. If you are not sure of a skill, then check with your teacher to ensure that you record, process or present your data correctly.

Put into practice

Think of as many focuses for your enquiry as you can for the following enquiry topics:
- inequality
- sustainability
- settlement.

Put into practice

When thinking about the theme of place, what areas could you study locally? (Cynefin)

55

Key terms

- **Enquiry question:** a question that is posed to be answered by a geographical investigation.
- **Hypothesis:** an idea or statement that is suggested so that it can be proved or disproved.
- **Predicted outcomes:** what you expect the findings to be.

Put into practice

The following enquiry questions/hypotheses are broad. Can you rewrite them to make them more specific?

1. Environmental quality varies from one area to another.
2. Does coastal erosion change along the coastline?
3. Migration has a positive impact on UK communities.

Brain break

For each of the following topics, list five different geographical themes in which you could carry out a fieldwork investigation:

- sustainability
- diversity
- mitigating risk
- change over time.

2.1.2 Posing enquiry questions

How to pose enquiry questions and understand their role

Deciding on **enquiry questions** is the first (and arguably most important) decision that you will make. It forms the basis on which the whole of your investigation will be focused. The role of the enquiry question is to provide a specific focus for the fieldwork investigation and provide a measure of how successful the enquiry is. It provides an aim and structure to the investigation.

There are different ways in which you could pose an enquiry question.

- Set a **hypothesis** to prove or disprove. This involves creating a statement, such as 'There is more erosion at point X compared to point Y on the Gower coastline'.
- Set an enquiry question to which your investigation will aim to find the answer to, for example, 'Is there more erosion at point X or point Y on the Ceredigion coastline?'

Plan, design and justify enquiry questions

Once you know the topic within which your enquiry focus is based, you need to start thinking about designing your enquiry question. Be careful not to make your enquiry question too broad. For example, if the topic that you are investigating is place and space, and your teacher has told you that this will be set in an urban environment, a broad enquiry question might be: 'How does the quality of the urban environment change?'

This is too vague and will make collecting data more difficult. Which urban environment? Where might the change be happening? It is better to make enquiry questions specific to the factor and location. A better enquiry question would be: 'How does the quality of the urban environment change in Cardiff city along a transect?'

In addition to the main enquiry question or hypothesis, some geographers choose to include sub-questions which break down the main question into smaller more specific ones. The answers contribute towards the main question. Two or three specific sub-questions are sufficient, and can help you identify what data you need to collect.

Geographical enquiry questions need to be justified. Is the enquiry question/hypothesis looking at a geographical concept? Is it a valid topic that can be measured and carried out in the timescale provided? Is it specific or broad? It is important to include a justification to show that the questions are a valid piece of geographical research.

Predicted outcomes

Predicted outcomes show the reader what you expect your findings to show, often in relation to geographical theories. They illustrate that you have a good level of geographical knowledge and understanding of the topic you are investigating. It doesn't matter if the actual outcomes are different, but predicting outcomes shows that you can apply your knowledge. The diagram below illustrates what typically happens along a river's course, but all models are theoretical and real geography is often 'messy'.

Examples of characteristics in the upper course:

- steeper land
- narrow valley floor
- narrower river channel
- angular bed load
- larger bed load
- smaller discharge.

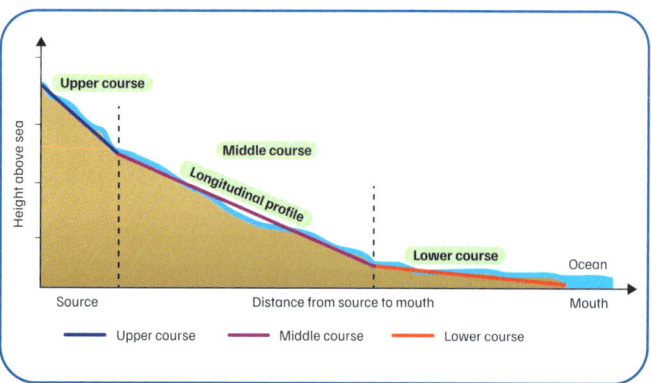

▲ Predicted changes along the long profile of a river

Examples of characteristics in the lower course:

- flatter land
- wide valley floor
- wider river channel
- more rounded bed load
- smaller bed load
- larger discharge.

2.1.3 Using maps to locate and plan the enquiry

When planning your geographical enquiry, it is important to consider and use relevant information sources so that it is clear to the reader what the locational context of your investigation is. One way this can be done is by using **Ordnance Survey (OS) maps**. These maps provide accurate and detailed information for the whole of the UK and therefore can provide vital information about your study area.

When using OS maps, it is important to include the following information:

- title
- key
- scale
- north arrow.

In fieldwork, OS maps can be used to locate the sites of data collection. Apart from enabling the reader to know exactly where the data was collected (so that it could be replicated in the future if necessary), it also allows you to observe key influencing features around the area, which you might not have noticed when on site.

Key terms

- **Four-figure grid reference:** *four numbers that are used to locate a grid square on a map.*
- **Ordnance Survey (OS) map:** *a detailed map which is produced by the British government's map making organisation.*
- **Six-figure grid reference:** *six numbers that indicate exactly where in a grid square something is located on a map.*

▼ *Ordnance Survey map of data collection sites on the river*

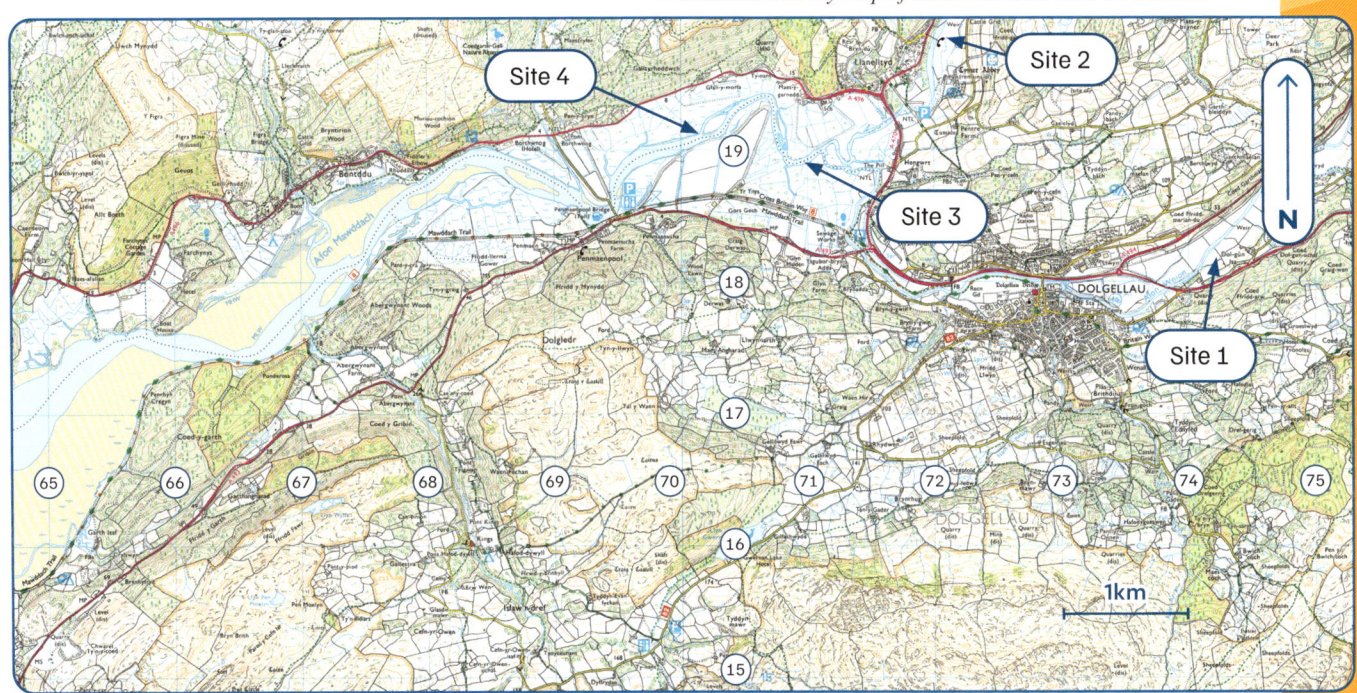

Labels versus annotation

When using OS maps to plan your enquiry, you could add labels or annotations to the map. Labels are shorter, more concise and generally highlight a feature or point of interest. Annotations add a little explanation or detail about the feature.

Put into practice

Suggest why it is important to include a title, key, scale and north arrow when using maps.

Put into practice

- Give the **four-figure grid reference** for site 1 and site 2.
- Give the **six-figure grid reference** for site 3 and site 4.
- Create a label that could be added to the map pointing to the forested area at Tyn-Y-Graig in grid square 6717.
- Create an annotation that could be added to the map pointing to the town of Dogellau in grid square 7317.

Using relevant geographical information systems (GIS) data

Key terms

- **Geographical Information Systems (GIS):** *a computer system that analyses, edits and displays geographical data.*

It is also helpful to look at **Geographical Information Systems (GIS)** data to help plan a geographical investigation. GIS combines data (e.g. air temperature, population figures) with maps to see spatial distributions of 'layers' of data. It allows you to 'switch' on or off different data layers depending on what you need to see.

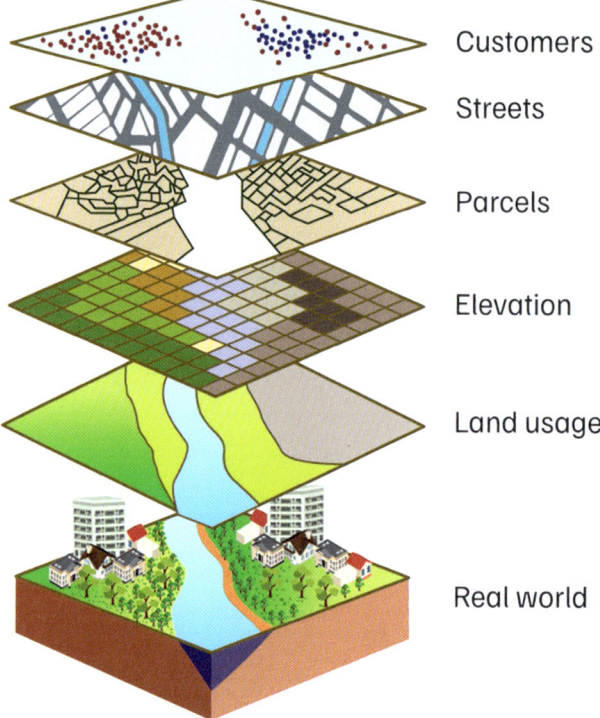

Ace your revision

Bing.com/maps allows you to view, cut and paste Ordnance Survey maps.

Spotlight

Many governments use GIS data in their planning, including natural disaster responses, road systems, building designs and the management of waste systems.

GIS can help in the planning of investigations as it can indicate where there might be differences within an area which could be worthy of investigation. For example, looking at temperature data across a city would indicate where urban heat islands might be found. When interpreting a GIS image it is important to know what 'layers' are represented in the image. Try adding or removing different features to see if it increases your understanding of the area. When using GIS it is important to look for spatial patterns and relationships between the different layers, e.g. is there a correlation between crime levels and population density?

William Roy

Born in 1726, William Roy was a young engineer who was given the job of drawing a small-scale military survey map of Scotland. It was his work which led to the establishment of the Ordnance Survey in 1791.

Put into practice

Think about the topic that your geographical investigation will be based on. Research relevant GIS data which will provide you with information about possible data collection sites.

Put into practice

Three common types of GIS images are natural colour, panchromatic and colour infrared (CIR). Find out the advantages of each.

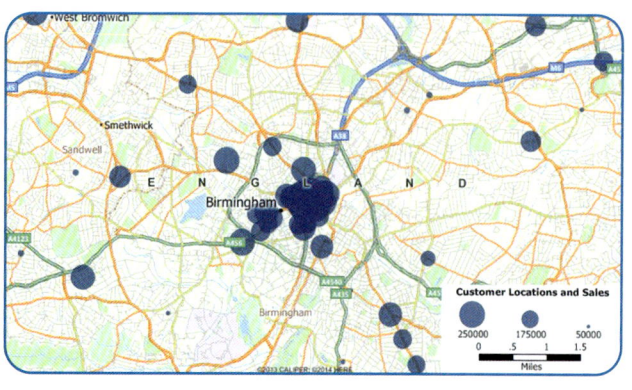

◂ *GIS map using proportional circles to show customer locations*

2.1.4 Risk and constraint considerations

When carrying out observations and data collection, it is important to think about the risk and constraint considerations in terms of you (the geographer), the public and the environment.

> **Key terms**
> - **Level of risk:** *how likely it is that the risk will occur.*
> - **Risk assessment:** *a way of highlighting potential hazards and reducing risk.*

Risk considerations

When geographers collect their primary data, they often go into environments that they are not familiar with. To keep themselves safe and to keep the environment from being affected, it is important to carry out a **risk assessment** so that the **level of risk** is reduced. To assess the level of risk you can use a simple grading system such as:

- Low = unlikely to happen/little impact to identified people.
- Medium = possible/moderate impact to identified people.
- High = likely to happen/significant impact to identified people.

Below is an example of a risk assessment.

Example of a simplified risk assessment for urban fieldwork

Activity being carried out _____

Date of activity _____

Location _____

Risk to health and safety	People at risk	Level of risk probability/significance	Measures to reduce risk level
Road traffic accident while travelling to location	Driver, students and public	Medium	Ensure the driver is qualified to drive the vehicle and that they are not distracted by passengers during the journey.
Danger from traffic while collecting data	Students and the public	Medium	Remind students about road safety; pick data collection locations that do not involve crossing busy roads.
Students getting lost in an unfamiliar place	Students	High	All students to be given a map with times and locations of meeting points. Students to be given an emergency number to call if they are lost. Students to always be in a group of at least 2 people.
Altercations between students and the public	Students and the public	Low	Remind students to always be polite and that members of the public do not need to answer questions if they do not wish to.
Damage to the environment – litter, graffiti	Community that lives there	Low	Remind students that they are to leave the environment as they found it and dispose of all litter appropriately.

Ace your revision
Include a risk assessment of your primary data collection procedures in your enquiry write up.

 Spotlight
Some centres use a risk matrix to help assess the level of risk for their fieldwork. See page 115.

Put into practice
Remember to include risks to yourself and risks to the public/environment. Include who is at risk, the level of risk and how to reduce the risk.

Key terms

- **Diversity:** *people from a range of social, cultural and economic backgrounds.*
- **Ethical considerations:** *a set of principles that are used to guide research/data collection activities.*
- **Human rights:** *basic rights and freedoms that belong to everyone.*
- **Sympathetic geographer:** *a geographer that considers members of the public and the environment when they are carrying out data collection.*

Put into practice

Create a list of ethical considerations when investigating migration into an area. Why must each of these be considered?

Ace your revision

When designing a questionnaire to investigate deprivation, you must be sensitive to people's personal circumstances. For example, avoid asking questions about a person's annual salary as this could cause offence. Instead, ask questions, such as 'Does your level of disposable income allow you to access social amenities?'

Malala Yousafzai

Born in 1990 in Pakistan, Malala Yousafzai is a **human rights** activist for female education. In 2012, she was shot by Taliban gunmen. She survived the shooting, which made her one of the world's most famous teenagers and greatly highlighted the discrimination against women and education in many countries.

How we can be sympathetic geographers

When geographers collect data, it is important that they leave the study site unchanged – their visit should have no impact. Being a **sympathetic geographer** will limit any changes to the environment, public, local businesses, etc.

To be sympathetic geographers, it is vital that **ethical considerations**, human rights and **diversity** are taken into account. If you are designing questions to ask the public, the questions must be sensitive to diversity, and you must ensure none of the questions could cause offence. For the data to be a true sample you must also ensure that the full diversity of the community is reflected in the population you survey.

Constraint considerations

It is also important to recognise what is practical to achieve when collecting data. There may be things that you would 'like' to achieve, but this does not mean that it is practical to do so. There are key factors that should be considered.

- **Accessibility** – is it safe to go to the identified site? For example, if surveying a river, is it safe to enter the water at the desired location, or is the river too deep or fast flowing or the bank too unstable or inaccessible? Is the site on private land? Do you need to gain permission from the landowner?
- **Availability of secondary data** – secondary data can be a vital part of geographical research in terms of comparing data over time or reinforcing the findings from primary data. However, if your key question/hypothesis relates to a change over time, it is important to find out what secondary data is available if you are going to use it as a comparison. For example, using a previous year group's data to look at change in footfall in an urban area.
- **Availability of equipment** – some data requires specialist geographical equipment, e.g. soil temperature probe, flowmeter, clinometer, etc. When planning your enquiry, it is important to check what equipment your school has available.
- **Time** – the time available to collect fieldwork data is often limited and needs to be considered when designing the data collection methods.
- **Travel** – the method of travel and time it takes is often one of the biggest constraints in planning geographical fieldwork. If you are based near the location, then travel will not impact the enquiry as much. If you are travelling by public transport, is it practical to take bulky fieldwork equipment with you?

Ace your revision

When including your constraint considerations in your report, make sure they are not generic, e.g. we didn't have time. Be specific.

Spotlight

Every time a teacher takes learners off-site, a risk assessment needs to be completed.

Now try this

Fieldwork plan

Topic of enquiry _____

Key question _____
_____

Sub-question (s) _____
_____
_____

Predicted outcomes _____
_____
_____

Wider geographical theories that relate to the topic	OS map locations of possible study sites
	GIS that are relevant to the study area

Factors to be considered in the risk assessment:
_____
_____
_____
_____

Chapter 2.2 Collecting evidence

AO2 AO3 AO4

🗝 Key terms

- **Conclusions:** *summary of your findings.*
- **Target population:** *target audience/group of people.*
- **Representative:** *showing what you intend to collect.*

**your revision**

Using sub-questions can help support your enquiry. Aim to use a maximum of three sub-questions.

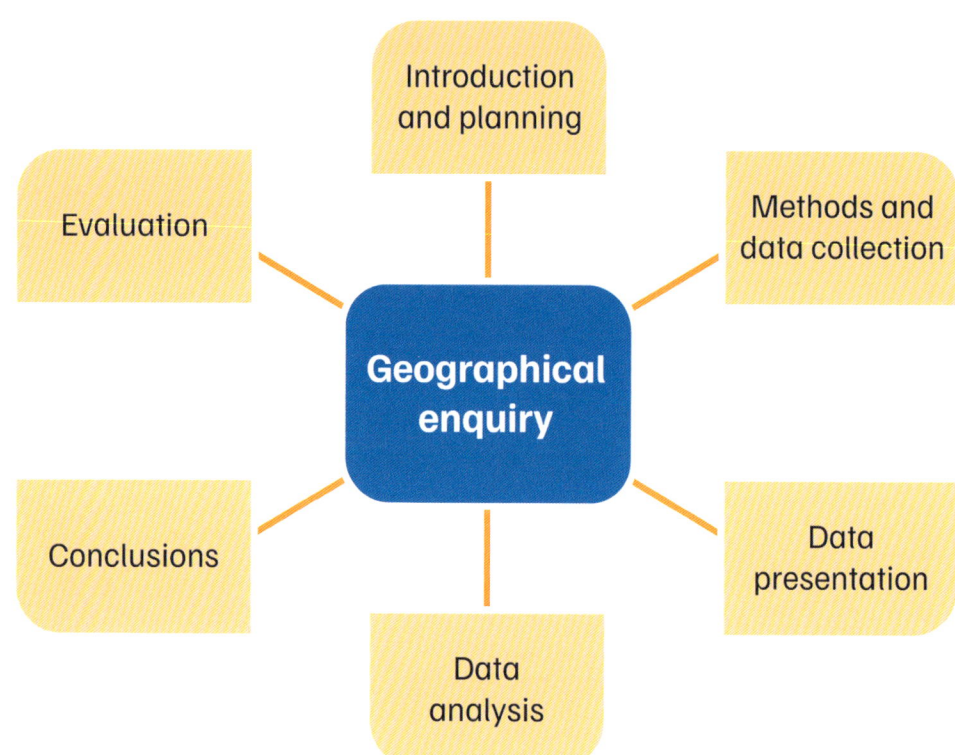

2.2.1 Selecting locations and sampling

Choosing the right location for your data collection is important to how successful your data collection will be, and how well you will be able to answer your hypothesis/enquiry question. There are several ways you can choose the best location, including GIS, OS maps or smart phone apps such as Google Maps.

Understand the importance of choosing data collection locations

Make sure you choose sites that:

1. are suitably linked to your hypothesis/enquiry question
2. are safe to access
3. allow you time to get there and back to your school
4. give you the opportunity to complete your data collection
5. allow you to use your existing resources/equipment within that area
6. provide facilities such as toilets or food.

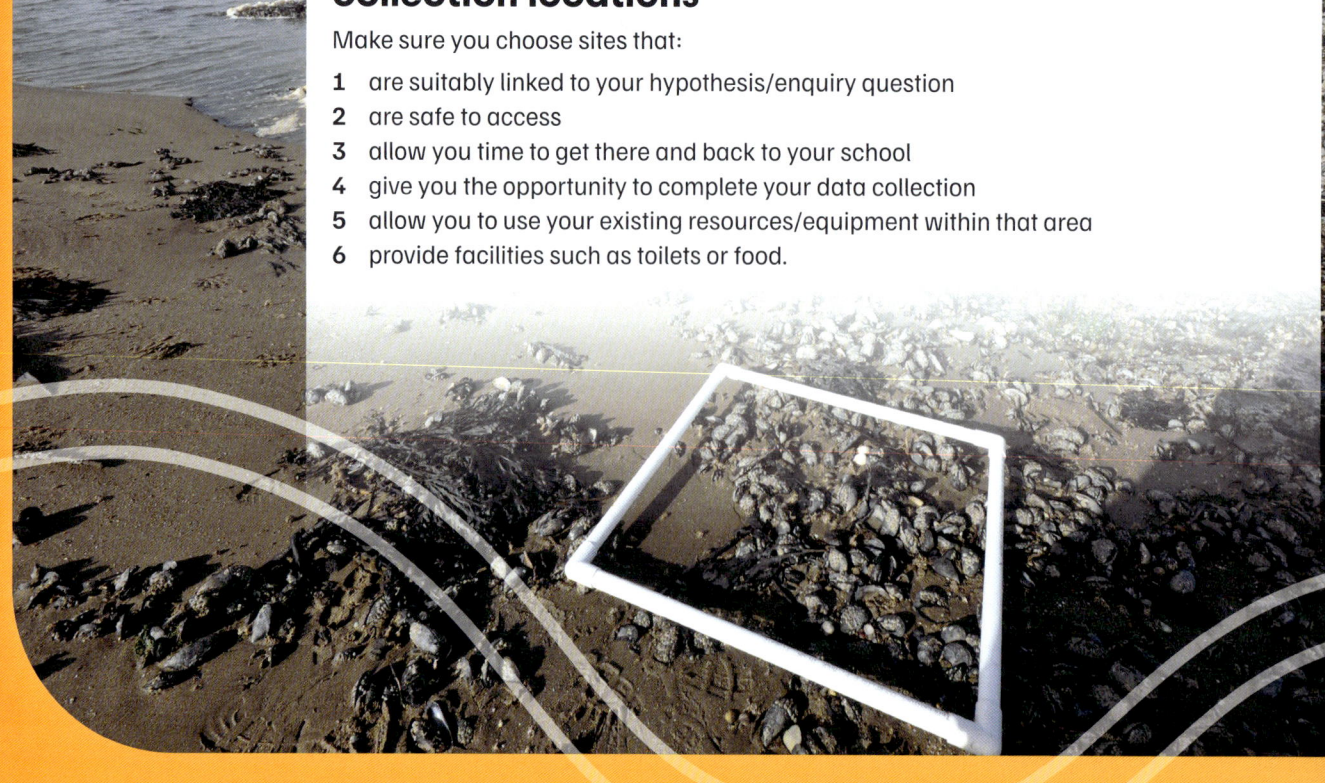

Understand the importance of obtaining representative and inclusive samples

It is important that any data collected is **representative** of the **target population** or area as part of the study, so that decisions and **conclusions** are well informed and accurate. Having a good amount of data can also allow you to complete some statistical work to see if your hypothesis is correct.

It is important to obtain a representative and inclusive sample to enable you to:

- gain a greater insight into the target group population, e.g. age, gender, ethnicity
- ensure an appropriate method for sampling is used, e.g. systematic, opportunistic
- create smaller sub-groups within the data that can be further examined.

▼ *Importance of obtaining a representative and inclusive sample*

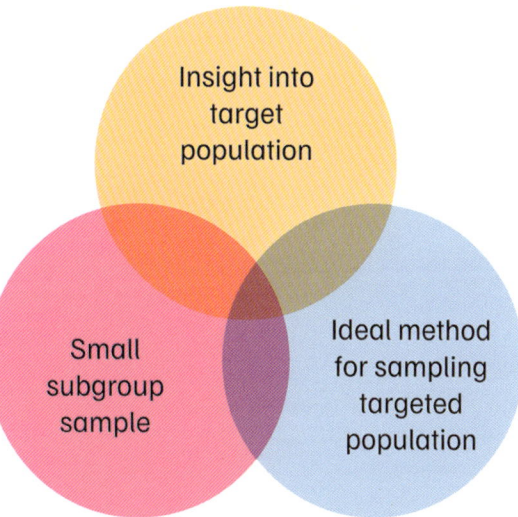

Spotlight

The target population or audience in Geography is the group or type of people your study is trying to find out about. For example, in an investigation looking at how elderly people feel about crime in their area, the target audience is elderly people.

Understand the process of sampling

Why sample?

There simply isn't time to collect every piece of data in every square metre of land, therefore we need to sample the areas we visit.

▼ *What factors affect sample size?*

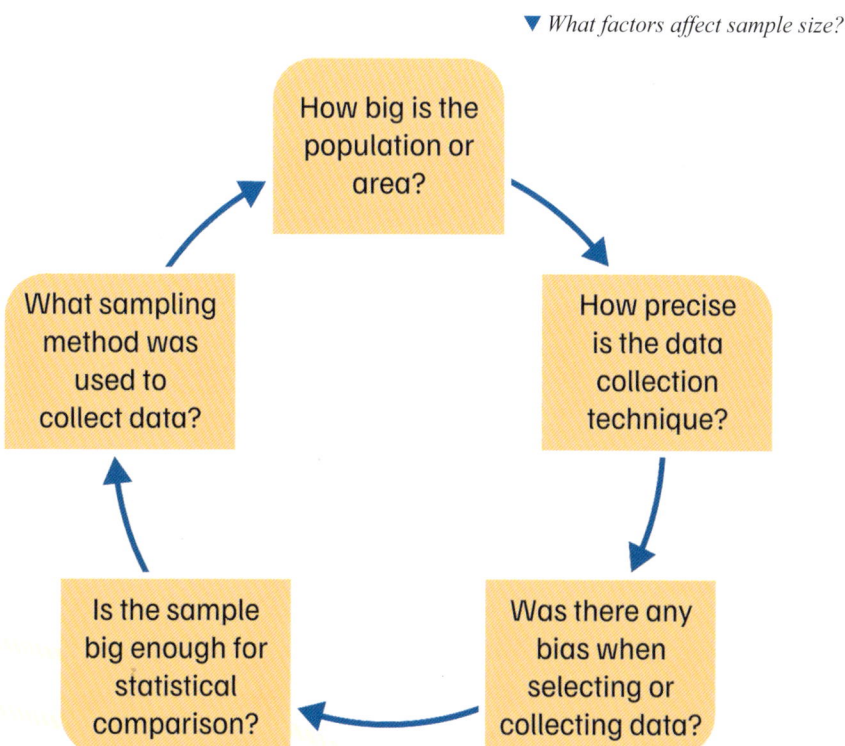

Key terms

- **Bias:** *influence that is unfair on the results.*
- **Random sampling:** *choosing information with no set pattern.*

Spotlight

An example of random sampling in Geography would be standing on a street and asking passers by a questionnaire.

Choose and justify data collection sites within a given area, sample size, sampling method

Sample size:

In Geography, the sample size refers to the number of times an observation is carried out. Having a sample size that is too small can lead to anomalies and make it difficult to identify patterns or trends. An anomaly is a result that is unexpected.

Sample method:

There are a few different ways of collecting data.

- *Random sampling*

Choosing a person to answer your questionnaire by chance (at random). Another example is choosing a pebble to measure roundness by randomly picking up pebbles along the transect of the beach with no set method.

Advantages

- Useful when investigating large sample populations.
- It avoids **bias** as no particular person is targeted.

Disadvantages

- It does not represent the overall area as only some data is sampled randomly.
- Some sites or social groups may not be accessible to the person collecting data so cannot be chosen at random and are therefore actively avoided.

- *Systematic sampling*

Collecting data in an ordered way with a system, e.g. collecting data every 5 m or every 5th person.

Advantages

- This allows you to repeat your method to gain further data and shows a consistent approach.
- Repeatable by any other group.
- Can be used to look for trends between data and location along a transect.

Disadvantages

- Some sites may not have a chance to be sampled and are therefore not included.
- You can sample too many times at one site, which may not always be helpful if you are collecting data for data sake. For example, there would be no need to collect every pebble on a beach to study what type of beach it is.

- *Stratified sampling*

Dividing sampling into sub-groups, for example dividing people into different age categories.

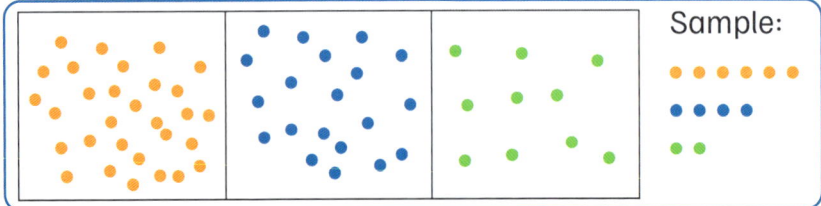

Advantages

- Can be used as a method for collecting data alongside other sampling methods.
- Can make comparisons between data sets.

Disadvantages

- Can be time consuming as you must categorise your findings, and it is not always possible to put findings into specific categories.
- If you are sampling a population, you must make sure you have up-to-date data and that the available population fits your chosen categories.

- **Opportunistic sampling** (sometimes called emergent sampling)

Used when sampling opportunities are limited, so you have to take the opportunities that are available. For example, when studying longshore drift with high tide, there is a limited choice of areas that can be measured.

Advantages
- Flexible design to collect data.
- Quick to complete.
- Useful where opportunities to gather data are limited and you might have to take data from the small environment or population you have access to.

Disadvantages
- The sample might be biased as it doesn't represent the entire target population.
- Difficult to repeat this method for future fieldwork.
- Possible volunteer bias or self-selection bias. This means that people select themselves to take part rather than being selected at random or systematically.

> **Key terms**
> - **Opportunistic sampling:** taking the opportunities to collect data when sampling opportunities are limited.

Choosing the right data collection site within your geographical location

There are several things you need to think about when you decide on sites to sample within your geographical location for your data collection.

- Does your chosen geographical location have your target population available? For example, if you are looking at the impact of students on an area, have you visited an area occupied by students?
- Is it safe to collect data from different sites in the geographical location? If you choose a beach location, can you access sites along the transect safely?
- Can you access the sites at your chosen geographical location?
- Is the geographical location close enough for you to get to and back in a suitable time?
- Is the geographical location relevant to your hypothesis/investigation question?

Choosing sample size

- It is important to consider finding a balance between accuracy and how feasible collecting the sample data is.
- Ensure enough data is collected for any statistical calculations, e.g. mean, median, mode, range, percentages.

Look at the image of Swansea's Oystermouth Road. If investigating a change over time, consider having a sample large enough for a clone town survey or beach transect with variation in rock type, so that the area is represented well.

> **Put into practice**
> Explain the reasons for your chosen data collection sites.

> **Put into practice**
> Using this image of Swansea's Oystermouth Road, design a data collection method to investigate land use change along the transect of the road, or a beach profile study of Swansea Bay.

Footpath alongside beach to safely carry out a transect study of changes before and after the regeneration looking at building use.

Car park for safe drop-offs

Beach transect to look at coastal processes

◀ *Fieldwork location for regeneration in Swansea along the waterfont area*

Key terms

- **Bi-polar survey:** environmental quality survey measuring on a scale of positive versus negative, e.g. pollution, graffiti, vegetation.
- **Primary data:** information collected first hand by you.

2.2.2 Methods of collecting primary data

Primary data is a very important part of geography fieldwork. It is collected first hand and for the first time so a hypothesis or question can be answered.

Design primary data collection sheets

Primary data collection sheets are used for collecting information to solve a specific problem or question. The data is collected first hand and not by other people.

▼ *Tips for designing your primary data collection method*

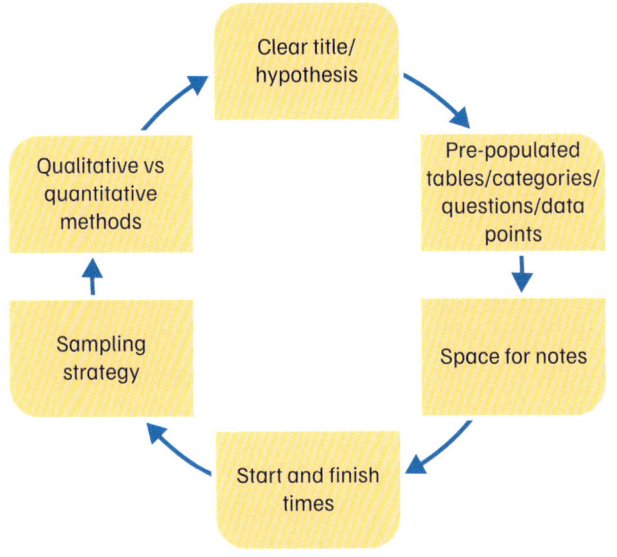

Ace your revision

Make sure you give specific reference to your own investigation and what you did during the data collection stage.

Example of primary data collection tool – environmental quality survey (EQS)

These are sometimes called **bi-polar surveys** because they have two scales of measurement.

Plus and minus scale indicates levels of environmental experience. Neutral value is important if the responder is indifferent between the two experiences.

Negative experience	-3	-2	-1	0	+1	+2	+3	Positive experience
Noisy								Quiet
Built environment is poorly maintained								Built environment is well maintained
Pavements and roads are poorly maintained								Pavements and roads are well maintained
Fumes/unpleasant smells								No fumes/unpleasant smells
Ugly views								Picturesque views
Litter evident								No litter
Graffiti and vandalism evident								No graffiti or vandalism
Dog fouling evident								No dog fouling
Street furniture overcrowds the area								Street furniture is not intrusive
Flowerbeds and trees are absent								Flowerbeds and trees are present
							TOTAL SCORE	

Number of categories should not be exhaustive to ensure it is specific to the enquiry and to keep the responder engaged.

The descriptions should be the opposite of each other to enable the responder to compare their views.

Total score allows for comparison between different locations.

Select and use fieldwork equipment to gain accurate and reliable results

There are some key things you need to think about when selecting fieldwork equipment to get the best results.

- Safety – do you know how to use the equipment in order to reduce harm?
- Basic equipment – what do you already have in school that you can use quickly and without additional cost? There may be equipment in your science department or a neighbouring school.
- Have you tested out your existing equipment?

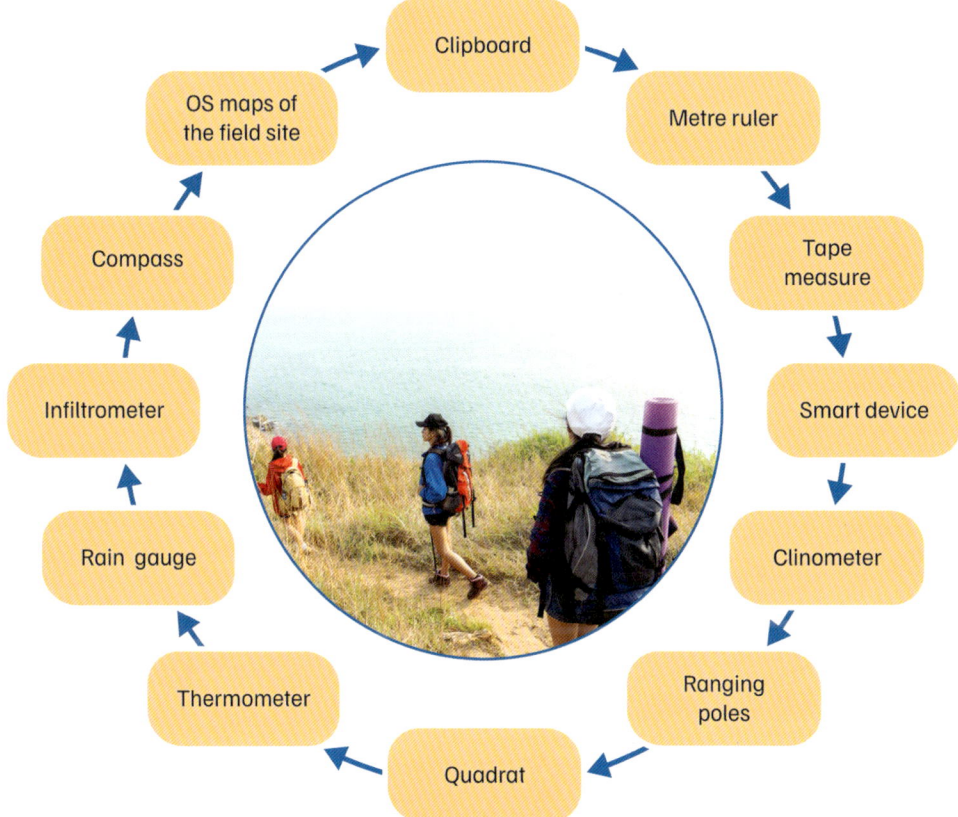

Clipboard → Metre ruler → Tape measure → Smart device → Clinometer → Ranging poles → Quadrat → Thermometer → Rain gauge → Infiltrometer → Compass → OS maps of the field site → Clipboard

Spotlight

Dos and don'ts of fieldwork

- Do a pilot study to check the area before you visit on the actual day.
- Check the equipment works and you have spare batteries.
- Practice using the equipment if possible around the school grounds so you know how to use it.
- Check the unit of measurement is set the same across each piece of equipment.

Put into practice

Copy and complete the following table to illustrate why you are using your selected equipment.

What are you measuring?	Why are you measuring this?	How are you going to measure this (equipment)?	Do you have this equipment in school?	Where are you using this equipment?	Why is this equipment suitable?
Windspeed	To compare changes between locations	With a digital anemometer	Yes	At 5 sites around the school	It will give an accurate reading in m/s

Key terms

- **Census:** *a periodic government count of key data, e.g. income of a household.*
- **RICEPOTS:** *residential, industrial, commercial, entertainment, public building, open space, transport, services.*
- **Quantitative data:** *numerical based information. It is thought to be more factual as it can be counted and measured. This type of data is objective and less descriptive than qualitative information.*

Equipment

Choosing the right equipment is very important to provide reliable data results. The Royal Geographical Association has some useful advice on equipment you will need for your fieldwork.

Select and use quantitative data collection techniques

Quantitative data involves the use of numerical data. Collecting this information can be useful when converting it into graphs for analysis. Quantitative data includes the following.

- Questionnaires
- Tally charts
- Traffic counts e.g. cars or pedestrians
- Environmental quality surveys
- Office for National Statistics (ONS) census data
- Velocity and discharge data (rivers)
- Temperature
- Wind speed
- Land use survey (GOAD map)
- **RICEPOTS** survey (land use categorising).

Code	Types of land use	Further information
R	Residential	Flat, terraced house, semi-detached house, bungalow, detached house
I	Industrial	Light manufacturing, heavy industry, chemical, extraction/mining
C	Commercial	Food, take-away, personal services, department stores, homeware and furniture, garage, market, specialist shop, office, vacant
E	Entertainment	Hotel, sports centre, gym, theatre, cinema, bar, restaurant, café
P	Public building	Education, library, hospital, place of worship, police station, ambulance station, fire station, welfare
O	Open space	Farmland, park, cemetery, unused land, derelict, sports field
T	Transport	Bus station, taxi rank, car park, railway station
S	Services	Financial, business, medical, estate agents, dental

Spotlight

Make sure you check your equipment before you leave school. For example, do the batteries work in the measuring devices?

Check all the devices are set to the same unit of measurement for reliability.

 Did you know

A compass diagram helps to show variations in different factors that affect perception of place.

Put into practice

This is a compass diagram for collecting and displaying data. Using a scale of 1–7 (7 being the best score), plot your findings from your investigation onto the compass diagram wheel.

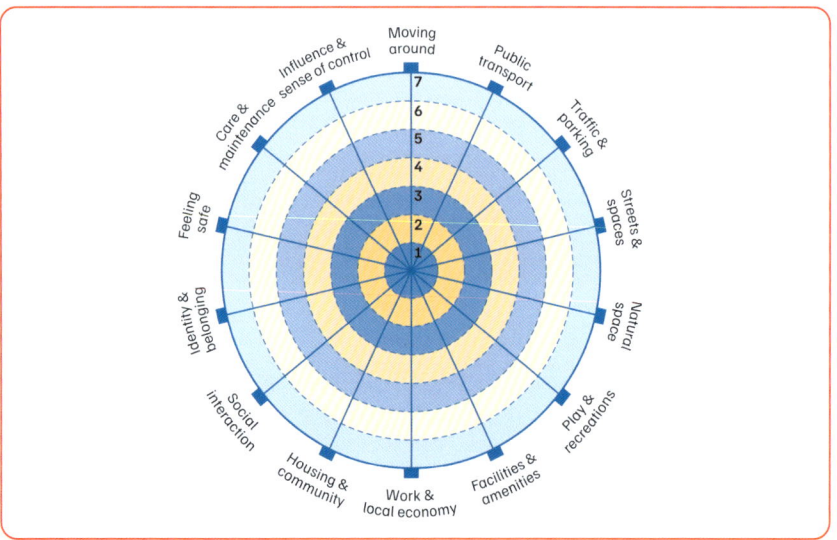

Did you know

GOAD maps were invented by Charles Goad to show different types of buildings and their uses. The maps were originally developed for fire insurance companies to assess fire risks.

Select and use qualitative data collection techniques

There are a range of **qualitative data** collection methods you can use in your geography fieldwork which look at human behaviour or our **perception** of something.

- Interviews
- Focus groups
- Observation studies
- Coding documents and paperwork
- Surveys e.g. Likert survey, which uses a scale to measure people's opinions with options such as 'strongly disagree', 'disagree', 'neither agree nor disagree', etc.
- Word cloud/wordle
- Sketch maps
- Photographs
- Perception studies

> **Key terms**
>
> - **Perception:** *opinion of something.*
> - **Qualitative data:** *non-numerical, thoughts, feelings, opinions, descriptive.*

▲ *Example of a wordle or word cloud*

Justify the choice of the data collection methods used

When deciding on your data collection methods you need to think about:

1. the sampling method you will use to collect your data, e.g. random sampling or systematic sampling
2. the primary and secondary data you should collect and how it will help you answer your enquiry sub-questions
3. the type of data: qualitative or quantitative
4. the equipment you need to collect the data
5. any factors that could stop you collecting data.

> **Put into practice**
>
> To what extent has the regeneration of Cardiff Bay made it a great place to work?

Example of qualitative data collection tools

This wheel is an example of a data collection tool for human geography-based investigations. You can tick when you see evidence of each factor that represents a place; the more ticks in each category, the stronger the evidence for that feature.

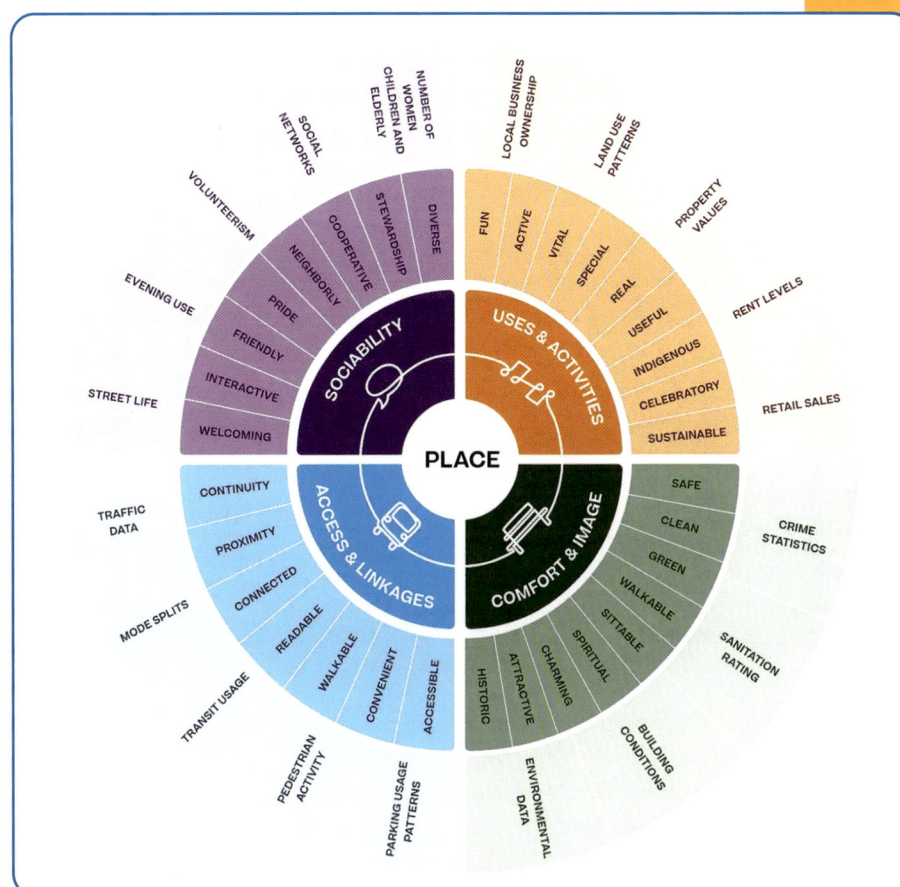

Key terms

- **Secondary data:** *information you have gathered from another source.*

2.2.3 Methods of collecting secondary data

In Geography it is important to have a range of data from different sources so you can justify your findings and produce an outcome that is valid (meaningful) against your hypothesis/enquiry question.

Find, select and use relevant secondary data

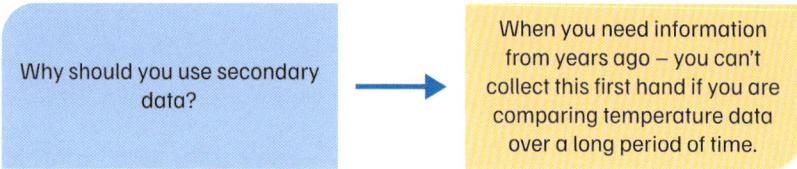

Why should you use secondary data? → When you need information from years ago – you can't collect this first hand if you are comparing temperature data over a long period of time.

When using **secondary data**, it is really important to think about these key factors if you want the most valid outcome to your investigation:

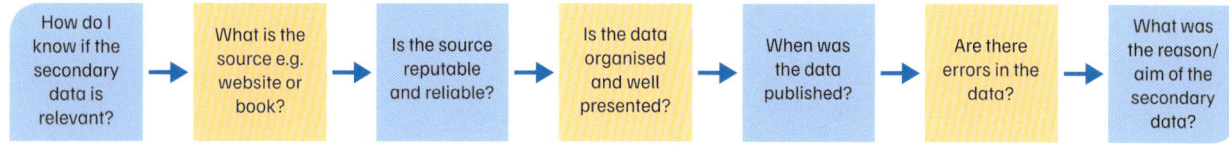

How do I know if the secondary data is relevant? → What is the source e.g. website or book? → Is the source reputable and reliable? → Is the data organised and well presented? → When was the data published? → Are there errors in the data? → What was the reason/aim of the secondary data?

Spotlight

Secondary data is useful if gathering primary data is challenging. For example, if you need climatic data from 10 years ago.

You should make sure the secondary data you use adds value to your investigation. Use these thought bubbles to help you evaluate your secondary data.

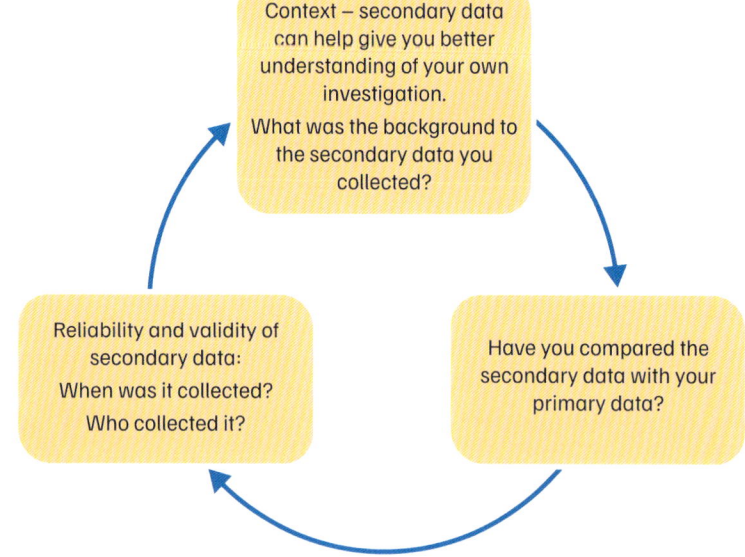

- Context – secondary data can help give you better understanding of your own investigation. What was the background to the secondary data you collected?
- Have you compared the secondary data with your primary data?
- Reliability and validity of secondary data: When was it collected? Who collected it?

Where can you find good secondary data?

You can find secondary data in the following places:

- maps
- government reports
- textbooks
- peer data
- census data
- newspaper articles
- house price data
- ArcGIS (interactive online digital mapping software)
- old photographs
- crime data, e.g. Police UK database
- river data from different years, e.g. Natural Resource Wales (NRW)
- GOAD maps, which show land use and buildings, available from the local council planning department.

Advantages of secondary data	Disadvantages of secondary data
Less time consuming than collecting data by hand	Difficult to avoid bias as you don't know how the data was collected
Good to show comparisons with your own data	Could be out of date
Shows change over time	May not cover the exact area you visited
Sources can be reliable, e.g. government	May not be completely relevant to your study, e.g. if the sampling method was different to yours

What is validity?

To make sure your data is valid, you must ensure it comes from a reputable source. **Validity** refers to how well your data helps you to answer your hypothesis and reach a trustworthy conclusion.

What is reliability?

Reliability refers to how consistent your results and conclusions are.

Secondary data can be unreliable if you are unsure of the source (where it came from) or it is out-dated and not relevant anymore. You can use the questions below to decide if your data or source is reliable.

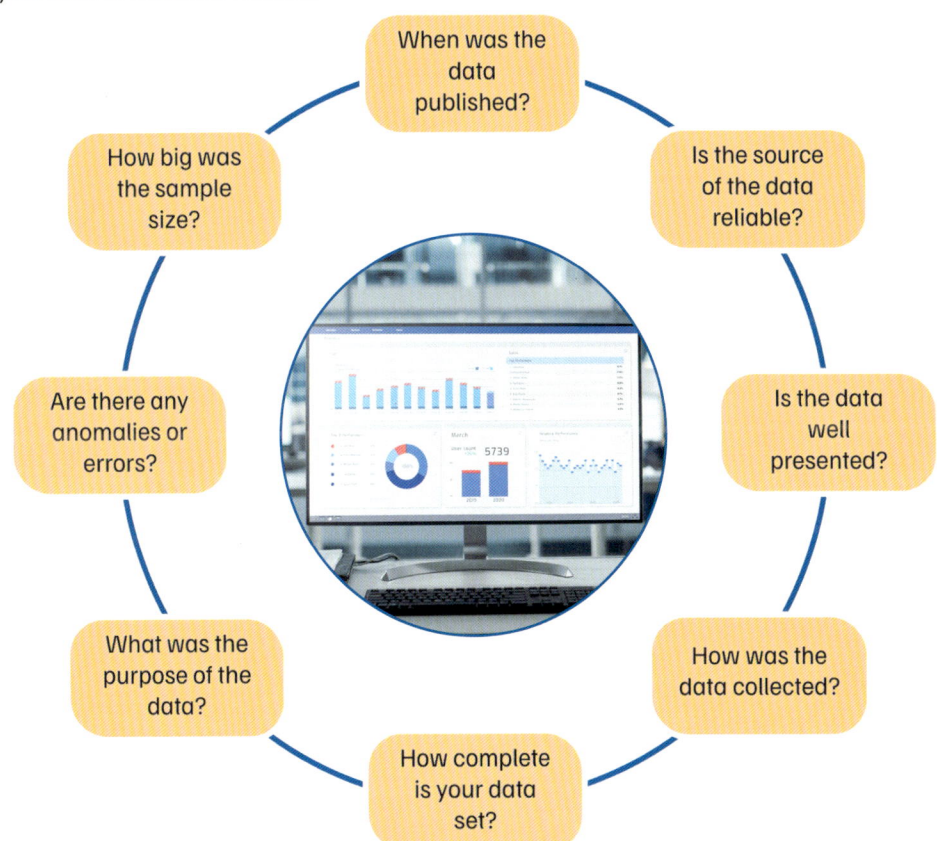

How to improve reliability in your investigation

- Repeat the data collection at a different time as the environment can change with the seasons. Be sure to stick to the same methods and points of data collection.
- Collect other types of data as this could make your conclusions more valid.
- Visit a different site with the same objective, e.g. sand dune formation in Merthyr Mawr (Ogmore) and Oxwich, Gower.
- Collect data from more sites in the same area, e.g. more transects when examining types of buildings on a street near a regenerated area, or more sand dune measurements.

Key terms
- **Reliability:** *how consistently sound something is.*
- **Validity:** *how factually sound something is.*

Ace your revision
Remember to reference where you got your secondary data from, so it doesn't look like primary data.

Fiona Sheriff
Fiona is an author of *100 Ideas for Secondary Teachers: Geography Fieldwork* and an award-winning Geography teacher.

Put into practice
Think about your own secondary data for your enquiry. Where did you get it from? How do you know it is valid? What date was it written? Who wrote it?

Chapter 2.3 | Processing and presenting evidence

AO2 AO3 AO4

🔑 Key terms

- **Continuous data:** *data that can take any value, it cannot be grouped.*
- **Discrete data:** *information that can be grouped into distinct groups/categories. It is also referred to as discontinuous data.*
- **Scale:** *the ratio between the distance measured on a map and the distance measured on the earth's surface.*

Spotlight

The satnav in a car is constantly making scale calculations to provide a visual map of the area and the distance left to travel.

Put into practice

For the following set of data, calculate the mean, median, mode and range.

56, 27, 38, 12, 19, 29, 27, 34, 43, 19, 27, 30

Give one type of data set where it might be helpful to apply the following statistical techniques:

- interquartile range
- percentage increase/decrease
- ratios/proportions.

2.3.1 Selecting and using appropriate quantitative and qualitative techniques

Once primary and secondary data have been collected, it is important to process and present data in a way that helps to see patterns or trends. There are many different ways of processing primary data. Some methods can be applied to most data while others are specific to the type of data collected.

- **Distance on maps** – on every map there will be a **scale**. Simply measure the distance from the two points on the map and apply this to the scale. For example, if using a 1:25,000 OS map and the distance you have measured is 8 cm, the 'real world' distance would be 8 × 25,000 = 200,000 cm or 2,000 m

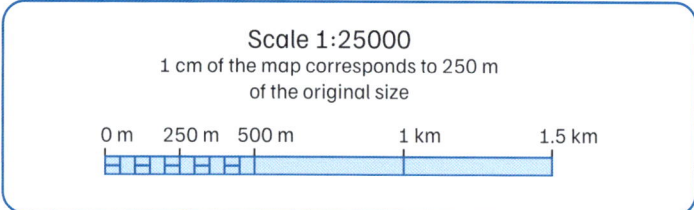

- **Median, mean, range and mode** – These are common statistical techniques that can be applied to most sets of data.

Technique	Definition	How to calculate
Median	The value located at the midpoint of the data	Put the data points into order. The middle value is the median. If there is an even amount of data points, then take the average of the two points in the middle
Mean	The average value of the data points	Add up the data point values and divide by the number of data points
Range	The difference between the maximum value and minimum value in a data set	Subtract the lowest value from the highest value
Mode	The value of the data point that occurs most frequently	Put the values in order, count how many times each value occurs. The data point that occurs most frequently is the mode

- **Percentages** – sometimes it is helpful to convert your data into percentages, e.g. when comparing data from two different sized data sets.
- **Other relevant techniques** – there are many other statistical techniques that could be used to help interpret geographical data, but their use will depend on the type of data that has been collected. Some of these might include:
  - interquartile range
  - percentage increase/decrease
  - ratios/proportions.

2.3.2 Selecting and using appropriate presentation methods for quantitative and qualitative data

Geographical data may be presented in a variety of ways. Selecting an appropriate technique is important to ensure that it enhances the visualisation of patterns or trends.

Selecting and using graphical techniques

Technique	Example	Advantages	Disadvantages
Bar graph		Easy to construct and interpret. The trend can be seen more easily than in a data table. Useful for discrete data	Can only be used with discrete data. If representing a lot of data, they can be cluttered. Trends can be exaggerated or minimised if the scale is inappropriate
Line graph		Easy to construct and interpret. Useful for comparing continuous data. Clearly shows trends. Simple to understand	Not very helpful at displaying percentage data. Trends can be exaggerated or minimised if the scale is inappropriate
Pie chart		Very good at illustrating a proportion of the whole. Comparison between the different factors is easy. Easy to interpret	More difficult to compare two sets of data. Does not show change over time. More difficult to construct compared to line and bar graphs
Histogram		Good for displaying a large data set. Good at visualising distributions. Useful when comparing data sets	Only useful for continuous data. Cannot be used to compare multiple sets of data
Scatter graphs		Illustrates the correlation between two variables. Able to apply a best fit line for missing data points. Can be used to see if the relationship is positive or negative. Useful to show the spread of data. Easy to identify anomalies	Only shows the relationship between two data sets. Difficult to interpret if the correlation is not strong
Star and radial graphs		Visually effective at showing patterns. Can compare multiple sets of data for the same factors. Easy to interpret	Takes slightly longer to construct compared with other techniques. Only helpful with certain types of data

The type of graph you select will depend on the data. Is it **discrete data** or **continuous data**?

Spotlight

Choropleth maps are often used during general election campaigns to show the predicted outcome of voting by region in a country.

Ace your revision

Selecting an inappropriate graphical technique to display data will lead to a loss of marks in your assessment.

Put into practice

Select an appropriate type of graph to display the following data sets. Explain your choices.
- The land area of deforestation by country in one year.
- Six factors of environmental quality across four sites in a city.
- Pebble size and distance downstream along a river.

Put into practice

For each of the mapping techniques described, provide an example of primary data that could be displayed in this way. Evaluate how appropriate the technique is for that data.

Selecting and using mapping techniques

Technique	Example	Advantages	Disadvantages
Choropleth map		Easy to construct and interpret / A good representation of data over space / Useful for identifying spatial anomalies	Indicates that there is a sudden change at the boundary / Does not show differences within a 'zone' / Unable to identify the exact figures for each zone
Flow line map		Useful for showing movement of people or goods / Illustrates volume and direction / Easy to make comparison between locations	Often need to distort the actual distance to be able to plot all the data set / Often not able to see the actual data figure
Proportional symbols map		Good for seeing the differences between locations / Good for displaying large amounts of data / Easy to see the overall trend	Difficult to see the absolute data for each section / Often the size of the symbol can obscure the location / Symbols can often overlap on the map
Located bar graph map		Combines numerical data with spatial patterns / Easier to see spatial patterns in the data / Easy to compare bar graphs for different areas	Can only be used for discrete data / Can easily become overcrowded / Bars can cross into other areas

Presenting qualitative data

Qualitative data, by its nature, does not have a numerical value and therefore is not usually presented using graphs or maps.

- **Word clouds** – the size of the word represents how often it was used in a response during interviews.
- **Transcripts** – sections of transcripts from interviews or focus groups can be included, but ensure that these are put in quotation marks.
- **Field sketches** – a simple sketch of observations at a particular location. These are very good at helping the reader visualise an area and to give deeper meaning to any data collected. They can be annotated to increase understanding/detail.
- **Photographs** – like field sketches, photographs can add clarity and understanding to other data that has been collected. Annotating photographs increases the reader's understanding.

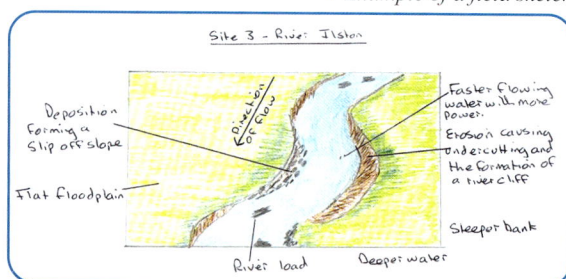

▼ Example of a field sketch

2.3.3 Referencing secondary data sources

How you present secondary data will depend on the format in which you were given it. Some secondary data may already be presented as a map (e.g. Office for National Statistics data) while other data might be in a raw format (e.g. data from a previous year's fieldwork). If you change the way you present the data, there are important things to remember.

- Do you have actual data values or relative values shown on a map?
- Does altering the data presentation method impact the pattern/trend that the data illustrates?
- If the raw data is not available, are you able to apply statistical techniques to the data?

It is important to consider whether the secondary resource is biased. Newspaper articles and social media can be a great source of information on a local topic, however they may include an opinion from the writer as well as the facts. When using secondary data, think about the following questions.

- Is the secondary data reliable? Was it collected in an accurate way?
- Does the writer/producer of the secondary data have a **vested interest**? Is there something for them to gain by presenting the article from a certain viewpoint?
- Who are the **stakeholders** mentioned in the secondary data and what viewpoint would they have that might influence the data?

It is very helpful to answer these questions in the evaluation section of your geographical enquiry to ensure that you have considered factors that could be influencing the data.

When including secondary data or quoting text from another document, it is important that it is referenced correctly – even if it is just a short quote. You should include a **bibliography** at the end of your work. For each piece of secondary data, you should include:

- the author's name
- the title of the document
- the year the data was collected or published
- the page numbers that you are referring to, if it is a long document
- the publisher's name.

Sometimes you may wish to **cite** a source within the main text of your document. You can do this by using quotation marks. After the quotation marks put the author and date of publication in brackets. Always cite work that you are quoting.

Key terms

- **Bibliography:** a list of the sources of information/data that is used in a study.
- **Cite:** identify the original source of the data or idea.
- **Stakeholders:** someone who has a vested interest in something.
- **Vested interest:** the thing that someone is likely to gain from a situation.

Ace your revision

You must have some element of secondary data in your fieldwork investigation report.

Put into practice

Plan the data processing and presentation techniques that you would use for both primary and secondary data for the following two fieldwork exercises.

1. A river study (primary data from three different sites – width, depth, speed of flow, bed load size and shape. Secondary data – last year's data collected by pupils).
2. An urban study (primary data – land use survey, pedestrian and traffic flows at five locations, quality of environment survey at five locations. Secondary data – newspaper article on the decline of the CBD).

Now try this

1. Look out of the classroom window and sketch what you see within the frame of the window. Add annotations that explain what you can see related to a geographical context.
2. Suggest how you can avoid bias with secondary sources as part of your fieldwork.

Chapter 2.4 Analysing and applying evidence

AO2 AO3 AO4

2.4.1 Selecting relevant data to answer the enquiry question

When selecting data, it is vital it helps to answer your main hypothesis or enquiry question. Always aim to have this in mind when you decide what information you will collect and from where.

Spotlight

For data to be relevant it must be:
- accurate
- complete with no gaps
- relevant to your study (ask yourself: Do I really need this?)
- timely (up to date)
- reliable.

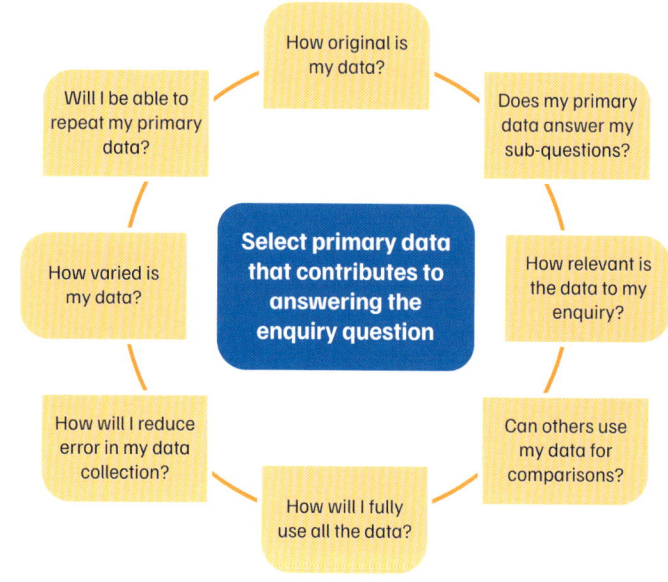

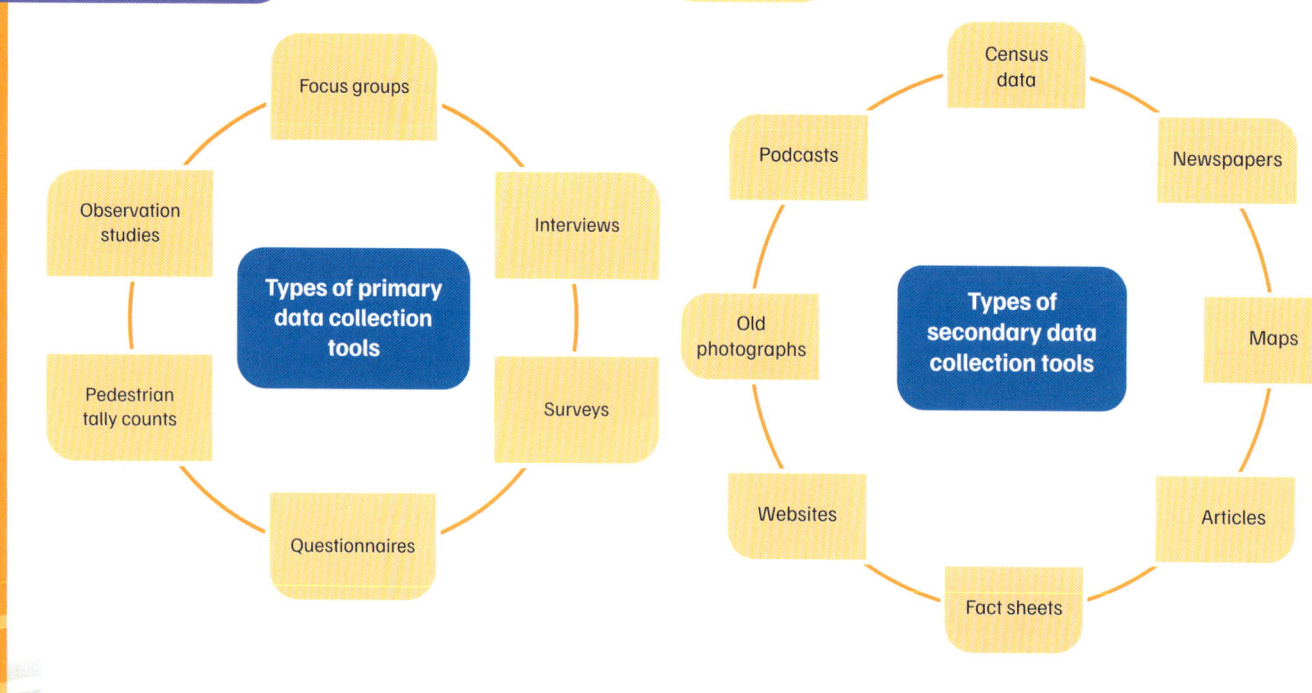

2.4.2 Identifying, analysing and interpreting trends and patterns

Analysing data involves trying to find patterns and trends in the information you have collected and seeing if it helps answer your main enquiry question. Geographers must do a number of things to analyse data (both primary and secondary) if they are to answer the main hypothesis or enquiry question.

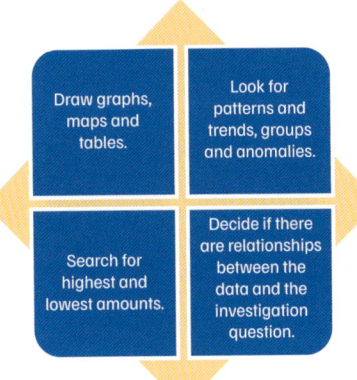

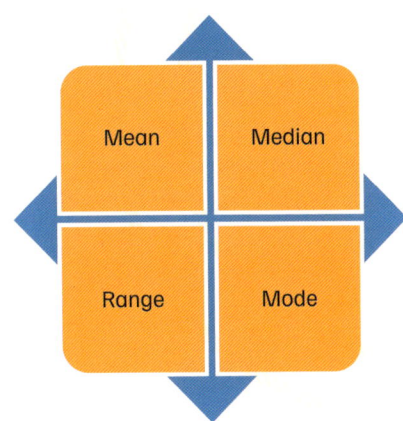

Ace your revision

You should always try to justify your analysis using qualitative and/or quantitative data.

- Look for anomalies in the data.
- What patterns can you see?
- How does the data link to your hypothesis/enquiry?

Put into practice

Describe the trend for average rainfall (mm) for the years of 2002 to 2012.

Year	Average rainfall (mm)	Rank
2002	300	9
2003	333	10
2004	122	2
2005	120	1
2006	267	8
2007	190	3
2008	335	11
2009	212	4
2010	233	5
2011	234	6
2012	256	7

Use data to interpret and justify described trends

Statistical analysis can be very helpful in spotting trends and patterns in data and seeing how relevant your prediction is to your hypothesis. There are a few ways you can carry out statistical analysis of your data and a few key things you can think about:

- highest versus lowest amounts
- anomalies (things that do not fit the expected pattern or trend)
- distance travelled
- flows or amounts.

Once you have identified your trends, it is important to justify them. Justifying trends and patterns in Geography helps to explain the 'why' behind patterns and variations in data. It is important that you include justification when analysing your data. This will help you to find reasons why the trend or pattern that you have observed is present. Try to think of as many reasons as possible.

Having data in a table allows you to rank order and complete some simple statistical analysis.

Proportional flow lines with quantitative data can show patterns of migration in the UK.

Hotspot analysis with GIS can identify clusters or high or low amounts of data, such as crime.

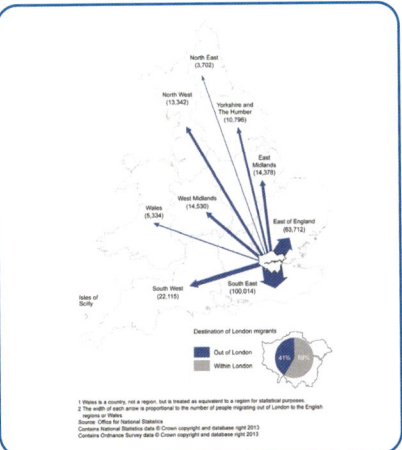

▲ Proportional flow lines

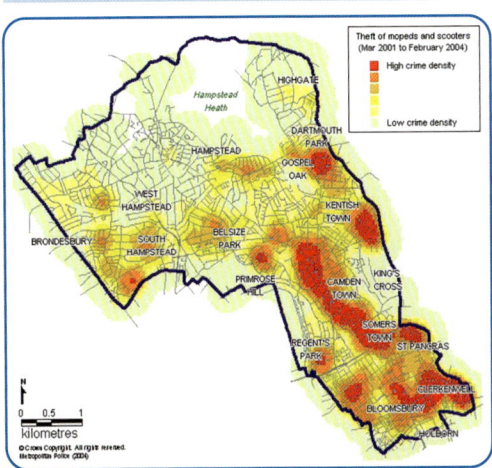

▲ Heat map showing crime levels

Spotlight

ArcGIS is a great tool for analysing key areas for patterns. Log on and have a look around your local area. The software is free if you have a personal or school-based account.

Chapter 2.5 Drawing conclusions

AO2 AO3 AO4

2.5.1 Drawing conclusions from fieldwork enquiries

Your conclusions should answer your main geographical enquiry question/hypothesis, as well as any sub-questions. You have done the research, presented and analysed the data, so what have you found out?

It is important to go back to your original enquiry question/s. If you included sub-questions, then try to answer these first. You can then use the answers to these questions to contribute to your conclusion of the main enquiry question/hypothesis. There are important things to remember when drawing conclusions.

- **Answer the hypothesis/main enquiry question**
  It is easy to become distracted by the data and answer a completely different question! Keep it focused.

- **Be selective in your data**
  You may have a vast amount of data, but it does not all need to be mentioned in the conclusion. Which data sets help you identify a trend or pattern in the data?

- **Reference data**
  It is important that you include some data in your conclusion. This may only be a very small amount (you don't need much) but it shows the reader that you are basing your conclusions on real data.

- **Justify your conclusions**
  Why have you reached these conclusions and what evidence have you found that indicates this pattern? Use your primary and secondary data.

- **Geographical concepts**
  Once you have stated your conclusion, how does it relate to the wider field of geographical research/knowledge? Is there a geographical theory that relates to your geographical study and do your conclusions agree or disagree with this theory? Remember that each location is unique and therefore has a unique set of influences upon it. If the results from your enquiry do not match geographical theory, then say so, but also include suggestions as to why this may be.

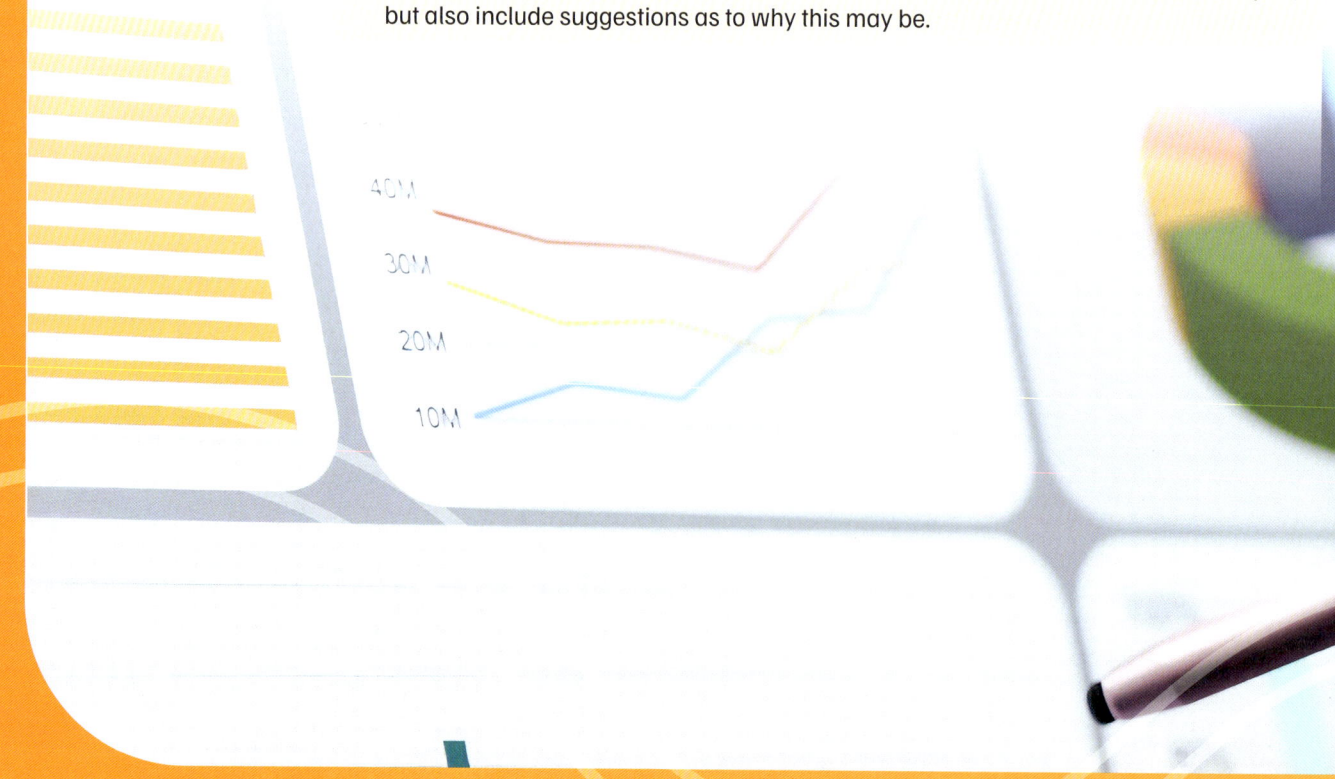

Remember, the wider geographical topics in which your enquiry will be based are:
- geographical flows
- sustainability
- change over time
- mitigating risk
- place and space
- inequality
- settlement
- use of transects.

Whichever one your enquiry is based in, research and understand the relevant geographical theories so that you can make reference to them in your conclusion.

Ben Fogle

Born in 1973, Ben is the United Nations Patron of the Wilderness and travels across the world to see the impact modern life has on people and the environment. He regularly campaigns on environmental issues.

Spotlight

Possible geographical concepts/theories that your fieldwork or enquiry might relate to include:
- sustainability – Egan's wheel
- mitigating risk – risk matrix for risk assessment
- settlement – bid rent theory
- inequality – GINI index
- geographical flows – Bradshaw model.

Ace your revision

Remember to talk about any anomalies you found in your primary data.

Try to think of reasons why some findings may not have matched what you were expecting at the start of the investigation.

Chapter 2.6 Evaluating techniques

AO2 AO3 AO4

🔑 Key terms

- **Evaluation:** *making a judgement/assessing something.*
- **Investigation:** *the process of finding out about a topic/issue.*

2.6.1 Evaluating each stage of the enquiry process

Why do students need to evaluate their investigations?

Being able to reflect on what you have done and why you have done it is important in Geography because it can open up other ideas you may want to investigate. It is also important to spend time thinking about the impact of what you have found out and how you could try and improve on the process next time.

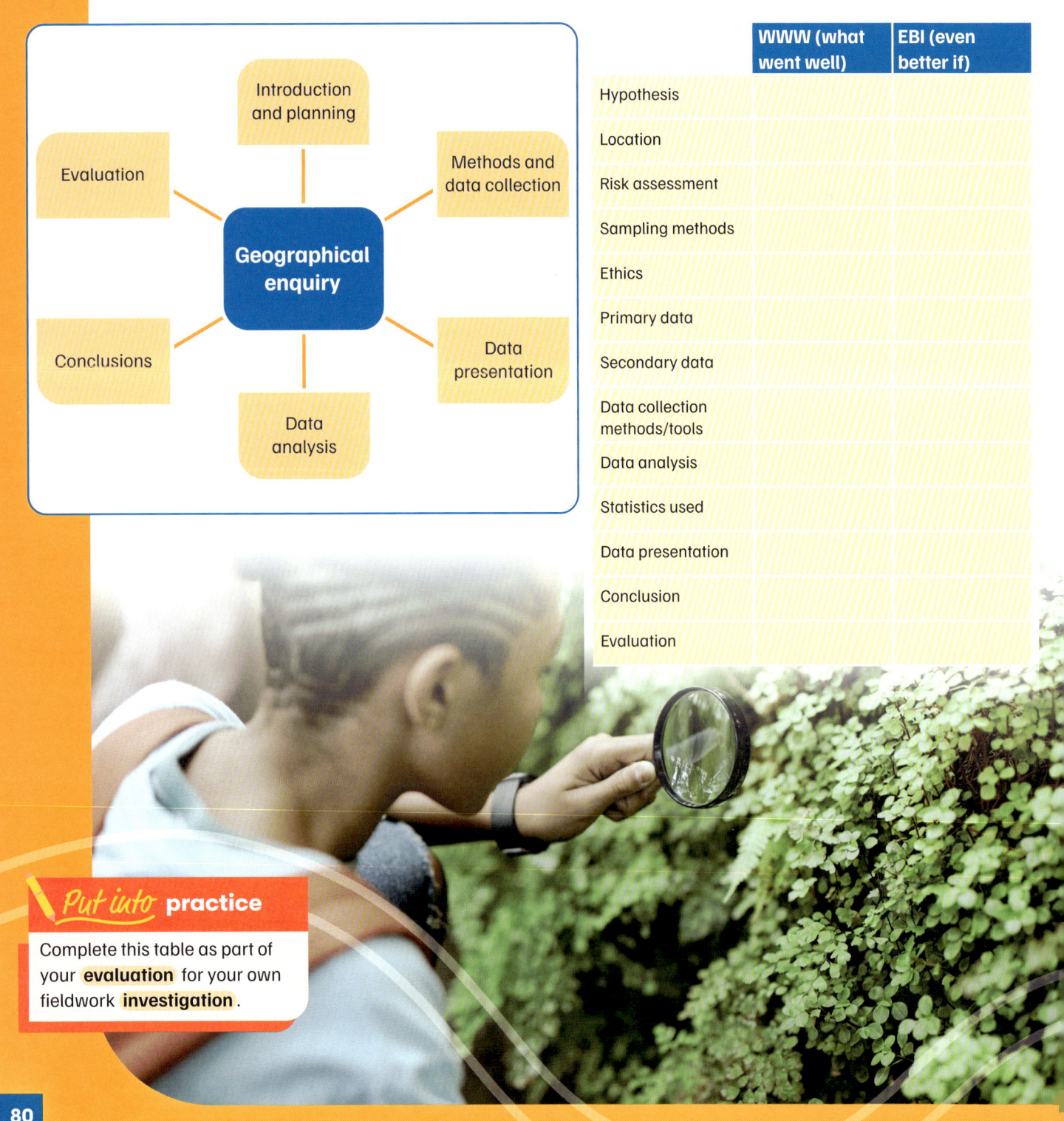

	WWW (what went well)	EBI (even better if)
Hypothesis		
Location		
Risk assessment		
Sampling methods		
Ethics		
Primary data		
Secondary data		
Data collection methods/tools		
Data analysis		
Statistics used		
Data presentation		
Conclusion		
Evaluation		

Put into practice

Complete this table as part of your **evaluation** for your own fieldwork **investigation**.

2.6.2 Identifying further areas of investigation/questions that could now be asked

It is always important to think about how your own fieldwork could be developed further – remember, a good geography investigation will always try to develop in a wider context and go a step further. These questions are useful in your evaluation.

- How could I improve my investigation?
- Could I compare my location to a different location?
- How could I improve the data collection, presentation or analysis?
- What new questions have arisen from my enquiry?
- Should I visit the same location at a different time of year?

Ace your revision

When evaluating in your enquiry, make sure you use the sliding scale of opinion.
- I completing agree…
- I somewhat agree…
- I disagree…

Identify geographical questions that have arisen as a result of your findings

Using a question matrix is a useful way of thinking of questions you want to ask about your investigation. They can help guide where you look for data and help you in your conclusion when you sum up your findings.

	Is? Does?	Has? Did? Was?	Can?	Should?	Would? Could?	Will?
What? Event						
Where? Place						
When? Time						
Which? Choice						
Who? Person						
Why? Reason						
How? Meaning						

The following questions could be generated using the question matrix.
- How could the time of year affect my data?
- What factors have affected the outcome of my investigation?

Put into practice

Write some questions about your own investigation that you can use to build on the enquiry.

Unit 2 recap

The six-stage enquiry process

You should be familiar with the six-stage enquiry process, understand how each stage supports the others and how to choose a topic and pose enquiry questions. You should be able to plan and design enquiry questions, justify them, predict outcomes, and link these outcomes to geographical knowledge. You must plan fieldwork using maps and GIS data, considering safety risks, ethical considerations, and restrictions on data collection.

Data collection

You must know how to select data collection locations, obtain representative samples, and understand sampling methods and factors influencing sample size. You should be able to design primary data collection sheets, use fieldwork equipment effectively, and justify your data collection methods. You must find, select, and use relevant secondary data, ensuring its value to your study.

Analyse and interpret

You should understand the importance of fieldwork and be able to analyse and interpret data to identify patterns and use it to justify trends.

Conclusion

Make sure you are able to draw conclusions that answer your initial questions. You should be able to reference broader geographical concepts such as sustainability, mitigating risk, place and space, inequality and settlement.

Evaluation

You must be able to evaluate all stages of the enquiry: planning, evidence collection, data processing, analysis and drawing conclusions. Also, you should be able to identify new areas for investigation and related geographical questions.

What factors affect sample size?

You should ask yourself these key questions when deciding on your sample size and what impact it will have on your investigation.

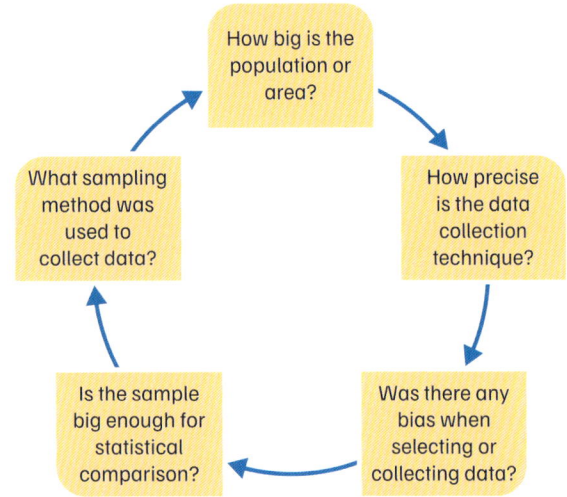

Key stages of fieldwork enquiries

Make sure you write about each stage to achieve top marks.

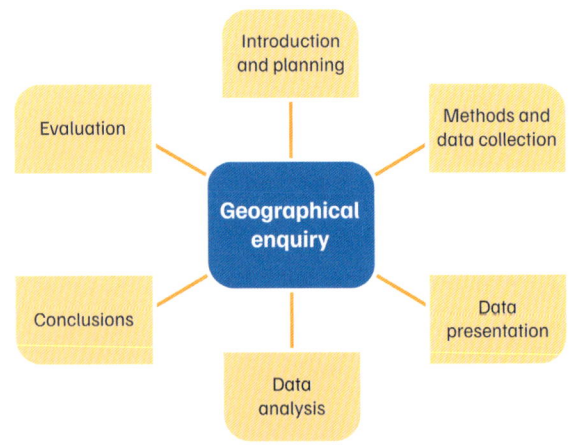

Data presentation

Make sure you can identify strengths and weaknesses of different ways to present data, and select appropriate qualitative and quantitative information.

Revision round up ▼

Your non-examined assessment is based on your research using the six-stage enquiry model.
All questions are based around this model.

1. Explain the role of the enquiry question.
2. Why is it important to include predicted outcomes at the beginning of the enquiry process?
3. Make a list of the features that should be included when using OS maps to locate the study sites.
4. Describe the benefits of using geographical information systems (GIS) when planning a geographical enquiry.
5. Draw a template for a risk assessment to collect fieldwork data.
6. Copy and complete the following table on sampling techniques.

Sampling type	Description	Advantages	Disadvantages
Random			
Opportunistic			
Stratified			
Systematic			

7. Explain the difference between primary and secondary data.
8. Describe what quantitative data is and give an example.
9. Describe what qualitative data is and give an example.
10. Name five sources of secondary data.
11. Name four methods of processing data.
12. Identify the strengths and weaknesses of the following graphical data presentation techniques:
    - line graphs
    - bar graphs
    - pie charts
    - located bar graphs
    - scatter graphs.
13. Identify the strengths and weaknesses of the following mapping techniques:
    - choropleth map
    - flow map
    - proportional symbols map.
14. Explain why a bibliography should be used when using secondary data.
15. Describe what information should be included in the analysis section of the geographical enquiry.
16. What questions should you consider when analysing data?
17. How do you ensure that your data analysis is focused on the enquiry questions?
18. Explain how you would structure a conclusion to a geographical enquiry.
19. What sections of the geographical enquiry should be considered in the final evaluation stage?
20. Why is it good practice to consider further geographical questions in your evaluation?
21. Which section of your enquiry should you reference to wider geographical theories?

Unit 3
Our Dynamic and Diverse World

It is estimated that there are 199 million tonnes of plastic waste currently in the earth's oceans.

Introduction
During this unit you will explore why we get the weather that we do, and how and why it is changing. You will find out what is threatening our oceans and why inequalities exist in Wales and beyond.

Did you know ! The lowest temperature ever recorded in Wales was -23.3°C. It was recorded in Rhayader in 1940.

The assessment:
This unit is assessed by a written examination and is worth 30% of the qualification. It has a total of 90 marks.

Assessment objectives

The assessment objectives assessed in Unit 3 are:

AO1 Demonstrate knowledge and understanding of places, people, environments and processes at a variety of scales.

AO2 Apply knowledge and understanding of geographical terms, skills and concepts to different contexts.

AO3 Analyse, evaluate, or make judgements from a variety of sources, synthesising where appropriate.

Contents

In Unit 3 you will cover the following:

Chapter 3.1: The geography of inequality 86
3.1.1 Regional inequalities in Wales and the UK 86
3.1.2 Measuring development to classify countries 94
3.1.3 The development gap 96
3.1.4 Reducing the development gap 98

Chapter 3.2: The highs and lows of our weather 100
3.2.1 Weather and climate 100
3.2.2 Factors affecting temperature 102
3.2.3 Factors affecting rainfall 104
3.2.4 Global atmospheric circulation 106
3.2.5 Low pressure weather systems – depressions 108
3.2.6 High pressure weather systems – anticyclones 110

Chapter 3.3: Wild weather 112
3.3.1 Global hazards caused by extreme low pressure 112
3.3.2 Global hazards caused by extreme high pressure 116

Chapter 3.4: Continual climate change 118
3.4.1 Natural causes of climate change 118
3.4.2 Human causes of recent climate change 121
3.4.3 Evidence that our climate is changing 123
3.4.4 Consequences of climate change 125

Chapter 3.5: Managing global challenges 130
3.5.1 Managing climate change 130
3.5.2 Managing threats to our oceans 132

By the time we're finished you will...

- be able to describe how development is measured and how the development gap can be reduced
- understand the hazards created by extreme low and high pressure systems
- be able to suggest sources of evidence of climate change
- be able to apply understanding of the challenges caused by climate change and threats to our oceans.

85

Chapter 3.1 The geography of inequality

AO1 AO2 AO3

🔑 Key terms

- **Deindustrialisation:** *the closure of previous industries, e.g. manufacturing, coal mining.*
- **Economic:** *money, finance.*
- **Global:** *worldwide.*
- **Impact:** *a consequence of an action or event.*
- **Inequality:** *differences in standards of living.*

3.1.1 Regional inequalities in Wales and the UK

Regional inequalities are a major issue in the UK and Wales, with wide economic and social disparities across the nation – disparities are differences or imbalances within a particular factor such as healthcare. The UK government is attempting to address this by introducing a 'levelling up' programme, which is a series of policies and ideas focusing on funding areas most in need.

What is inequality?

Inequality refers to different standards of living and can be linked to social, **economic**, environmental or political factors. Inequality in the UK dates back as far as the 19th century and has been made worse by **deindustrialisation**.

There are different kinds of inequality, some examples are shown below.

Gender Inequality
Decision making that favours men over women

Political Inequality
Laws that favour some groups over others

Economic Inequality
The differences between different groups in terms of their income and wealth

Inequality of Opportunity
Some groups have more opportunities as a result of their background

Inequality of Access
Unequal access to services such as healthcare and education

Ace your revision
Make sure you compare regional inequalities across the UK using statistics, facts and figures.

Now try this

1. Explain why people living in rural areas often have poorer access to services, such as mobile signal and broadband connectivity, than people living in urban areas.

Winnie Byanyima

'The scale of global inequality is quite simply staggering.'

Winnie is the executive director of the Joint United Nations Programme on HIV/AIDS (UNAIDS), under-secretary of the United Nations and a global leader for equality. She leads the United Nations' fight to end the AIDS pandemic by 2030.

▼ *Features of inequality*

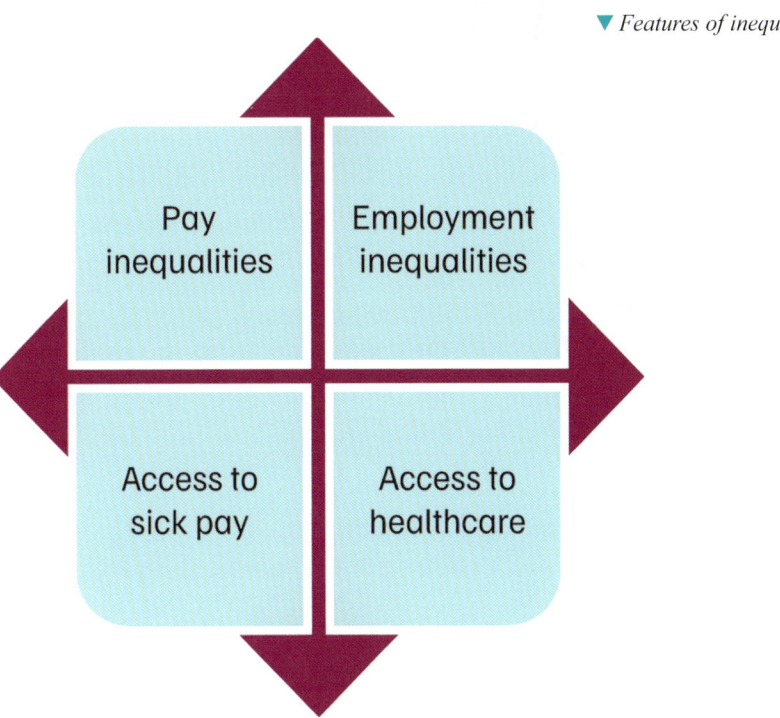

Pay inequalities: can lead to social exclusion.

Employment inequalities: can lead to lower wages and lower skilled jobs.

Access to sick pay: those in lower paid jobs often have poorer access to healthcare and sick leave.

Access to healthcare: geographical location and socio-economic status can lead to inequalities.

▼ *Factors leading to inequality*

Physical Features
The geographical features of an area, such as mountains, coastlines and climate.

Infrastructure
Different levels of technology, roads, railway, key buildings such as hospitals.

Standard of Living
Access and ability to purchase food, water, gas, electric.

Education
The better the quality of education with more specialist teachers, the better the standard of living for young people.

Spotlight

The UK has some of the most severe regional inequalities anywhere in the world, yet it is the sixth richest **global** economy.

This photograph shows differences in the quality of housing in an area of London. You can see high-rise flats in the background and more affluent terraced houses in the foreground.

Ace your revision

When answering 'Describe' exam questions, remember to use the following in your answer:
- highest versus lowest amounts
- anomalies
- key
- named places.

Put into practice

- List one group that is at risk of inequality.
- Describe the types of inequality that group may face.
- Explain the **impact** of inequality on Wales and the UK.

Patterns of inequality in Wales and the UK

Inequality in Wales and the UK is a complex issue with deep roots, shaped by economic, social, and political factors. Patterns of inequality can be seen in a range of areas, including income, education, health, and access to opportunities. The wealthiest 1% hold a disproportionate share of the nation's wealth, while those in lower income brackets often struggle with rising living costs.

	Wales	UK
Education	588,000 school children in full time education daily (2021)	8.7 million (2023)
Investment	In 2021–2022, Wales had 43 investment projects. In 2022–2023, Wales had 47 investment projects	In 2023, the UK had a total of 985 investment projects; 736 of these being new projects
Religion	2021 Christian 43% No religion 46% Muslim 2.2% Hindu 0.4% Sikh 0.1% Jewish 0.1% Buddhist 0.3%	2021 Christian 46% No religion 37% Muslim 6.5% Hindu 1.5% Sikh 0.8% Jewish 0.5% Buddhist 0.4%
Race	2021 White (Welsh, English, Scottish, Northern Irish or British): 91% Black (Welsh, African, Caribbean): 1.7% Asian: 2.9%	2021 White: 82% Black: 4.0% Asian: 9.3%
Rural and urban locations	2021 Rural population: 33% Urban population: around 80%	2021 Rural population: 18% Urban population: 83%
Services (e.g. broadband connectivity and mobile coverage)	9.8% employed in the services sector (2021) Ofcom's 2024 report indicates that 68% of Welsh homes have access to full-fibre broadband.	57% employed in the services sector (2021) Ofcom's 2024 report indicates that 69% of UK homes have access to full-fibre broadband.
Employment	2021 75% aged 16–64	2021 75% for people aged 16–64

What are the physical causes of inequalities?

Danny Dorling

'Since the Great Recession hit in 2008, the 1% has only grown richer while the rest find life increasingly tough. Inequality is more than just economics. It is the culture that divides and makes social mobility impossible.'

Professor Danny Dorling is a British social geographer with links to Oxford University. His work includes studying divided cities and inequality in the UK.

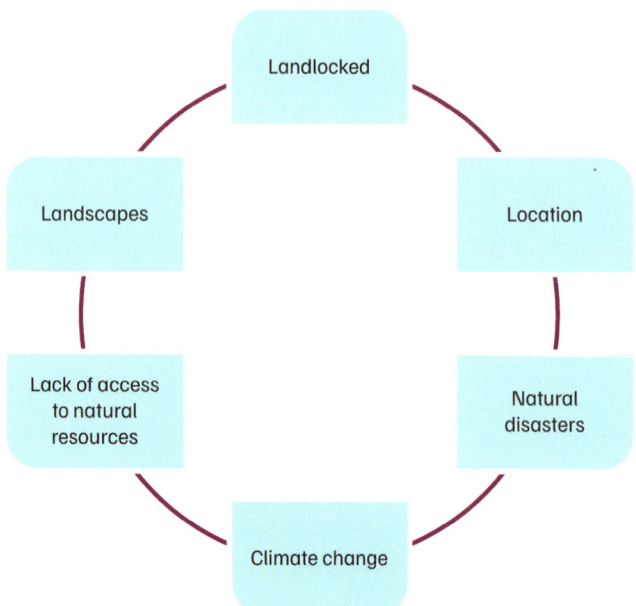

- Landlocked
- Location
- Natural disasters
- Climate change
- Lack of access to natural resources
- Landscapes

- Being **landlocked** could mean you have poor access to coastal water, which could be used for fishing or trade.
- **Natural disasters** can deter transnational companies (TNCs) from wanting to invest for fear of their businesses being destroyed.
- **Lack of access to natural resources** can lead to a reliance on importing goods, which means other countries could charge a higher tariff (tax) to import them.
- **Climate change** can lead to an increase in desertification, causing crops to fail. For many LICs, this is the staple source of profit in trade with other countries.
- **Geographical location** can affect inequality. For example, the south of the UK experiences greater economical investment in its cities leading to greater employment compared to the north of the UK.
- **Landscapes** can affect inequality by certain areas being more isolated geographically than others, for example upland areas have a more challenging terrain, making it harder to build infrastructure.

What are the human causes of inequalities?

- **Access to housing** can lead to inequality in several ways. Rising house prices are forcing more people to rent as housing is unaffordable. Those people who own more property tend to have the most wealth. In 2023, the IFS said that housing costs are rising for low income households.
- **Communications** can lead to inequality when there are differences in how people access, process, and act on information. There is a digital divide across the UK and in rural areas where broadband is limited or non-existent.
- **Access to healthcare services** can lead to lower death rates and fewer long term health issues, which means a more work-ready population and fewer people in hospital.
- **Demographic inequalities** can lead to economic disparities between different groups. For example, amongst ethnic minority communities in 2024 in the UK, the median hourly wage was 14.8% lower compared to white employees.
- **Transport:** the rising cost of train tickets, petrol and bus fares means people on low incomes might struggle to get to their daily jobs.
- **Pay inequalities** can affect the economic growth of a country. A consequence of pay inequality is economic deprivation as people will be unable to afford basics, such as food and education.
- **Employment inequalities:** people working in lower paid jobs compared to those in higher paid employment can face disparities in wealth and earnings. However, those employed in higher skilled, higher paying jobs in other sectors might experience lower levels of inequality. South Wales Valleys (Blaenau Gwent, Merthyr Tydfil) have some of the highest unemployment and economic inactivity rates in Wales.
- **Industrialisation** can create a class divide and limit social mobility. People might be limited in employment opportunities as manufacturing-based jobs pay far less than service-based jobs. Environmental damage can also be a side effect of industrialisation, for example Tata Steel, Port Talbot.

What are the consequences of inequality in the UK?

- **Segregation** – people being forced to live and work away from others, e.g. in LICs we often see people living in informal settlements.
- **Perceptions of people** can be driven by social class and income, and are affected by inequality. Perceptions can vary depending on background, experience and wealth.
- **Regional variations in wealth** – this can lead to poor health due to a lack of investment in services, and lower educational attainment due to higher paying teaching jobs being in the south of the UK (teachers are paid more to be recruited to Inner London). People with a higher income and economic security are more likely to be able to afford a house compared to lower income residents who may remain within the rental market for longer.

Key terms

- **Demographic:** *statistical data relating to the population.*
- **Enclaves:** *areas surrounded by another community or place.*
- **IFS:** *Institute for Fiscal Studies.*
- **Income:** *the amount of money per person, such as gross national income.*
- **LICs:** *low income countries.*

Fun fact

Did you know, King's College London said that the 'UK has an unusually centralised state and a London-dominated economy.'

Fun fact

Did you know, according to GeoExpro, Africa is a continent with 54 countries, 16 of which are landlocked.

Spotlight

Aberdeen University said that ethnic segregation creates more physical distance between individuals and their jobs. In the UK, we sometimes see 'sink estates' or enclaves as ethnic minority communities are housed together in a concentrated area. The Guardian Newspaper (2023) said that 44% of ethnic minority people are in social housing compared to 16% of white people.

Key terms

- **Productivity:** how much output there is, e.g. people working, money made.

Put into practice

Using the map of disposable income by region in the UK and Ireland, describe the patterns of disposable income.

Spotlight

You can see from the map that the southeast of the UK is the wealthiest region. It has a median household wealth of £503,400, which is more than twice the median household wealth of the north of England. Source: Equalitytrust.org.uk

▼ *Regional variation in disposable household income across the UK (2021)*

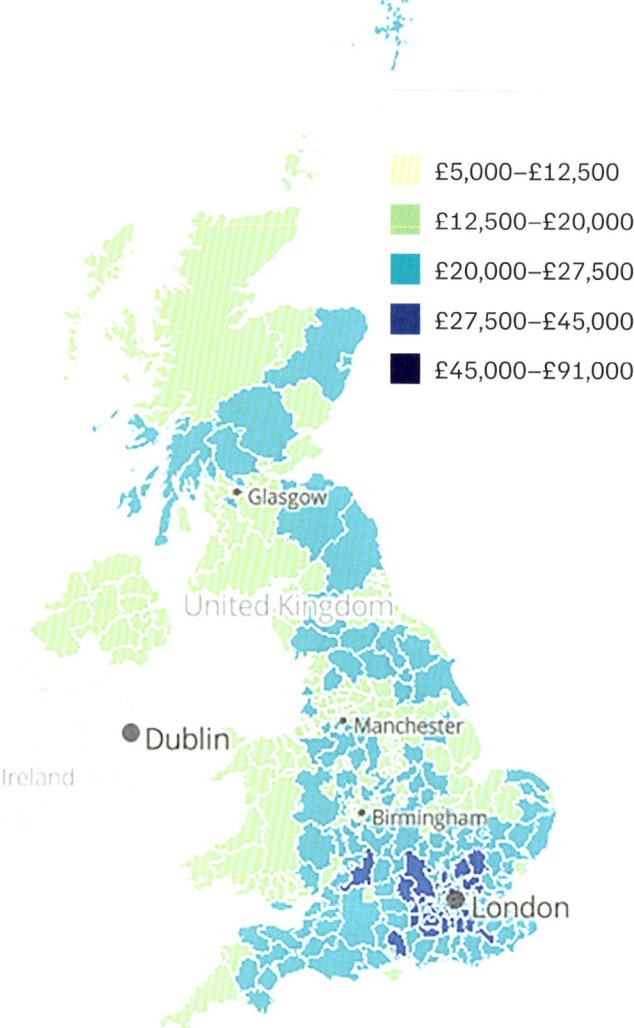

- £5,000–£12,500
- £12,500–£20,000
- £20,000–£27,500
- £27,500–£45,000
- £45,000–£91,000

The lowest income regions are mostly in urban areas such as the Midlands, the northwest and the northeast of England. You can also see from the map that Wales has low disposable income per person in Rhondda Cynon Taff (RCT). However, all parts of Wales have below average UK disposable income. The highest disposable income is in the south of Wales in urbanised/densely populated areas. Areas around London have the highest disposable income due to higher levels of **productivity**.

Similar regional variations can be found in employment, school performance and access to housing and services such as mobile signal. This is because the causes of inequality are often interlinked.

Spotlight

Aylesbury Estate, in Southeast London, is one of the UK's biggest housing estates with around 2,704 flats and 7,500 residents. There are concerns over the state of the physical buildings as well as public perception of the estate.

The impacts of inequality on Black, Asian and Minority Ethnic communities

The UK is becoming increasingly ethnically diverse with over 20% of the population being from ethnic minority communities. A report from 2024 highlighted the following points.

- Inequality has a significant negative impact on the health and education of minority ethnic communities.
- During the pandemic, Black and Asian communities experienced approximately 23% more deaths than other ethnic groups.
- Black communities have higher rates of unemployment, often more than twice that of white communities.
- Higher rates of racism and discrimination are experienced by ethnic minority communities.
- Ethnic minority communities are 2.5 times more likely to be in poverty than white communities.

What is the Welsh Government doing to sustainably reduce inequalities?

Being sustainable means using resources responsibly, so they are available for future generations. The Welsh Government is aware of the need to manage Wales and its resources so that future generations can continue to live healthy, prosperous lives in an environment that can sustain them.

The Welsh Government has a series of action plans to help target different key areas of Welsh life.

1. Economic action plan
2. Race equality action plan
3. Strategic equality plan 2024–2028
4. Net zero strategic plan
5. Health and social care plan
6. Improve public transport
7. Improve representation of different groups
8. Meet the Sustainable Development Goals (SDGs)

▼ The Welsh Government's seven well-being goals

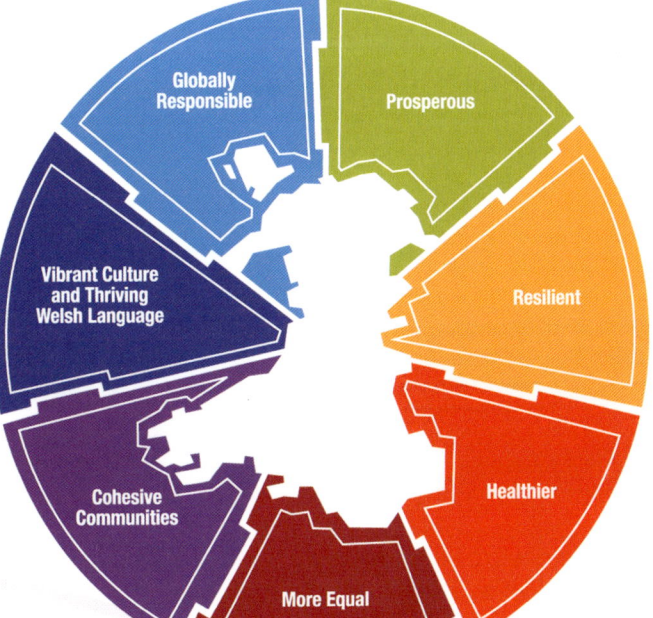

Spotlight

Net zero is a target of balancing out greenhouse gas emissions by reducing emissions where possible and introducing methods to absorbing them from the atmosphere.

Ace your revision

It is really important that you know how the Welsh Well-being goals link to Unit 4, which focuses on sustainability.

Spotlight

Cambridge University said reducing inequality is essential to reducing climate change. 'People on lower incomes can be more restricted in the things they can do to help reduce their carbon footprint.' Charlotte Kukowski – Cambridge University, Departments of Psychology and Zoology.

Rachel Reeves

The Chancellor Rachel Reeves told parliament, 'We will provide the funding required to begin tunnelling work between Old Oak Common and Euston. This will catalyse private investment into the local area, delivering jobs and growth.'

Rachel Reeves is the Chancellor for the British government (2024) and Labour MP for Leeds West and Pudsey.

Put into practice

Complete your own research into how the Welsh and UK governments are trying to reduce inequality. What other ideas and strategies can you find out about? Maybe try making some flash cards or mind maps on this.

What is the UK government doing to reduce inequalities?

The UK government is committed to reducing inequalities across the country by focusing on Sustainable Development Goal 10 (SDG 10). This is one of the universal goals for member states of the United Nations. The goals aim to transform the world into a fairer place.

People on lower incomes are more limited in how they can reduce their carbon footprint and are more likely to be affected by the consequences of climate change. For example, people on lower incomes struggle to insulate their homes, buy electric cars and bikes, and cook more meat free meals. Therefore, more meat production is taking place for the lower income market.

Infrastructure project – HS2

The UK government is committed to delivering on the HS2 rail project – a high-speed railway that will stretch from London to Birmingham. The bullet trains will then continue north using the existing tracks. The aim of the HS2 rail project is to connect the north of the UK to the south at faster speeds, which would allow people to commute rather than leave the north of England to search for work.

In 2023, the Conservative Prime Minister, Rishi Sunak, said phase 2 of the HS2 train from Birmingham to Manchester and Leeds would be cancelled due to spiralling costs. This has created a lot of uncertainty for projects linked to it. In December 2024, the Labour government confirmed that only phase 1 would go ahead (London to Birmingham).

Advantages of HS2	Disadvantages of HS2
Provide a modernised transportation network, easing congestion on the railway lines	40% of benefits of HS2 will go to London (source: New Economics Foundation)
Create more jobs: estimated 25,000 jobs for constructing HS2 and 3,000 jobs for operating it. Many of these jobs will sit outside of London	The full costs of the HS2 are still not fully understood – could the costs continue to spiral?
Regeneration of northern areas previously disconnected from the south, creating a UK central hub for global businesses	Wales contributes to the building of HS2, but HS2 does not travel through Wales
Reduce journey times from London to Birmingham to 45 minutes	Government estimates the London to Birmingham leg will cost up to £66 billion

▼ *Proposed route of HS2 train*

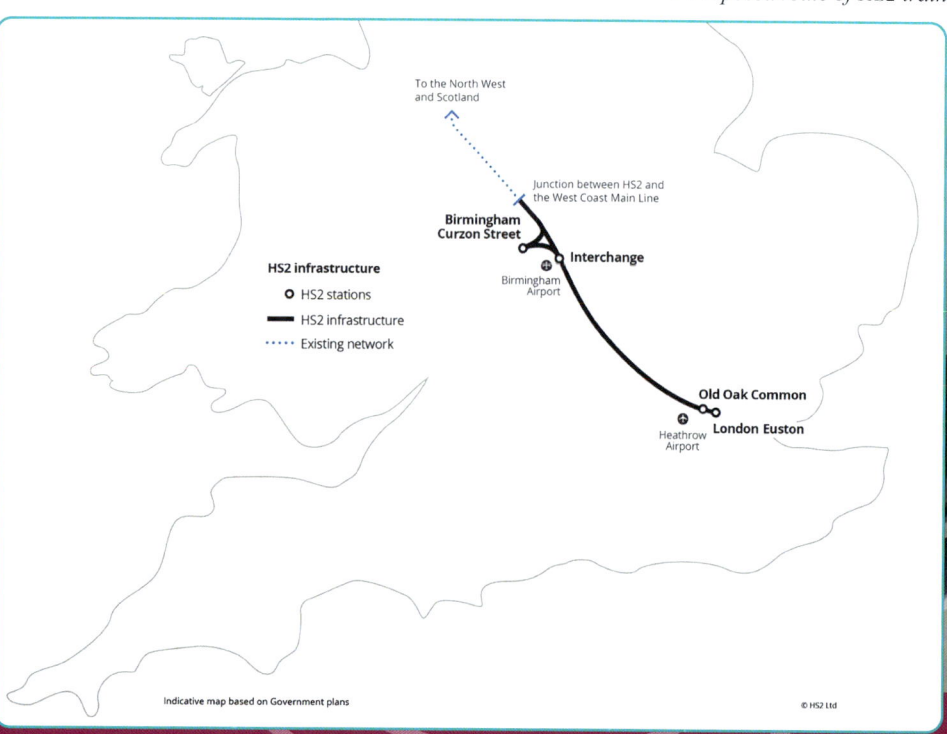

UK government strategies to reduce inequalities as part of the 'levelling up' agenda:
- increasing the minimum wage adding more staff to the NHS building more affordable housing
- securing greater private investment to the UK economy
- universal credit to support those on lower incomes
- improving infrastructure and connectivity, e.g. HS2.

Strategies to improve housing

In 2024, the Labour government set an ambitious target to build 1.5 million new homes in five years. The target included the provision of social housing and the improvement of the quality of housing. In Wales, the government committed £81 million in extra funding for social rented homes with the aim of building 20,000 new homes.

An example of a social housing project is the Merthyr Valleys Homes housing association, who are committed to building 40 homes on the hillside in Cefn-coed-y-cymmer, on the northwestern edge of Merthyr Tydfil. The aim is to ensure that enough affordable housing is available in the area.

Put into practice

Improvements to infrastructure and housing are just two ways in which the governments in Wales and the UK can reduce regional inequalities. Carry out some research to find out how the governments have introduced schemes to help:
- create employment
- improve education and public awareness
- improve race relations.

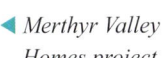
◄ *Merthyr Valley Homes project*

Put into practice

Study the information on this page and assess how sustainable the Merthyr Valleys Homes project is.

▲ *Local resident in Merthyr*

"Since the new houses have been built, I am concerned about the extra traffic congestion on the road leading to the new estate. It has added to my journey time and has also increased air pollution. I don't think this is sustainable for the area."

"I am thrilled with my new home as it is much warmer and more eco-friendly compared to my old rental house. The solar panels on the roof have cut my electricity bills."

▲ *Resident of Merthyr Valley Homes*

"I was out of work for the last 4 months, but this housing development has allowed me to get back to work so I can earn money to support my family."

▲ *Construction worker*

Key terms

- **Development continuum:** *a sliding scale of development terms.*
- **Gross domestic product (GDP):** *measures the monetary value of final goods and services.*
- **HIC:** *high income country.*
- **MIC:** *middle income country.*

3.1.2 Measuring development to classify countries

There are a range of indicators to help measure the development of a country which can be organised into four categories.

Simple: measuring one factor
Composite: measuring more than one factor
Qualitative: thoughts and feelings
Quantitative: numerical

- Balance of trade (BOT) – this shows the total value of exports versus imports in a certain period of time. This means a country is earning more from its exports than imports and is a sign of economic strength.
- Calorie intake – this could be a sign of food security in a country. In LICs, poor calorie intake is linked to poor economic growth.
- Employment sectors – the more people employed in tertiary and quaternary sectors, the more developed a country is thought to be. These sectors require higher levels of skill, pay better salaries and gather greater levels of investment from governments and outside companies.
- **Gross domestic product (GDP)** – this is the monetary value of goods and services in a country. However, not all work is paid work or shown in the country's GDP.
- Human development index (HDI) – takes account of literacy rate, gross national income (GNI) and life expectancy.
- Income levels – the amount of money a person or household earns over a certain period of time.
- Literacy rate – percentage of people who can read and write.
- Purchasing power parity (PPP) – this is a useful measure of development as it shows the price of specific goods in a country. The greater a country's PPP, the more developed it is thought to be.
- Urban population – this can be a sign of development due to investment in infrastructure and employment beyond traditional agriculture. By 2050 it is thought 7 in 10 people will live in urban areas.

Put into practice

Complete the table by organising these indicators of development into simple, composite, qualitative and quantitative.

Simple	Composite
Quantitative	**Qualitative**

Another useful way of measuring development is the sliding scale called the **development continuum**. It is often thought of as more realistic because it allows countries to move across different categories of development.

Development continuum based on GNI (source: World Bank, 2023)

The World Bank classifies countries by economic indicators such as income. You will need to know that countries are grouped into three main areas: high income country (**HIC**), middle income country (**MIC**) and low income country.

As of 2023, these countries can also be broken down further based on income levels.

- High income economies – gross national income of $14,005 per person or more.
- Upper-middle income economies – gross national income of $4,516–$14,005 per person.
- Lower-middle income economies – gross national income of $1,146–$4,515 per person.
- Low income economies – gross national income of $1,145 per person or less.

What are the advantages/disadvantages of classifying countries?

Advantages	Disadvantages
Can help provide an overview of a country's level of development	Can be subjective (biased) depending on how data was collected
Can help classify a country's development to provide levels of aid	Data can quickly become out of date
Can be used to help set targets for development, e.g. Sustainable Development Goals (SDGs) as agreed by the United Nations	Some data uses averages of a country so regional data is missed out

Now try this

Name of country	Income level
Australia	$63,150
Botswana	$8,340
Costa Rica	$14,260
France	$45,180
Japan	$39,350
Mali	$840
Singapore	$70,590

◀ Figures from World Bank open data 2023

1 Using the data table, calculate:
  A the range of GNI
  B the median of GNI.

95

Key terms

- **Colonialism:** *the practice of establishing control over a foreign territory and its people, often involving settlement, exploitation of resources and cultural domination.*
- **Development gap:** *the divide between the richer north and poorer south.*
- **Trade blocs:** *a group of countries that have agreed to reduce or remove trade barriers between themselves.*

3.1.3 The development gap

The **development gap** is a more crude way of categorising countries as it oversimplifies their grouping and does not always consider all factors.

What human factors have led to the development gap?

There are a series of human factors that have led to and increased the development gap.

- **War** – which can affect industries and populations.
- **Colonialism** – the historical impact of other countries invading or taking over.
- **Dependence on trade of primary goods** – often happens with LICs.
- **Corrupt political systems** or governments.
- **A lack of investment** by other countries or companies.
- **Famine** and a lack of food security.
- **Globalisation** – global trade tariffs, LICs are often restricted from gaining entry to **trade blocs** and therefore lower tariffs (taxes).
- **Outward migration** – people leaving their country or area for a better life.
- **Industrialisation** – countries that have more industries and transnational companies will develop stronger trade links and economies.
- **Urbanisation** – LICs are the fastest growing areas for urban development.
- **Demographic characteristics** – a large labour market can drive the economy of a country. Demographic covers gender and amount of people in ethnic groups, for example.

▼ *Development gap by income (2023)*

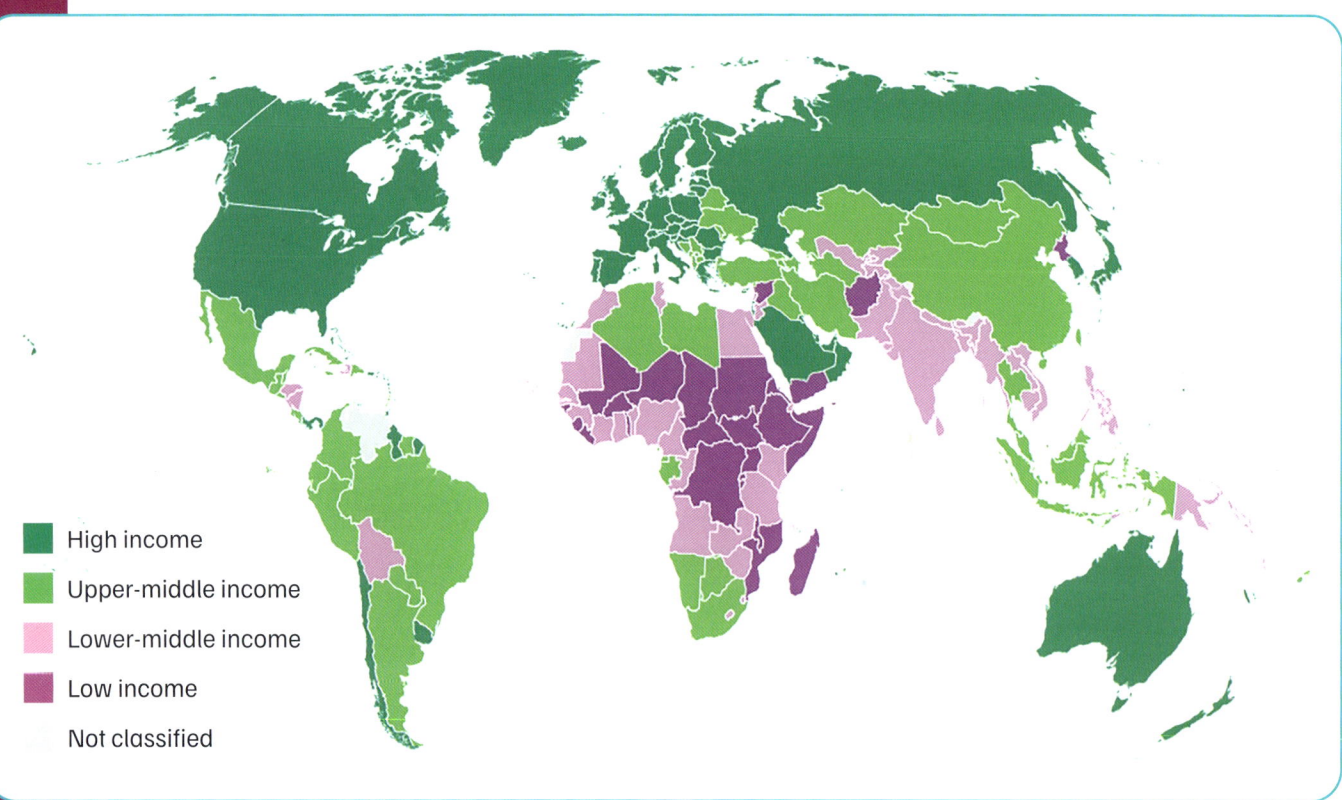

What impact has colonialism had on countries' development?

Colonialism has created uneven development because the production of goods and services is controlled by HICs who also take the profit. A good example of this is the looting of Africa. Colonial powers took advantage of many LICs to grow their own economies by exploiting resources such as gold, tobacco, diamonds and oil. They developed their own infrastructure and education systems with the profits. However, colonialism has had some positives, such as:

- improved infrastructure, e.g. Botswana
- improved relationships with some countries through investment by TNCs
- development of university systems using profits from De Beers Diamond TNC.

What physical factors have led to the development gap?

Countries with differing levels of development to the richest countries in the world often face harsh physical factors that affect their development and slow down growth.

Climatic issues:

- forest fires
- drought leading to famine and crop failure
- tropical storms
- poor access to water (insecurity)
- climate related disease, e.g. malaria.

Other natural factors include:

- natural disasters, e.g. earthquakes in Haiti
- geographical location – countries that are not landlocked and have access to coastal areas can build ports that help shipping and trade
- natural resources – a lack of natural resources makes it difficult to produce goods and services, leaving countries with a low economic base.

> **Did you know**
>
> The continent of Africa has 16 landlocked countries, which makes it challenging to gain access to water for farming once it is desalinated. The coastline can also be used for trade by building ports for shipping goods (import and export).

▼ *Haiti earthquake – how natural disasters affect development*

Now try this ▼

1. Physical factors have had a larger impact on the development gap than human factors. To what extent do you agree with this statement?

Key terms

- **Agencies:** *businesses or organisations.*
- **Aid:** *support in the form of money, people or resources.*
- **Fair trade:** *trade between countries that ensures a fair price is paid to farmers.*
- **MNC:** *multinational company.*
- **Strategies:** *key ideas to help improve or monitor something important.*
- **TNC:** *transnational company.*

3.1.4 Reducing the development gap

There are a range of ideas and **strategies** that governments and other **agencies** use to help close the development gap.

Aid

Aid comes in many different forms and for different reasons, so that a less developed country can try to make progress. What is important is a top-down approach from governments to communities. Types of aid include:

- bilateral aid – from one country to another
- multilateral aid – between several countries
- humanitarian aid (emergency aid) – in times of disaster
- tied aid – for projects linked to the donor country
- debt relief – e.g. wiping off debt in return for planting more trees
- voluntary aid – given freely by charities/non-governmental organisations (NGOs).

▼ *NGOs helping with disaster relief*

Spotlight

The FAIRTRADE Mark is used on products such as coffee and chocolate to show they have been more sustainably sourced from producers in lower income countries.

Put into practice

1. Examine the benefits and costs of using AID to help LICs.
2. Fair trade is the most sustainable strategy to help develop LICs. To what extent do you agree?

Fun fact

- There are more than 30,000 products with a FAIRTRADE Mark available worldwide.
- They exist in 120 countries.
- The first Fairtrade bananas were available to buy in the UK in 2000.

Advantages of fair trade	Disadvantages of fair trade
Farmers get to be part of a co-operative community and have a say in how they farm	Expensive goods compared to supermarket own brands
Less use of pesticides and less plastic pollution	Not all supermarkets sell fair trade goods
Profit is reinvested into local education systems	The range of goods is quite small, so the amount of profit is debatable

Fun fact

In 2008, Wales become the first Fairtrade Nation in the world!

To become a Fairtrade business, you have to apply for a Fairtrade Licence and meet important criteria when you are inspected. All goods must be produced in line with Fairtrade International's rigorous environmental, economic and social standards and a third-party person checks these standards are met.

Multinational (MNC) and transnational (TNC) companies

MNCs (sometimes called TNCs) bring both advantages and disadvantages when they enter a developing country to set up new factories and other types of infrastructure.

Advantages of MNCs	Disadvantages of MNCs
Much needed investment from the MNC into the developing country	Long hours and poor pay for workers
Workers learn new skills	Children often forced into labour instead of school
MNCs try to improve infrastructure, e.g. roads	Profit often leaves the developing country and returns to the developed country headquarters (HQ)

Spotlight

In 2013, the Rana Plaza textiles factory in Bangladesh collapsed, killing more than 1,100 workers and stopping supplies of textiles to other countries. It is likely the disaster was caused by poor safety conditions left unchecked by the MNC, and that workers were exploited by low wages and poor working conditions.

Tourism

Tourism can help LICs (low income countries) to develop as it is often their most valuable commodity.

▼ *The Maldives are heavily dependent on tourism*

Spotlight

Advantages of tourism to the Maldives:
- increase in GDP to $600 million a year
- profit from tourism makes up 90% of the government's income
- 11% of the population are employed in tourism.

Disadvantages:
- foreign ownership of resorts has created a loss of culture
- pollution from hotels goes into the ocean
- damage to the coral reef from trophy hunting scuba divers.

Now try this

1. Using the table of advantages and disadvantages of MNCs, explain the impact of MNCs on developing countries.
2. Evaluate which strategies for reducing the development gap have been most successful.

Chapter 3.2 The highs and lows of our weather

AO1 AO2 AO3

🔑 Key terms

- **Climate graph:** a graph which shows the main climate data of rainfall and temperature for an area.
- **Precipitation:** water falling from the atmosphere, e.g. rain, hail, sleet, snow.

3.2.1 Weather and climate

The difference between weather and climate

It is important to recognise the difference between weather and climate. Weather refers to the day-to-day conditions of the atmosphere, which can frequently change within a 24-hour period. Climate is the average weather conditions experienced in a place over a longer period of time, e.g. 30 years.

How the temperature and precipitation of Wales vary

The temperature and **precipitation** levels within Wales vary greatly both:

- spatially – where a location is
- temporally – in the same location at different times of the year.

The graphs below show monthly rainfall (blue bars) and temperature in Celsius (purple line).

✏️ Put into practice

Look at the **climate graphs** on the map and find the following:

- July temperature for Haverfordwest
- January rainfall for Welshpool
- the month of highest rainfall in Betws Y Coed
- the month with lowest temperature in Cardiff.

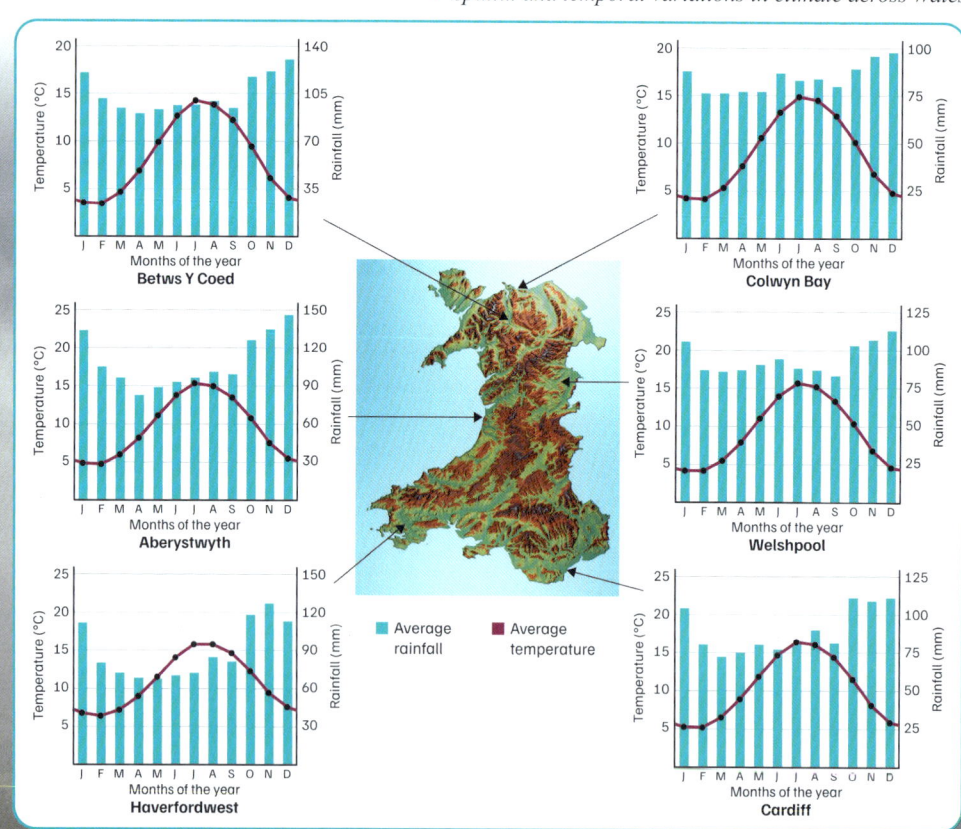

▼ *Spatial and temporal variations in climate across Wales*

The climate of Wales

Overall Wales' climate is maritime in nature – there is a fairly narrow temperature range, frequent precipitation and the weather is very changeable. As the graphs show, climate varies across Wales but there are common features we could use to describe the climate for the whole of Wales.

- The mean annual temperature is 7–11°C.
- The warmest month is usually July, the coldest months are January or February.
- May has the highest mean monthly sunshine total; December has the lowest.
- Rainfall occurs throughout the year, with the wettest period being October to January.
- Wales is one of the windier parts of the UK – with the strongest winds on high ground and at the coast.

Key terms

- **Maritime climate:** *a climate that is characterised by the large body of water that it is located near to.*

Derek Brockway

Born in 1967, Derek is a Welsh meteorologist who worked at the Met Office for 20 years. He became the main weather forecaster for BBC Wales in 1997 and regularly presents weather forecasts for the BBC on television and radio.

Ace your revision

The specification states that learners 'should know the climate of Wales'. Make sure you know some details, such as the warmest or wettest month, or temperature ranges. Stating simply that it has a **maritime climate** will limit your marks.

Fun fact

Blaenau Ffestiniog is not only one of the wettest places in Wales, but also of the UK. On average it receives 1,421 mm of rain a year.

Now try this

1. Describe how climate differs spatially across Wales for the locations shown on the map.
2. Using the climate graphs, summarise how the climate of Wales changes across the year.

Key terms

- **Air mass:** *a large body of air that has similar characteristics throughout such as temperature and humidity levels.*
- **Altitude:** *the height a location is above sea level.*
- **Aspect:** *the direction in which a slope is facing.*
- **Topography:** *the shape of the land.*

Put into practice

Explain the factors that affect Wales' climate.

3.2.2 Factors affecting temperature

There are many factors that influence temperature patterns in Wales.

- **Air masses** have a large influence on the climate of Wales and the rest of the UK. There are five air masses that influence the UK's weather. The name of the air mass indicates the weather characteristics it brings.

▼ *Main air masses influencing the weather in Wales*

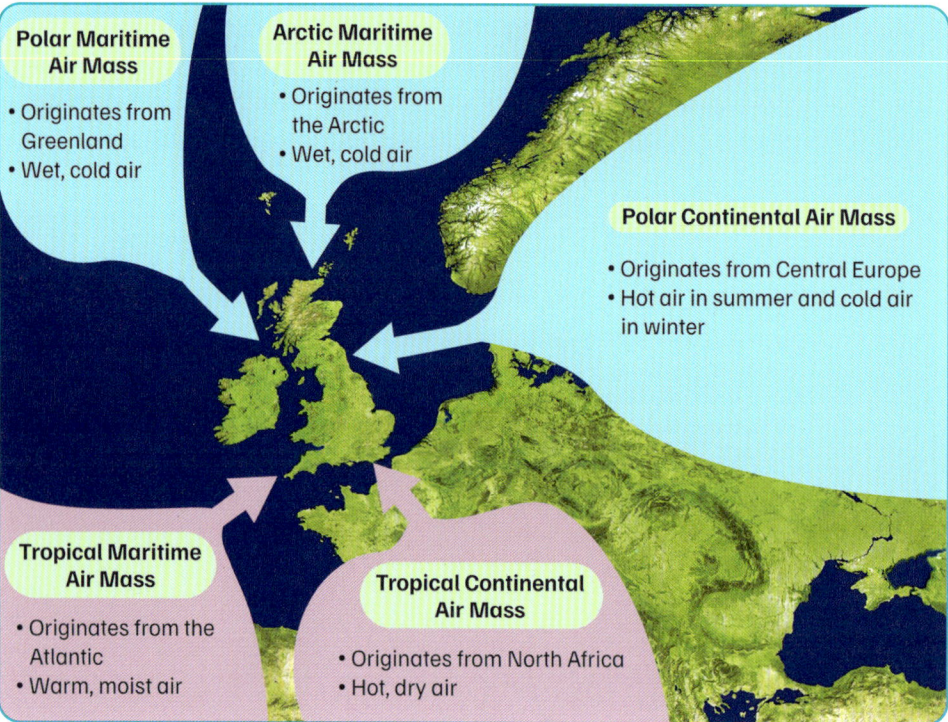

- **Altitude**: the **topography** of Wales varies greatly from stretches of coastline to numerous mountains. Altitude is therefore an important influencing factor on temperature for any location. Temperature decreases by around 1°C for every 150 m increase in altitude. There is a negative correlation between temperature and altitude.

- **Aspect**: this factor can make a significant difference to the temperatures a location receives. It is the difference between being in the shade or the direct heating effect of the sun. The sun rises in the east and sets in the west (travelling via the south) so south facing slopes in Wales experience warmer temperatures than north facing slopes.

▼ *Influence of aspect on temperature*

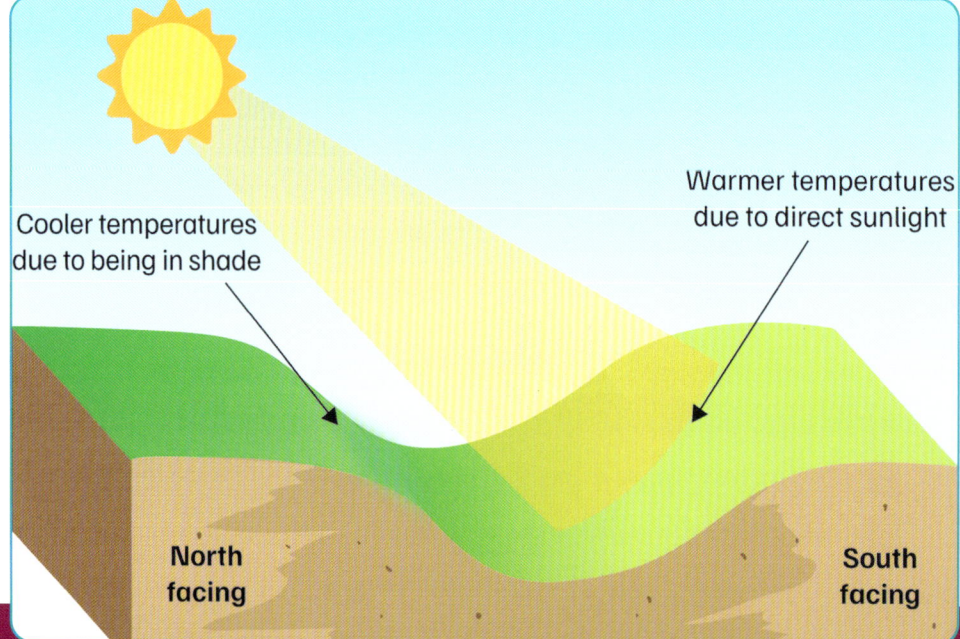

102

- **Latitude**: the closer to the equator a location is the hotter the temperatures are likely to be. The curvature of the earth influences the distance solar radiation travels before reaching the earth's surface and the surface area it heats up. Therefore, if latitude was the only influencing factor, south Wales would be warmer than north Wales.

▼ *The effect of latitude on temperature*

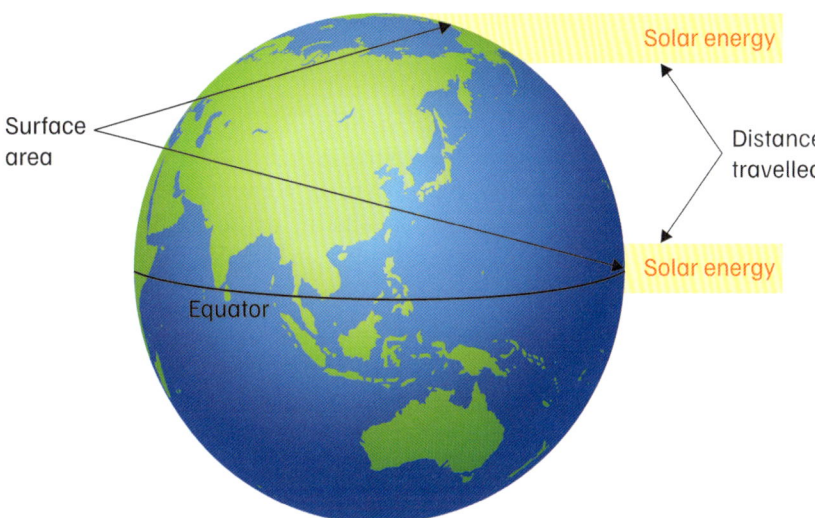

Key terms

- **Latitude:** *distance from the equator.*
- **Ocean currents:** *the large-scale movement of ocean water in a particular direction.*
- **Prevailing wind:** *the usual direction from which a wind blows for a certain location.*

Put into practice

Draw a mind map to include all the factors that influence temperature in Wales.

- **Ocean currents** affect temperature by warming (or cooling) the air above them. The main ocean current that affects the west of the UK (and therefore Wales) is called the North Atlantic Drift. This current brings a warm ocean current from the Gulf of Mexico in the South Atlantic. As a result, the western side of the UK experiences warmer temperatures in the winter compared to the eastern side.
- **Prevailing wind**: the prevailing winds for the UK come from the southwest. As a result, they bring warm air and increase temperatures in Wales.

▼ *North Atlantic Drift*

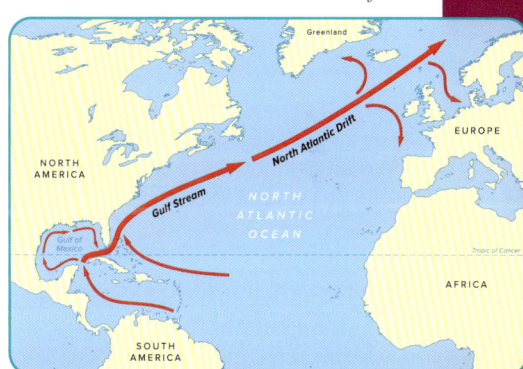

Now try this

1 Complete the following table to show how air masses affect temperatures in Wales.

Air mass	Temperature
Polar continental	
Tropical maritime	
Polar maritime	
Arctic maritime	
Tropical continental	

2 Give two reasons why latitude affects temperature.

3 Look at the climate graphs on page 100. Suggest reasons for the differences in winter temperatures for Haverfordwest and Welshpool.

Key terms

- **Condensation:** *when water vapour (gas) turns back to a water (liquid).*
- **Convectional rainfall:** *rainfall that forms due to the rapid heating of the earth's surface and the air above it.*
- **Frontal rainfall:** *rainfall due to weather fronts being created where warm and cold air meet.*

3.2.3 Factors affecting rainfall

When you are trying to understand patterns of rainfall in a location, it is important to understand how rainfall is formed, which in turn aids its forecast. For rainfall to occur there are two essential steps that need to take place:

- warm air rising
- condensation – water vapour in this warm air turns into liquid when it comes into contact with tiny particles or dust in the atmosphere.

There are three types of rainfall formation (caused by three different ways the warm air rises).

1. **Convectional rainfall** regularly occurs in tropical regions where air temperatures are hot and there are high humidity levels. In the UK, convectional rainfall happens in the summer after a period of very warm temperatures. Convectional rainfall is characterised by short periods of heavy rainfall often with thunder and lightning.

▼ *Formation of convectional rainfall*

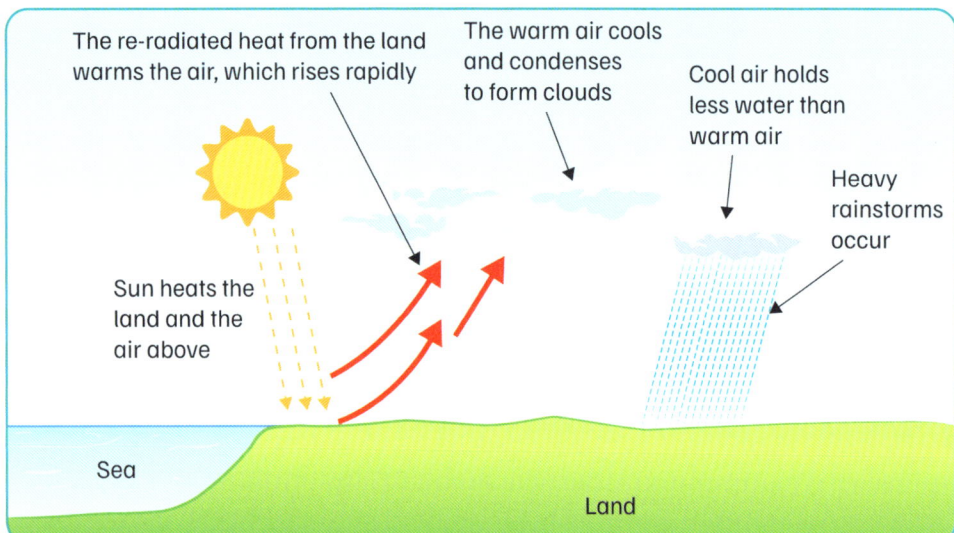

2. **Frontal rainfall** is frequent in Wales and the UK. It is created when a body of warm air meets a body of cool air. They do not mix, and the warm air rises over the cold air. The boundary line between the warm and cold air is called a weather front. Weather fronts form during low air pressure conditions.

▼ *Frontal rainfall formation*

Fun fact

The Met Office measures rainfall in official weather stations using a rain gauge. The gauge has a 12.7 cm diameter opening to collect the rain. The gauge is placed above ground level to avoid ground flow water entering it. A reading is taken and the instrument reset at 9 am every day in the UK.

3. **Relief rainfall** is also frequent in Wales. It is caused by air moving towards a mountain range, which forces the air upwards.

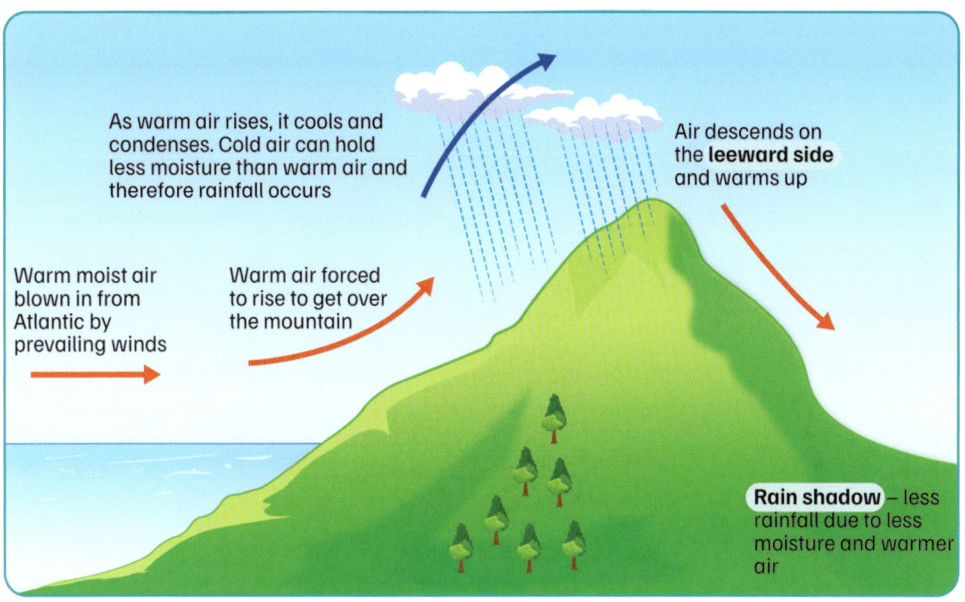

▼ *Relief rainfall formation*

Key terms

- **Leeward side:** *the side of a mountain that faces away from the prevailing wind.*
- **Rain shadow:** *an area which experiences less rainfall on the leeward side of a mountain.*
- **Relief rainfall:** *rainfall that is caused by a change in the height of the land.*

Put into practice

1. Explain why periods of intense heat can cause rainfall.
2. Explain why each side of a mountain range often experiences differing levels of rainfall.
3. Describe what happens when a body of warm air meets a body of cold air.

▼ *Relief rainfall in Eryri*

Ace your revision

A question may refer to a specific type of rainfall or provide a resource that indicates a rainfall type but doesn't name it. Make sure you know which type of rainfall the examiner wants you to talk about.

Now try this

1. What two factors are needed for rainfall to occur?
2. In convectional rainfall, is it the air heated by the sun or the re-radiated heat from the land that causes the air to rise?
3. Draw an annotated diagram to explain the formation of relief rainfall.

Key terms

- **Arid:** an area that receives little or no rain.
- **Ferrel cell:** mid-latitude atmospheric circulation which moves air in the opposite direction to the Polar and Hadley cells.
- **Global atmospheric circulation:** a global system of winds moving air between areas of high and low pressure.
- **Hadley cell:** a circulation of air that rises at the equator, travels north or south and sinks back to the earth's surface around 30° north or south. The air then moves back along the earth's surface to reach the equator before rising again.
- **Insolation:** the amount of solar radiation that is received at a location.
- **Polar cell:** the atmospheric circulation cell between 60° to 90° (poles) latitude in both hemispheres
- **Trade winds:** permanent prevailing winds that blow east to west in tropical regions.
- **Tropopause:** the boundary line in the atmosphere between the troposphere layer and the stratosphere layer.
- **Westerlies:** permanent prevailing winds found in mid latitudes (30° to 60°) that blow west to east.

Ace your revision

Make sure you know the degrees of latitude where the cells start and finish. You will need to put this detail into your exam answers.

3.2.4 Global atmospheric circulation

To understand why areas of low pressure and high-pressure form at different locations it is important to know how the global circulation of air in the atmosphere works. This is summarised in the diagram below.

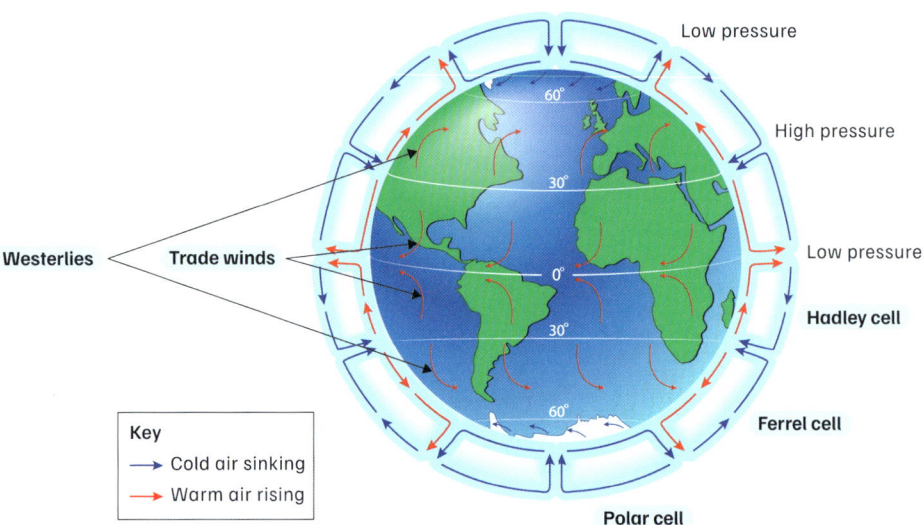

▼ *Global atmospheric circulation*

- **Low pressure (equatorial low) at the equator:** as there is more **insolation** at the equator (see page 103) the air heats up to higher temperatures and at a faster rate. As a result, the hot air rises creating an area of low pressure over the equator. We have already seen that air rising due to hot temperatures leads to convectional rainfall, which is a common feature at the equator.
- **High pressure (sub-tropical high) where the Hadley and Ferrel cells meet:** when the air that rises at the equator reaches the **tropopause** it is forced to move north or south. As it moves away from the equator it steadily becomes cooler and heavier. Around 30° north and south the air begins to descend. This descending air creates high pressure at the earth's surface, which brings **arid** conditions. At 30° N/S this air forms part of the Hadley cell and Ferrel cell circulations.
- **Low pressure (temperate low) where Ferrel and polar cells meet:** around 60° north and south we can see another area when air rises after meeting on the earth's surface. The air that descends around 30° latitude warms as it moves across the earth's surface and on meeting the cold air from the polar cell it begins to rise over the cold air. This again causes low pressure and brings frontal rain. This part of the global atmospheric circulation system has a major influence on the weather that is experienced in Wales and the rest of the UK and is the reason behind many of the low pressure systems the country experiences.

George Hadley

Born in 1685, George was an amateur meteorologist who suggested the way that circulation in the atmosphere could sustain the trade winds, which were vitally important for trading sailing ships at the time. His work led to the Hadley cell being identified. It was named after him in recognition of his earlier work.

Influence of axial tilt on global climate: The axis of the earth runs from the North to the South Pole, but it is not perpendicular (straight up and down). It has an axial tilt of around 23.5°. As a result, the angle at which the sun's rays hit the earth at different latitudes varies throughout the year. Different parts of the earth are orientated towards the sun at different times of the year and receive varying amounts of sunlight. This creates the seasons and the varying length of daylight hours.

In addition to influencing temperature and daylight hours, axial tilt will also have an impact on rainfall patterns. Nearer the equator, this results in a smaller seasonal shift in rainfall patterns, creating an intense rainy season and a drier season. Whereas around 30° north and south, the high pressure systems that are usually experienced are replaced by low pressure systems, which can bring rainfall to those normally dry areas.

Key terms

- **Axial tilt:** the angle at which the earth spins on its axis.

Fun fact

Summer is always warmer than winter due to the sun's rays hitting the earth at a more direct angle.

Put into practice

1. Make a revision card about the atmospheric air circulation. Draw on the cells and label them. Add in the direction of warm and cold air.
2. Identify the locations where high and low pressure are likely to occur.

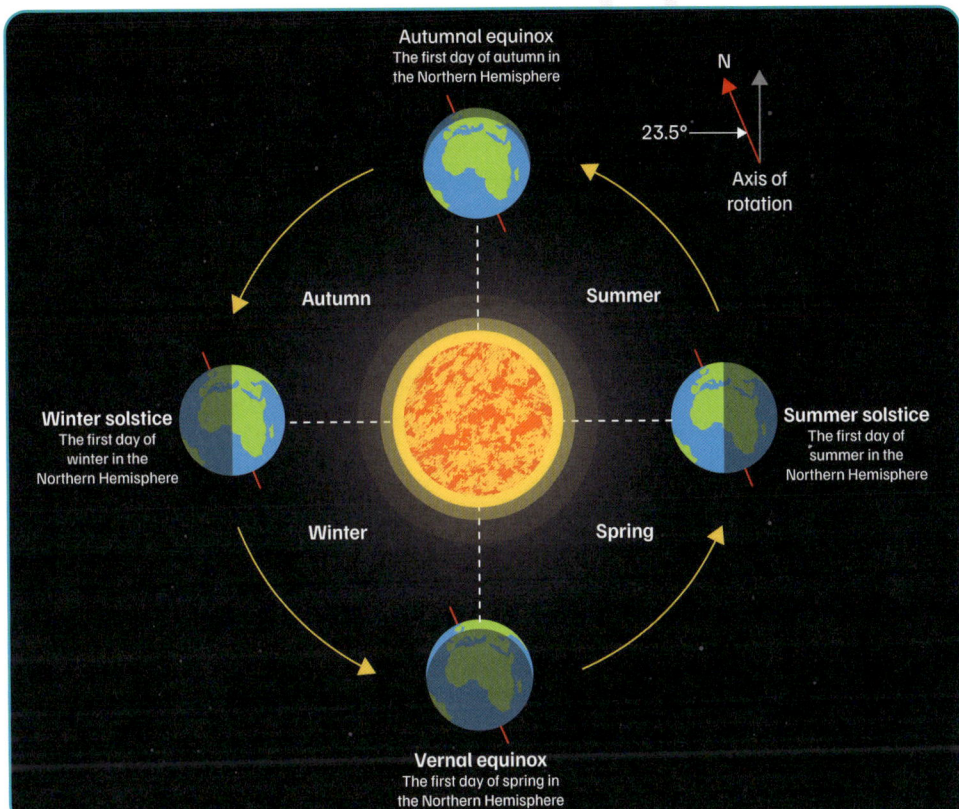

◄ *Influence of axial tilt on global climate*

William Ferrel

Born in 1817, William was an American meteorologist and teacher who studied many scientific papers of the time. He built on the work of George Hadley, writing an article on winds and current in the ocean, which was published in 1856. It discussed how the earth's rotation bent trade winds and the existence of three atmospheric cells in each hemisphere. The Ferrel cell is named after him.

Now try this ▼

1. Name the atmospheric cell that is responsible for low pressure systems at the equator.
2. Explain why the UK experiences lots of rainfall due to the global atmospheric circulation system.
3. Describe how, and explain why, the tilt of the earth has an impact on our seasons.

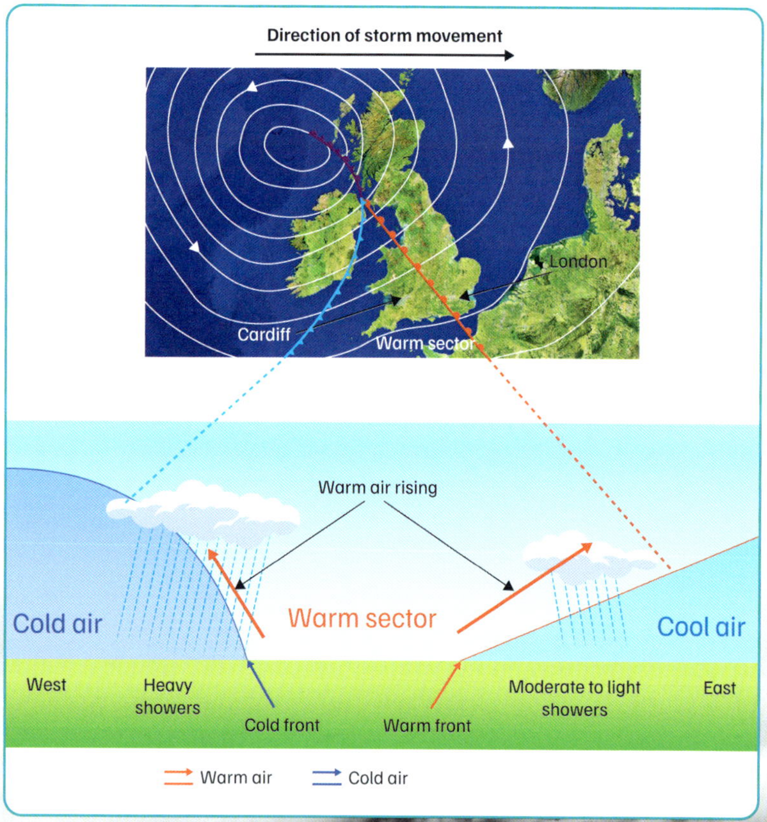

Key terms

- **Cold front:** *the boundary line between warm air and cold air when cold air moves forward and pushes underneath a body of warm air.*
- **Low pressure system (depression):** *where the air pressure is low, caused by rising air.*
- **Synoptic chart:** *a weather map showing air pressure which is used to predict the weather.*
- **Warm front:** *the boundary line between warm air and cold air where warm air is advancing.*

Put into practice

Using the image of the low pressure system, identify the following features:

A low pressure area
B occluded front
C clouds.

▼ *Low pressure system (depression)*

3.2.5 Low pressure weather systems – depressions

As we have already seen, **low pressure systems** (also known as **depressions**) are caused by a large amount of air rising. Due to the latitude of the UK, low pressure systems frequently cross the country from west to east. A **synoptic chart** of a low pressure weather system is characterised by the lowest pressure at the centre, with close isobars and **warm fronts** and **cold fronts**.

The weather conditions brought by depressions

The weather conditions brought by a depression can be described as:

- unsettled, with changeable weather and rainfall amounts
- high amount of cloud cover
- windier than high pressure with wind movement in an anticlockwise direction
- mild temperatures.

▼ *Synoptic chart and cross-section of a low pressure weather system*

How weather changes over time and space as the depression moves from west to east across Wales and the UK

The weather changes as different parts of a depression move across a location. Changes can be seen in different parts of the depression.

- **Air pressure** – air pressure lowers as the warm front approaches, reaching its lowest point in the warm sector, and then increases after the cold front passes.
- **Cloud cover and type** – as rising warm air is a key component of low pressure systems, they also create clouds. As the warm front approaches, cloud cover increases – in particular cirrus and stratus clouds. The clouds clear in the warm sector but build quickly with the approach of the cold front into large cumulonimbus clouds. Behind the cold front are cumulous clouds, which clear as the depression moves further away.
- **Precipitation frequency and intensity** – at the warm front there is drizzle and light rain. The warm sector is dry, and heavy rainfall occurs at the cold front. Behind the cold front there are showers which eventually clear.
- **Temperature** – as a depression approaches, the temperature will increase. It reaches its peak in the warm sector and decreases as the cold front approaches. After the cold front passes the temperature is significantly colder.
- **Wind speed and direction** – winds move in an anticlockwise direction in a low pressure system. The closer the isobars (pressure changes) are together, the stronger the wind speeds. The cold front is often associated with the strongest winds.

Key terms

- **Warm sector:** *the warm air between a warm front and a cold front.*

Put into practice

1. In a low pressure system:
   - do the winds blow clockwise or anticlockwise?
   - is the pressure lowest in the middle or on the edge of the weather system?
   - which comes first, the warm front or the cold front?
2. Add the weather characteristics to each section of the table below.

Behind the cold front	At the cold front	In the warm sector	At the warm front	Ahead of the warm front

Ace your revision

Ensure you know the different weather conditions for each part of the low pressure system.

Now try this

1. Describe the changing weather conditions experienced by London on page 108 as the low pressure system moves eastwards.
2. Explain why the UK experiences a lot of low pressure weather systems.

> **Key terms**
>
> - **Anticyclone:** *an area of high pressure where air is sinking.*

3.2.6 High pressure weather systems – anticyclones

High pressure systems (also known as **anticyclones**) are caused by a large amount of air sinking over an area. A synoptic chart of a high pressure system shows the highest pressure at the centre, the isobars are further apart than in low pressure systems and there is an absence of weather fronts. The weather conditions associated with areas of high pressure in Wales and the UK can be described as:

- stable – anticyclones stay over a location longer than low pressure systems
- lack of cloud cover
- low wind speeds
- dry weather.

▼ *High pressure synoptic chart*

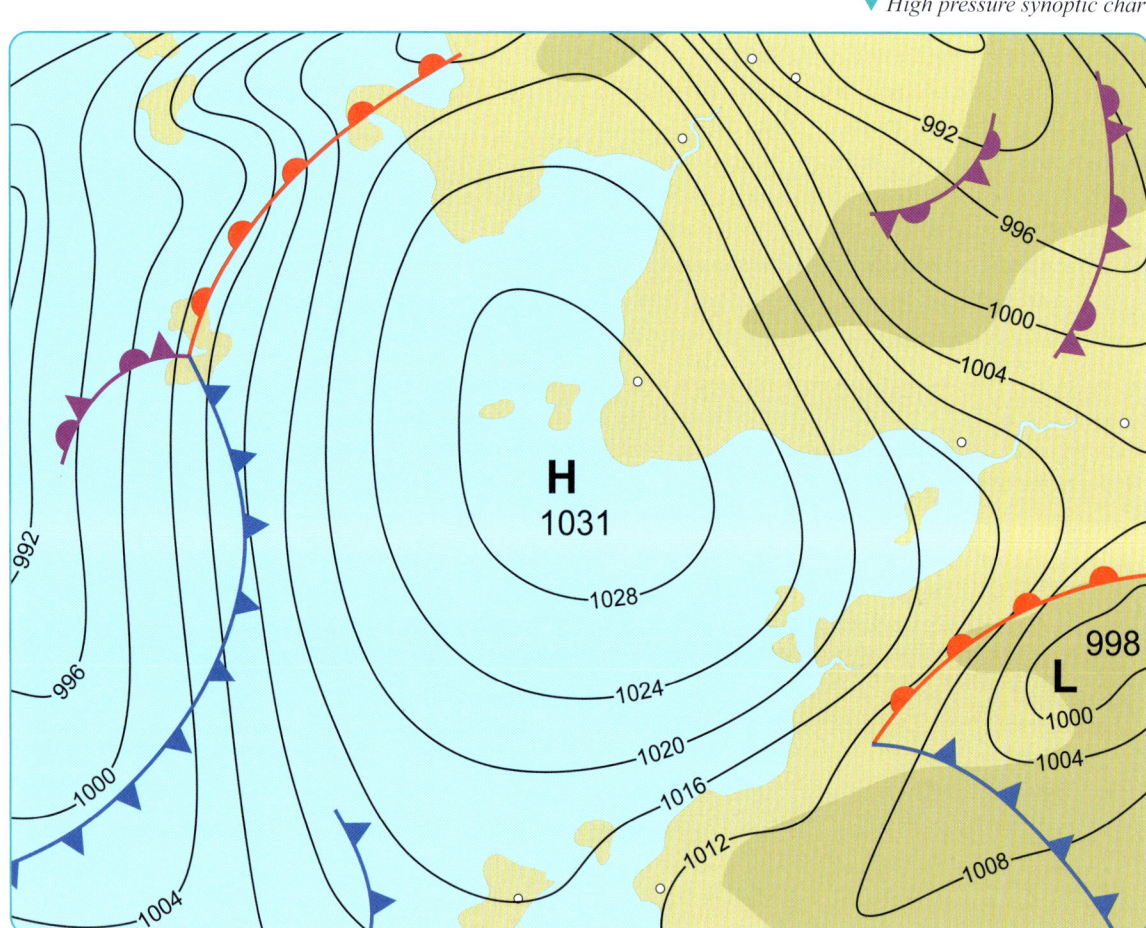

Summer and winter anticyclones

There are some similarities and differences with the weather experienced in anticyclones over the UK if they occur in summer or winter.

- **Air pressure** – the air pressure in anticyclones is usually above 1000 millibars both in winter and summer.
- **Cloud cover** – generally there is a lack of cloud cover in both summer and winter due to dry air descending rather than rising. In the summer, however, if the high pressure system brings extreme heat causing hot air to rise, then clouds will form, resulting in convectional rainfall. In the winter, fog can be caused by anticyclones due to cold temperatures forcing any moisture in the air to condense at a low (often ground) level.

- **Precipitation** – rainfall is not associated with high pressure systems as the air is dry and there are no weather fronts. However, in the summer high pressure systems can sometimes cause convectional rainfall due to long periods of heat causing hot air to rise.
- **Temperature** – this is where the most marked difference is seen. In summer, anticyclones bring hot weather to Wales and the UK due to clear skies. In winter, the clear skies lead to cold, crisp days as the lack of cloud cover enables the temperature to drop. This can lead to frost overnight.
- **Wind speed and direction** – wind speeds are very slow and often non-existent which can be seen by the widely spaced isobars in a synoptic chart. They move in a clockwise direction.

Ace your revision

Make sure you can describe the varying weather conditions between anticyclones in the summer and winter and be able to explain the reasons for these differences.

Put into practice

1. In a high pressure system:
   - **A** do the winds blow clockwise or anticlockwise?
   - **B** is the pressure highest in the middle or on the edge of the weather system?
2. Complete the following table to show the features of high pressure weather in the summer and winter.

	Air pressure	Cloud cover	Precipitation	Temperature	Wind speed and direction
Summer					
Winter					

Now try this ▼

1. Name two ways that you could identify a high pressure system on a synoptic chart.
2. Describe the common weather characteristics that are associated with high pressure systems in Wales and the UK throughout the year.
3. Explain why there are some differences in weather experienced under a high pressure system between summer and winter.
4. Heat waves are one example of summer anticyclones in Wales. Examine the impact of heat waves on people and the economy.

Chapter 3.3 Wild weather

AO1 AO2 AO3

3.3.1 Global hazards caused by extreme low pressure

Global hazards are often natural hazards that threaten people or the environment around them. As global temperatures increase, we are seeing more and more global hazards ranging from drought to tropical storms. Global hazards can be caused by extreme changes in high or low pressure.

The causes of low pressure hazards (physical and human)

Hot air rises to form clouds through the process of condensation. As part of this process, precipitation occurs bringing unsettled weather which is often associated with depressions. Low pressure encourages air masses to fill the space left by rising hot air, leading to changeable weather.

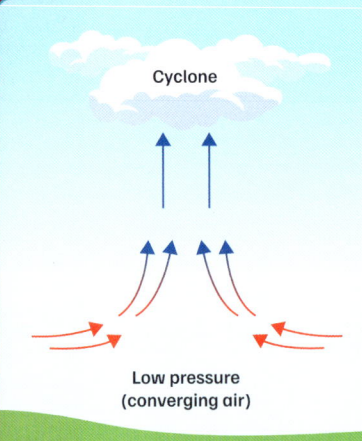

▼ *Air movement in a low pressure system*

Physical causes of low pressure hazards	Human causes of low pressure hazards
Rising and cooling of water vapour	Burning of fossil fuels, which generates greenhouse gases
Imbalance of heat across the world	Increase in cattle ranching, releasing methane
Ascending and descending air	Deforestation affects gases in the atmosphere
El Niño is a weather pattern in the tropical Pacific Ocean which causes warm sea temperatures and lower air pressure	

Impacts of low pressure hazards (social, economic and environmental)

Case study

Hurricane Sandy, Caribbean and United States east coast, 22 October–2 November 2012		
Social	Economic	Environmental
286 people were killed	It was estimated that the damage cost the city of New York $70 billion	1.5 billion tonnes of raw sewage leaked into the surrounding rivers, contaminating habitats
Nearly 2 million people in New York City experienced loss of power	Sea level rise contributed to $8 billion in damages	14 foot storm surges caused damage to the surrounding coastline
Nearly 1 million people lost mobile phone coverage/signal	Retail sales decreased by nearly 9% due to flooding damaging shops and products	80 mph strong winds

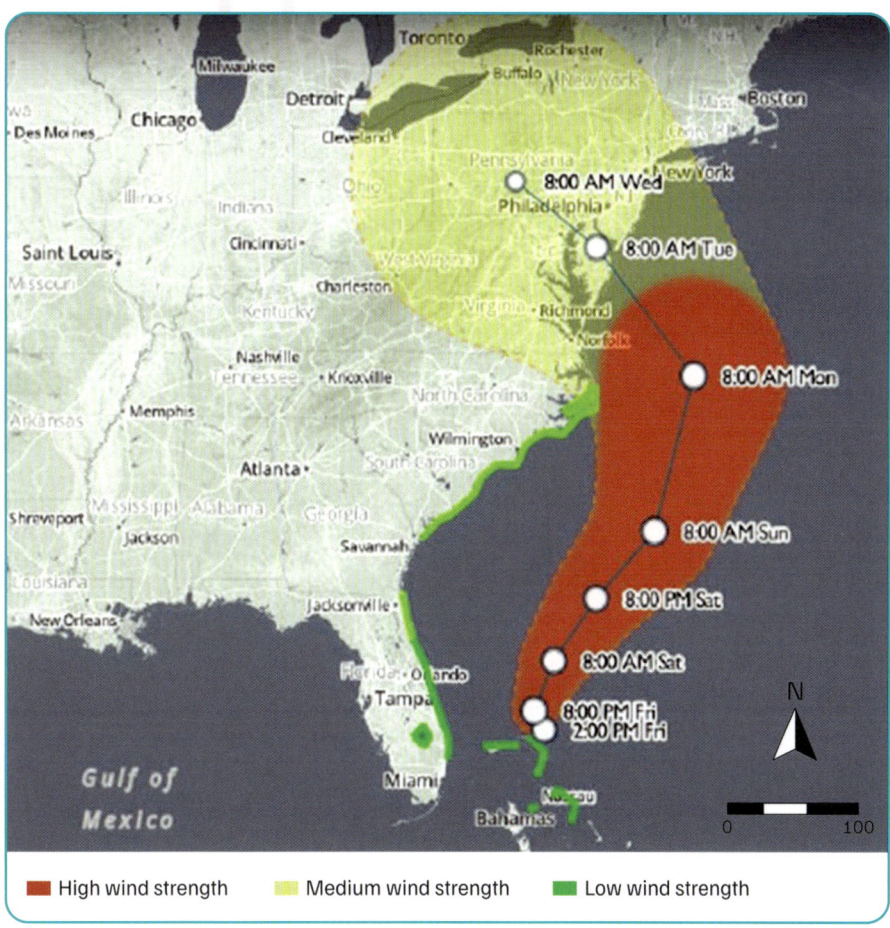

◀ Map of Hurricane Sandy

■ High wind strength　　■ Medium wind strength　　■ Low wind strength

◀ The aftermath of Hurricane Sandy

▼ People receiving food and clothes in Queens, New York, during Hurricane Sandy

Key terms

- **Mitigation:** *reducing risk or loss of a particular event.*
- **Park response model:** *a method of tracking how quickly a country responds to risk and the impacts at different stages of a disaster, also known as the disaster response curve (DRC).*
- **Risk matrix:** *a scoring system to classify levels of hazard risk.*

Put into practice

1. How would you improve the hazards management cycle in order to increase the levels of sustainability?
2. Which of the stages in the hazards management cycle will have the greatest impact on sustainability and therefore lower the risk?

Spotlight

The strength of climatic hazards can vary depending on population density, how strong and stable buildings are and how well prepared the community is.

Park response model ▶

Responses to low pressure hazards (emergency and future mitigation)

Countries can use the hazard management cycle to prepare for natural hazards. The cycle ensures each provision is taken care of in readiness for an emergency event. The better the preparation, the faster the recovery and, in theory, the lower the risk.

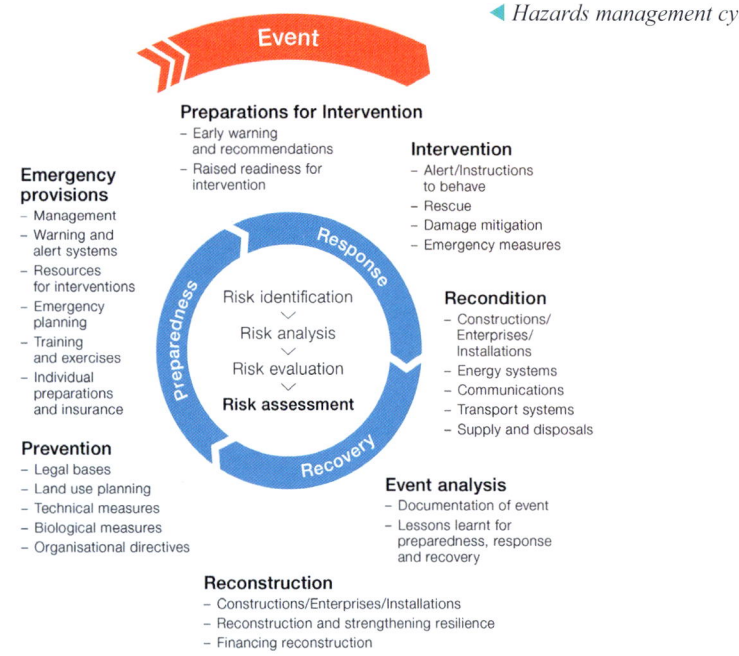

◀ *Hazards management cycle*

1. **Response** – provide immediate help, for example search and rescue crews. The faster a country's response and the more targeted their support, the more likely an area is to recover.
2. **Recovery** – rebuilding services and buildings. This relies on governments and other support agencies, such as charities, to help people get back on their feet quickly.
3. **Mitigation** – taking action to reduce the problem in the future. The better a country's planning for hazards, the quicker they can recover, and less damage might be caused.
4. **Preparedness** – educating people and developing community resilience. If people are aware a hazard could happen and know what to do, the more likely they are to survive.

The **Park response model** helps to show how important the recovery phase is in a disaster and the impact of the disaster recovery on a community's quality of life. The better the response to a disaster, the stronger and faster the recovery will be for that area.

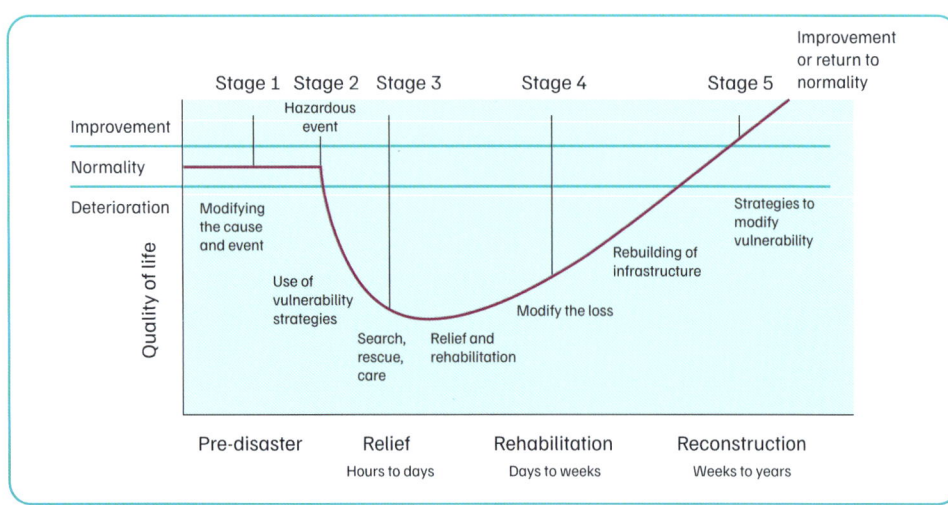

A risk matrix

	Impact				
	Insignificant 1	Minor 2	Significant 3	Major 4	Severe 5
Almost certain 5	5	10	15	20	25
Likely 4	4	8	12	16	20
Moderate 3	3	6	9	12	15
Unlikely 2	2	4	6	8	10
Rare 1	1	2	3	4	5

Probability (y-axis)

Very low | Low | Medium | High | Very high | Extreme

Scoring system for a risk matrix

- **1-4: Acceptable** – no further action needed apart from ongoing checks and maintenance
- **5-9: Adequate** – might need further intervention and support
- **10-16: Tolerable** – needs urgent reviews of measures in place
- **17-25: Unacceptable** – immediate response needed

Using a **risk matrix** to consider the probability versus impact of a hazard is another useful method that can be used by geographers to manage the risks of natural disasters.

Risk matrix ratings – probability

- Rare – unlikely to happen
- Unlikely – possible occurrence
- Moderate – likely to happen
- Likely – almost certain to happen
- Almost certain – will happen

Risk matrix ratings – impacts

- Insignificant – won't cause any serious impacts
- Minor – might cause some injuries but with minimal impact
- Significant – might cause injuries that will need emergency services to help
- Major – will cause injuries and issues that need definite intervention from professionals
- Severe – will result in death

For example, for Hurricane Sandy, if you take the possible risk of storm surges as **almost certain (score of 5)** and the impact as **significant** due to local population and housing being affected **(rating 3)**, this would give an overall risk matrix score of 15.

Responses to Hurricane Sandy

How quickly you respond to a low pressure event can mean the difference between saving lives or adding to the fatalities. Hurricane Sandy is a good example of how the government, NGOs and local people tried to respond to one of the most devastating events in history.

Responses to Hurricane Sandy included a mix of government, local community and NGOs using a top-down/bottom-up approach in order for strategies to be effective and for everyone to have ownership.

Now try this

1. Find a tropical storm case study that you want to use for your exam. Using the risk matrix template, write down five risks people faced and score them.

2. Using the response diagram for Hurricane Sandy, evaluate the different types of actions taken and how effective they were.

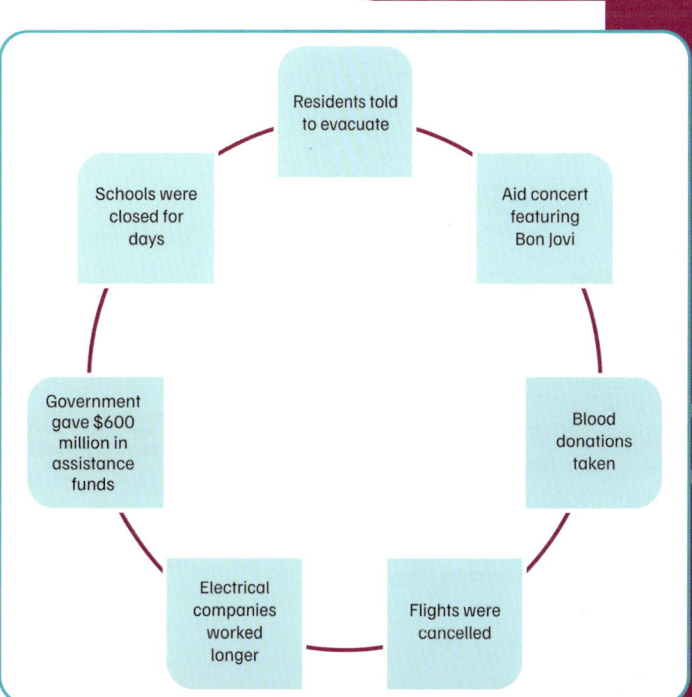

Responses to Hurricane Sandy ▶

(Residents told to evacuate; Aid concert featuring Bon Jovi; Blood donations taken; Flights were cancelled; Electrical companies worked longer; Government gave $600 million in assistance funds; Schools were closed for days)

Key terms

- **Coriolis effect:** *the earth's rotation.*
- **Equilibrium:** *balance.*
- **Severity:** *how bad the impact of something is.*

3.3.2 Global hazards caused by extreme high pressure

Global hazards can also be caused by high pressure, for example, droughts, forest fires and heat waves. Humans can increase high pressure hazards as a result of their actions. This can have a negative impact on weather events around the world.

Human causes of high pressure hazards	Physical causes of high pressure hazards
Deforestation can lead to reduced water storage in lakes and rivers	Descending air can lead to dry, hot weather in summer
Water supply diverted for cotton plantations to supply cotton for the fashion industry, which has led to disruption of the Aral Sea and disruption to seasons in the area	Change in direction of the trade winds
Burning more fossil fuels increases temperature due to disruption to the ozone layer	**Coriolis effect** – earth's rotation which can affect air circulation causing it to deflect winds and ocean currents

Nature prefers **equilibrium**, and we have upset that balance with intense human interaction. Human-induced climate change has led to a greater **severity** of high and low pressure. The atmospheric and ocean circulation is affected by disruption of the transfer of heat within the tricellular model.

▼ *Factors affecting the impact of high and low pressure systems*

▼ *Air movement in high pressure*

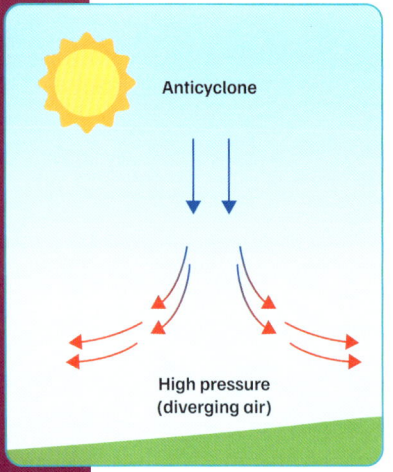

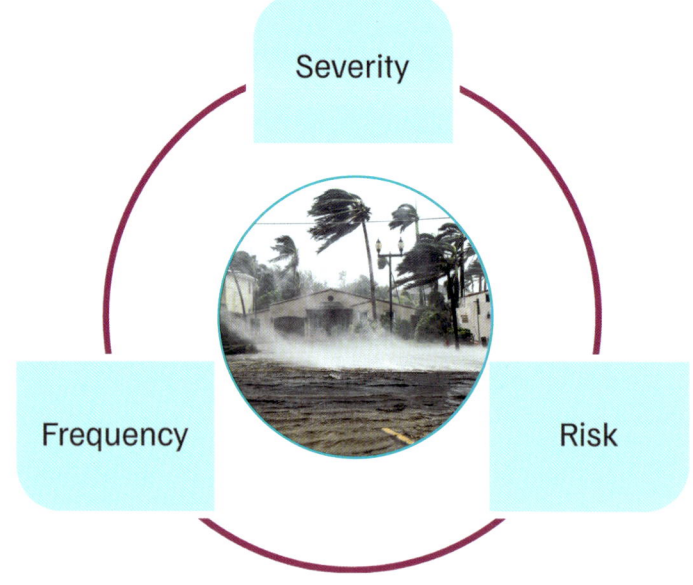

Spotlight

Australia reviews its water sources every year due to the high temperatures it experiences. This is called the Murray-Darling report.

The greater the frequency of events such as tropical storms, the more severe the impacts experienced are. As a country struggles to recover from previous events, the population, environment and economy are at greater risk from future events.

Physical causes of high pressure	Human causes of high pressure
When jet streams merge together	Burning fossil fuels releasing carbon into the atmosphere
Coriolis effect – the earth's rotation causing air to move towards the right in the northern hemisphere	Warming of the ocean temperatures as a result of surface run off containing chemicals from activities such as mining, leading to warming of the oceans

Impacts of high pressure hazards (social, economic and environmental)

Social impacts	Environmental impacts	Economic impacts
Death	Low rainfall	Loss of property
Dehydration	Wildfires	Loss of businesses
Communication systems destroyed	Heat waves	Insurance costs to repair/replace items
Injuries from fire	Drought	Government aid

Responses to global hazards caused by high pressure

Responses to geographical hazards should include emergency responses as well as planning for future mitigation in case these events happen again.

Emergency responses (short-term)	Long-term responses (mitigation)
Evacuation of areas at risk of high pressure hazard, e.g. drought	Constructing new buildings that are made from materials that are durable (long lasting)
Search and rescue teams looking for people	Dam building to ensure water stores are maintained
Banning the use of hose pipes	Developing more efficient use of irrigation for farming, e.g. hydroponics
Digging new wells, e.g. Oxfam help to do this	Water transfer schemes (Wales transfers water to England)
Emergency water trucking (EWT) – Oxfam help to provide temporary water trucks to rural areas	Desalination plants to use sea water that is filtered and cleaned (but the power used to run desalination plants may add greenhouse gases to the atmosphere)

▼ *EWT response in Somalia*

▲ *The stool of sustainability shows how environmental, social and economic factors support sustainability*

How sustainable are responses of a specific global extreme high pressure weather event?

If sustainable responses to high pressure hazards such as drought are done well, it can limit population exposure to this hazard by up to 70%. When evaluating how sustainable human responses are to high pressure hazards, it is important to consider the impact on social, economic and environmental areas of life.

 **Ace your revision**

In your exam, you might be asked to explain the impacts of high pressure systems. Use connectives to help drill down explanations of each point, for example:

This leads to... furthermore, a consequence of this is... as a result of this, I think...

Chapter 3.4 Continual climate change

AO1 AO2 AO3

🔑 Key terms

- **Eccentricity:** *a measure of how circular or oval the earth's circulation of the sun is.*
- **Elliptical:** *when the earth's circulation of the sun appears more oval.*
- **Obliquity:** *the angle of tilt of the earth's axis from vertical.*
- **Orbital precession:** *the extent to which the earth 'wobbles' on its axis as it turns.*

3.4.1 Natural causes of climate change

The climate naturally changes, going through periods of warming and, at other times, periods of cooling. These periods will differ in their duration and are caused by different factors.

Milankovitch cycles

Milankovitch cycles are changes in the way the earth moves in its orbit around the sun, on its axis and how it turns.

- **Eccentricity** – the earth's orbit of the sun varies from being almost circular to being **elliptical**. When the orbit is more elliptical, there is more variation in distance between the earth and the sun. As a result, there is a greater difference in the solar radiation received. This leads to a difference in the length of our seasons. If eccentricity reduces, the length of the seasons becomes more even. Currently the earth's eccentricity is approaching its most circular orbit, which means the length of the seasons is even.

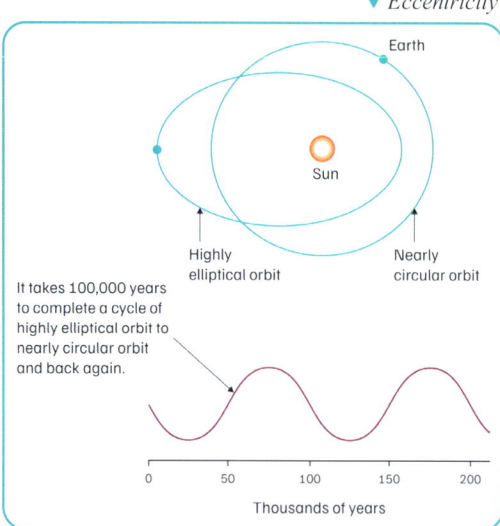
▼ *Eccentricity*

- **Obliquity** – the angle of the axis of the earth's rotation varies between 22.5° and 24.5°. When the angle is greater we experience more extremes in the seasons. This is because in the summer, when the hemisphere is tilted towards the sun, it is closer to the sun and receives more heat. Periods when the angle of tilt is larger are linked to ice melting, whereas a shallower tilt leads to periods of ice accumulation.

- **Orbital precession** – as the earth rotates around its axis, it wobbles due to the gravitational effects of the moon and sun. This wobble makes the difference between the seasons more extreme in one hemisphere and less extreme in the other.

Even though each of the Milankovitch cycles move independently of each other, when taken together they have an influence over the climate of the earth across long timescales.

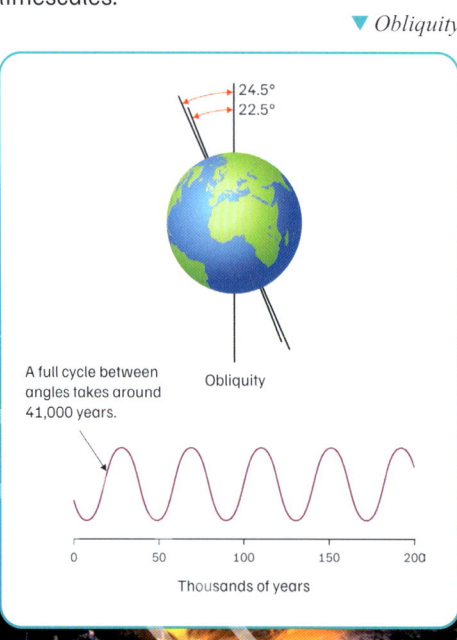
▼ *Obliquity*

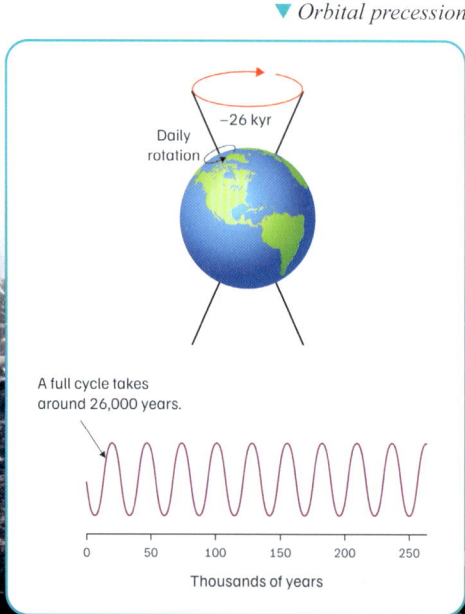
▼ *Orbital precession*

Milutin Milanković

Born in Serbia in 1879, Milutin was a mathematician, astronomer and climatologist. His work on the position of the earth in relation to the sun (Milankovitch cycles) helps to explain why the earth has experienced previous periods of climate change (glacial and interglacial periods) together with a prediction of when this will happen in the future.

Fun fact

Currently the southern hemisphere is seeing greater extremes between the seasons, but in around 13,000 years' time this will change to the northern hemisphere seeing greater extremes.

Sunspots

The amount of solar radiation emitted by the sun can naturally vary. Sunspots are darker, cooler areas on the sun's surface (caused by a concentration of magnetic field lines). Sunspots are actually intense storms on the surface of the sun and can lead to solar flares.

Scientists believe the impact of sunspots on climate change is minimal. The individual sunspots on their own don't affect climate, but it's the solar activity that can affect temperature as it radiates towards earth. During periods of low sunspot activity, the sun emits less energy, which can lead to cooler temperatures. The greater the level of sunspot activity, the warmer temperatures will be. Increased sunspot activity also increases the intensity and frequency of the northern lights, making them more visible.

▼ *The northern lights*

Spotlight

The number of sunspots varies through a natural cycle of around 11 years. It is thought a period of cooling known as the Little Ice Age (1650–1850) may have been due to sunspots reducing the amount of solar radiation reaching the earth. The solar energy can reach the earth and increase global average temperatures by 0.05°C to 0.1°C.

Did you know

There is a solar cycle prediction panel that meet to look at evidence of solar cycles because they effect spacecraft and radio communications.

Key terms

- **Glacial period:** *a period of time, thousands of years, where temperatures are colder and glaciers advance.*
- **Interglacial period:** *a period of time, thousands of years, where temperatures are warmer and glaciers retreat.*
- **Quaternary period:** *a period of geological time which covers from 2.58 million years ago to the present day.*

Fun fact

The eruption of Krakatoa in 1883 is still one of the world's largest ever volcanic eruptions. The volcanic eruption was so loud that it was heard 3000 km away in Australia. The volume of ash produced was so large that it blocked out the sun, which resulted in a lowering of global temperatures for around five years.

Put into practice

1. Describe the eccentricity cycle of the earth.
2. What are sunspots?
3. Give the main characterisitcs of a glacial climate and an interglacial climate.

Volcanic eruptions

Volcanic activity can have an impact on climate in a couple of ways.

- When a volcano erupts it emits gases including carbon dioxide, which is a greenhouse gas. This will reinforce the greenhouse effect and can lead to an increase in temperatures.
- When large volcanoes erupt, a vast quantity of volcanic dust is ejected into the upper atmosphere. This can be transported large distances from the eruption site. It can reflect incoming solar radiation so that the amount of solar radiation received at the earth's surface decreases. This will cause a decrease in temperature. The eruption of Mount Pinatubo in the Philippines is thought to have had a slight temporary cooling effect on global temperatures.

Comparing glacial and interglacial climates to today

When we look over longer time scales, we can see marked differences in climate. The following graph shows the difference in temperatures.

▼ *Global temperatures over the last 400,000 years (**Quaternary period**)*

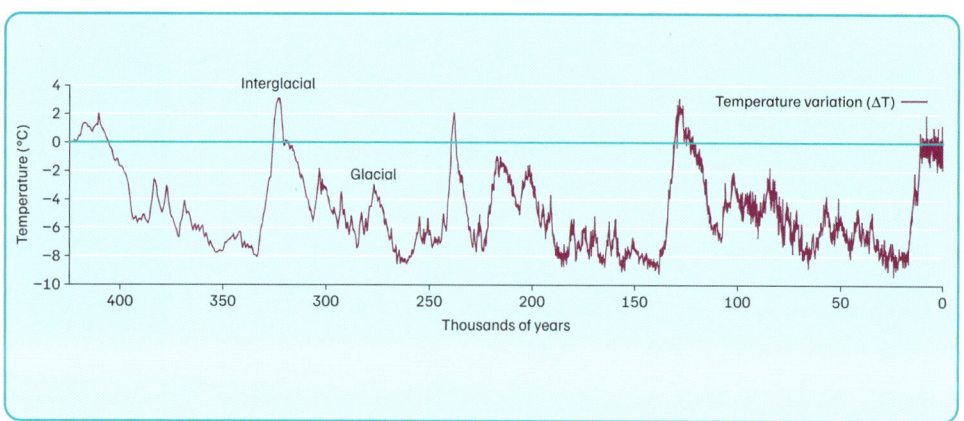

From the graph we can see that during **glacial periods** the average temperature varies between 0°C and -9°C, and during **interglacial periods** the average temperature ranges between 0°C and 3°C. Glacial periods last longer (70,000 to 90,000 years) than interglacial periods (10,000 years). We are currently in an interglacial period that has lasted 11,000 years so far.

Interglacial periods experience more rainfall than glacial periods because much of the water in the hydrological cycle in glacial periods is locked up in vast ice sheets. As a result, in glacial periods the climate is very arid, with about half of the amount of rainfall that we experience today. The current warming period (interglacial) is overwhelmingly driven by human action as it is warming at an unprecedented rate.

Now try this

1. Explain how orbital precession impacts climate.
2. Evaluate whether volcanic eruptions may have more of a warming or cooling effect on climate.
3. Describe how today's climate compares to those of a glacial and interglacial climate.
4. To what extent do you agree that the current period of global warming is unquestionably linked to physical causes?

3.4.2 Human causes of recent climate change

The natural greenhouse effect

The **greenhouse effect** is a natural process where heat is trapped in the earth's atmosphere. This process warms up the earth's atmosphere and enables life to exist on earth.

> **Key terms**
> - **Greenhouse effect:** *a natural process that traps heat in the earth's atmosphere.*
> - **Greenhouse gases:** *gases that trap or absorb heat.*
> - **Re-radiated:** *when short-wave radiation from the sun is absorbed by the earths' surface and re-emitted as long wave heat radiation back into the atmosphere.*

▼ *The greenhouse effect*

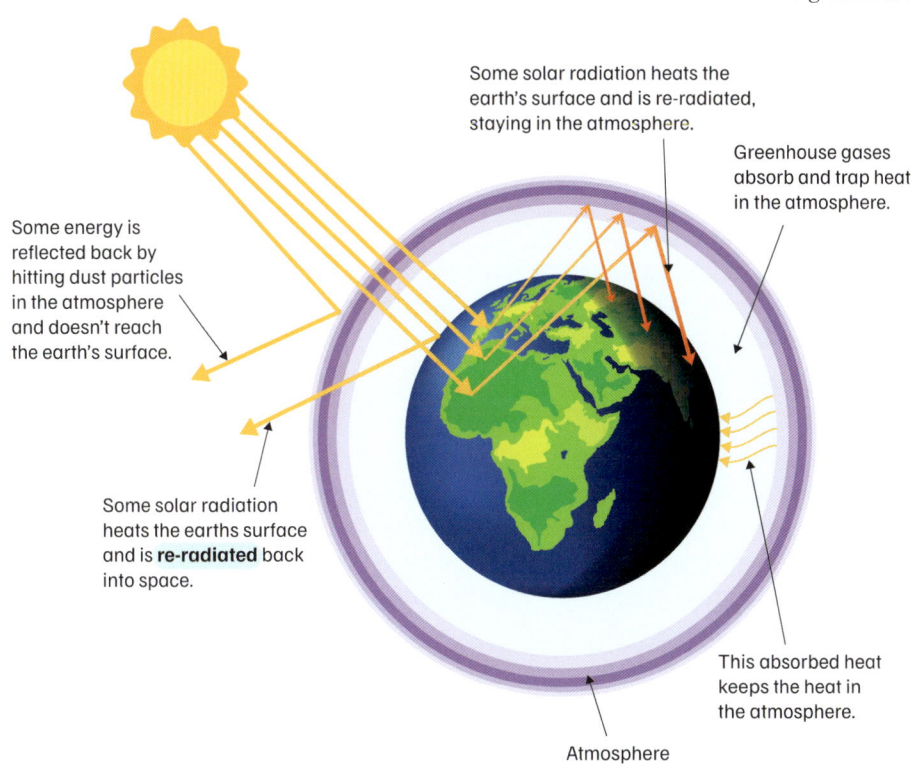

Cows produce methane when they burp.

The **greenhouse gases** that occur naturally in the atmosphere include:

- **carbon dioxide** – produced during respiration, natural forest fires, volcanic eruptions and decomposition of plants
- **nitrous oxide** – present through the nitrogen cycle, e.g. bacteria breaking down material in soil and emissions from oceans
- **water vapour** – present in the atmosphere due to the hydrological cycle
- **methane** – produced in wetland habitats, digestive processes of some animals (termites and cows) and microbes in oceans.

121

Ace your revision

When discussing the greenhouse effect in an extended answer, ensure that you mention it is a natural process that is 'enhanced' or 'increased' by human activity.

Eunice Newton Foote

Born in 1819, Eunice was the first scientist to be able to confirm that water vapour and carbon dioxide could absorb heat. Even though a man named John Tyndall is credited with 'discovering' the greenhouse effect, it is actually the work of Eunice Foote that enabled him to do so.

Human enhanced greenhouse effect

Many human activities increase the amount of these greenhouse gases in the atmosphere and therefore increase or enhance the greenhouse effect. This leads to a greater amount of warming than would naturally happen.

- **Carbon dioxide**
  - **Burning fossil fuels** – fossil fuels (such as oil, coal and gas) are fossilised remains of animals and plants that lived millions of years ago. When burnt they release the carbon that was stored in the organism.
  - **Deforestation** – forests are often referred to as carbon sinks or the 'lungs of the world' because trees absorb carbon dioxide through photosynthesis. When trees are cut down, this stops the absorption of carbon dioxide and increases the amount in the atmosphere. If these trees are then burnt, deforestation has a further impact because the carbon that was stored in the tree is released into the atmosphere.
- **Methane**
  - **Landfills** – as large amounts of waste decompose, they release methane.
  - **Farming (cattle)** – cows produce methane through their complex digestive systems. Methane is released when they burp.
- **Nitrous oxide**
  - **Industrialisation** – nitrous oxide is produced as a by-product of many manufacturing processes, e.g. the production of nylon fibres.
  - **Farming (crops)** – most arable farmers use artificial fertilisers to speed up and increase the growth of crops. These fertilisers are often nitrogen based which bacteria in the soil convert to nitrogen dioxide.
  - **Fuel combustion** – when fossil fuels are burnt for fuel, they release nitrous oxide.

Put into practice

1. Make a copy of the greenhouse effect diagram on page 121 and add numbers to indicate the order of the labels shown.
2. What is meant by the term 'enhanced greenhouse effect'?
3. Create a table like the one below to indicate how each of the named gases can be increased in the atmosphere.

	Carbon dioxide	Methane	Nitrous oxide
Naturally occurring			
Human activity			

Now try this

1. Explain the process that keeps heat in the earth's atmosphere.
2. Look at the image of forest fires and explain why this human activity might have an impact on the greenhouse effect.
3. Of the human activities mentioned on this page, evaluate which is the most unsustainable.

▲ *Forest fires*

3.4.3 Evidence that our climate is changing

There are many pieces of evidence that show our climate is changing. It is important to look at both long-term and short-term evidence in order to understand how the climate is changing.

Long-term evidence

- **Ice core data** – an ice core is a section of ice drilled out of an ice sheet or glacier. It shows layers as each season of snow has fallen and been frozen to form ice. The ice often has gas bubbles trapped in it, which represent the atmospheric conditions at the time the layer was created. Analysing the chemicals in these gas bubbles gives an indication of the climate at the time.

Short-term evidence

- **Dendrochronology (changes to tree rings)** – as a tree grows, its trunk gets wider. When the tree is cut down, a series of rings can be seen in the trunk. Each ring represents a year of growth. The width of the ring indicates the amount of growth and is an indicator of climate. A wider ring indicates a warmer, wetter climate.
- **Intergovernmental Panel on Climate Change (IPCC)** – the IPCC is an organisation put together by the United Nations to assess data in relation to climate change. It looks at the data from thousands of organisations around the world to assess the current extent and future risks of climate change and the adaptations communities may need to make.
- **NASA Science** – NASA collects scientific data to provide climate change evidence and support communities in adapting to its effects. The types of data they can provide are sea level change observations from space and one of the most reliable sources of surface temperature analysis (GISTEMP).

▼ *An ice core from Iceland, showing layers of ash from eruptions over the centuries*

▼ *Dendrochronology – measuring the width of tree rings*

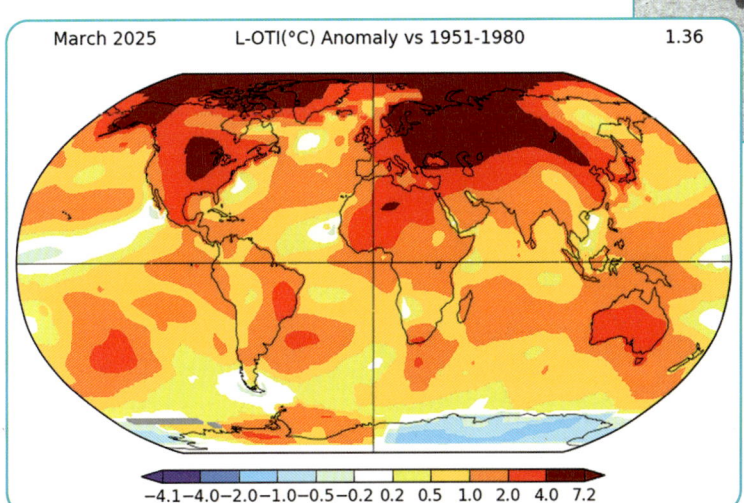

▼ *NASA surface temperature analysis map*

Key terms

- **Thermal expansion:** *when a liquid is heated, it expands in size.*

Fun fact

If the whole of the Antarctic ice sheet melted, then global sea levels would rise by 58 m.

Keeling Curve

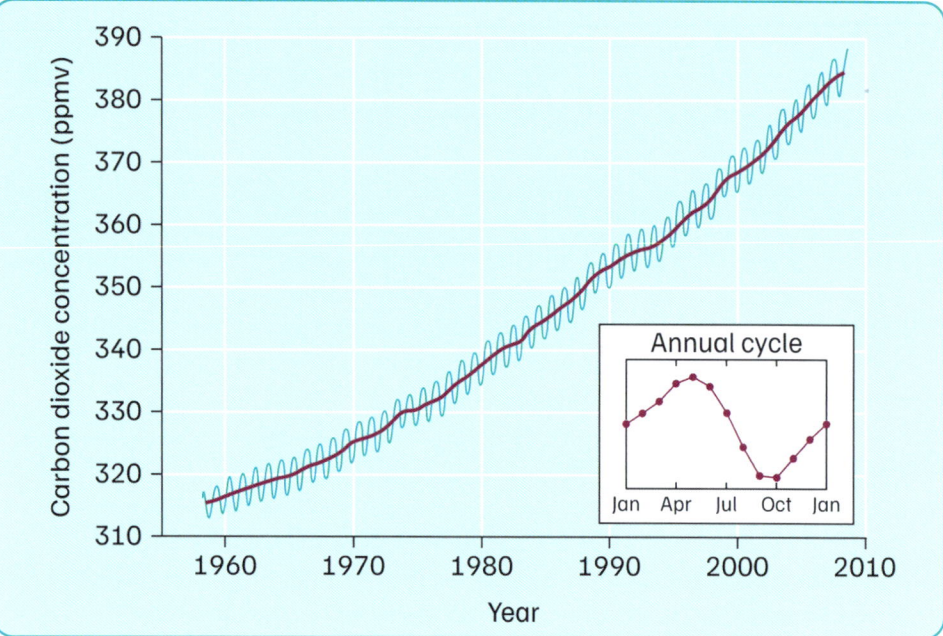

- **Keeling curve** – this is a graph which shows the seasonal variation of carbon dioxide recorded at the Mauna Loa Observatory, in Hawaii, from 1958 to the present day. As carbon dioxide is a greenhouse gas, it is logical to think that as the amount of carbon dioxide in the atmosphere increases, so will the surface air temperature.
- **Retreating glaciers, ice caps and sea ice** – the expansion or reduction of the size of glaciers and ice caps is a good visual method of identifying climate change. If temperatures are increasing, then these will retreat at a faster rate. For example, the ice caps on the top of Mount Kilimanjaro in Tanzania have melted by around 80% since 1912.
- **Sea level rise** – in warmer climates global sea levels rise due to **thermal expansion** and the release of water from melting ice caps and glaciers. Monitoring sea levels through sea gauges, and more recently satellites, enables comparisons to be made.

Charles David Keeling

Born in 1928, Charles worked at the Mauna Loa Observatory in Hawaii and was involved in measuring seasonal variations in carbon dioxide levels. His work was able to contribute towards confirmation of the theory that human activity was enhancing the greenhouse effect.

Put into practice

1. Why should climatologists look at both short- and long-term evidence of climate change?
2. Suggest reasons why the Keeling Curve oscillates every year.
3. Describe two ways in which warmer temperatures lead to sea level rise.

Now try this

1. Explain why ice cores provide data that other forms of climate change evidence do not provide.
2. Describe how tree rings provide evidence of climate change.

3.4.4 Consequences of climate change

The impacts of climate change are wide and varied. Some of the impacts are shown below.

Impacts of climate change in two contrasting places

There are different types of contrasting environments that you could compare when looking at the impacts of climate change. Some examples include:

- two countries at different stages of the development continuum
- an island country compared to a continental country
- a country with a coastline compared to a landlocked country
- two regions within the same country.

Ace your revision

When answering a question on the impacts of climate change make sure you highlight which impacts are on the environment and which are impacts on people.

Put into practice

1. Annotate a world map to highlight an area of the world for each of the impacts shown in the diagram below.
2. Research and write a one-page summary of the impacts of climate change on:
   - two countries at different stages of the development continuum
   - a country with a coastline compared to a landlocked country
   - two regions within the same country.

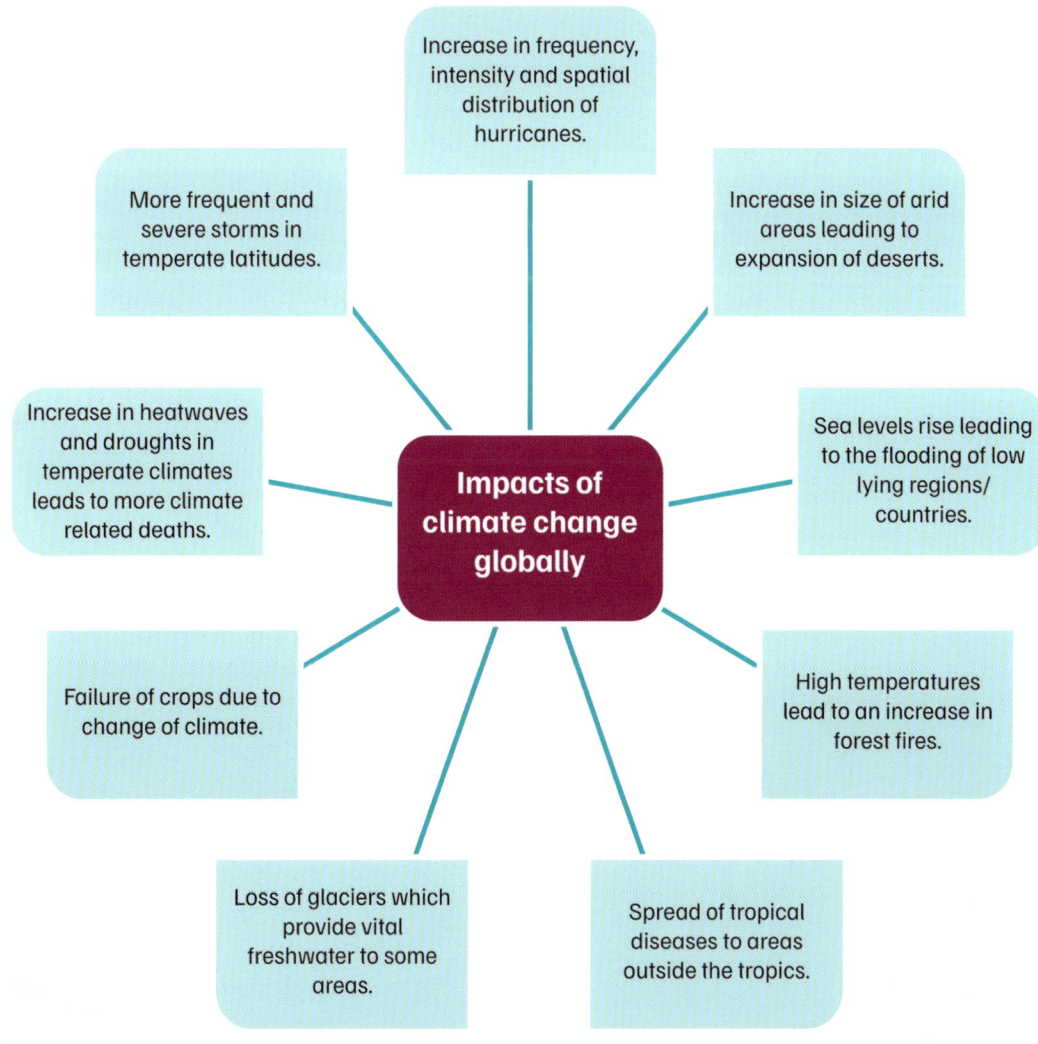

Impacts of climate change on an island country and a continental country

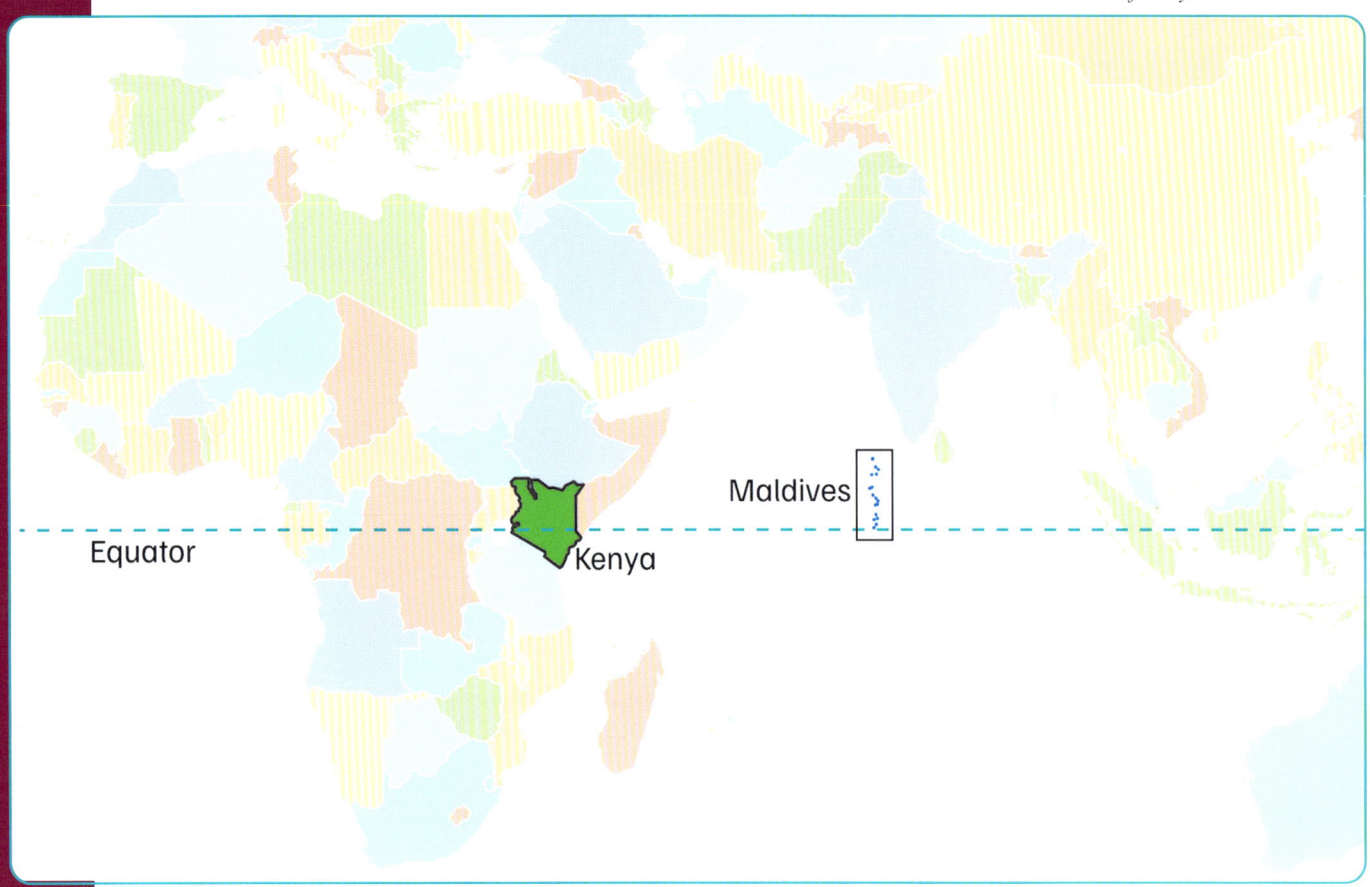

▼ *Location of Kenya and the Maldives*

Island country – Maldives

Impacts of climate change on the Maldives

- One of the smallest countries in Asia, the Maldives is home to half a million people.
- Tourism is the major industry with over half a million visitors each year. They come to see the coral reefs and spectacular sea life.
- Composed of around 1,200 islands but only around 200 are inhabited.
- The highest point of land is 2 m above sea level and is extremely vulnerable to the effects of climate change.
- Warmer ocean temperatures lead to the death of coral reefs and sea animals that depend on them.
- According to the World Bank, 'with future sea levels projected to increase in the range of 10 to 100 cm by the year 2100, the entire country could be submerged'.
- The Maldives has put together a National Adaptation Programme of Action, that attempts to alleviate many of the threats the Maldives faces.
- A large sea wall has been built around the capital Male.
- In 2008, the Maldivian president announced plans to purchase new land in India, Sri Lanka, and Australia for when much of the country is submerged.

▲ Inhabited Maldivian island

◀ Abandoned Maldivian island

▲ Sea wall built around Male, the Maldivian capital

Spotlight

1.8 billion people are at risk of severe flooding due to climate change.

Continental country – Kenya

Impacts of climate change on Kenya

- Kenya is home to around 55 million people. It is a country of contrasts – cities to rural villages, tropical coastline to high mountains.
- Tourism and farming are the major industries. Nearly 2 million people visit Kenya each year. They mainly come to see the wildlife and landscapes.
- Kenya exports around $190 million foodstuffs a month.
- Global warming will lead to increased severity and frequency of droughts, which will impact Kenya's ability to grow/rear and export food.
- Poor crop growth will lead to famine and the displacement of people from rural areas.
- Much of Kenya's coastal areas are on low lying land, which means they are vulnerable to sea level rise and storm surges.
- Kenya is aiming to ensure that within the next 20 years, 100% of energy generation will be from renewable fuels.

▲ *Rhinos in Nairobi National Park, Kenya*

▲ *A dried up dam in Kajiado, Kenya 2022*

Put into practice

Use the information on pages 126–128 plus your own research to complete the following table.

Impact of factor on the country	Kenya	Maldives
Sea level		
Temperature		
Rainfall		
Water resources		
GDP		
Infrastructure		
Tourism		
Ecosystems		
Location of population		

Now try this ▼

1. Give two impacts of climate change on the environment and on people.

2. Evaluate the impacts of climate change on two contrasting places that you have studied.

Chapter 3.5 Managing global challenges

AO1 AO2 AO3

 **Key terms**

- **COP:** The United Nations conference of the parties.

 Ace your revision

Remember to use real-life case studies of named places/events wherever possible, especially for 6- and 8-mark questions.

Spotlight

Management at global level. **COP** 27 was the 27th United Nations Annual meeting on climate change where it was decided that funding (run by the World Bank) would be available to support poorer nations with the impacts of climate change.

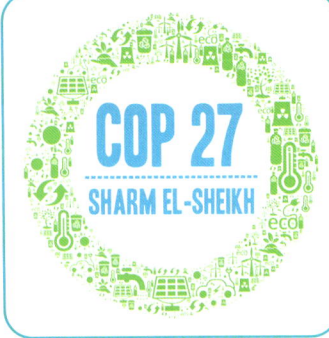

3.5.1 Managing climate change

Climate change is a severe threat to the earth and its functions. The choices we make in the next few years will have long lasting effects on our future and for the generations to come. According to the IPCC report in 2018, if temperatures continue to rise by 2°C, there will be many adverse impacts on our oceans, marine wildlife and human existence.

How are people managing the impacts of climate change?

To tackle the growing issue of climate change, a top-down approach from the government and bottom-up approach from local communities is needed. There are a range of strategies and policies already being used to try and mitigate for the serious issues we are facing. These can be divided into three levels: local, regional and global.

In 2022, the Welsh Government set up a programme to restore national peatlands over a 5-year period. It is estimated that this plan will reduce carbon emissions by 8,000 tonnes. This is an example of management at a national level.

▼ *Peat bog in Bannau Brycheiniog*

▲ Solar panels near Seville, Spain

Fun fact

Seville has a solar panel field that has enough panels to power 3,000 homes regionally. Solar panels help manage climate change by reducing greenhouse gas emissions and replacing fossil fuels with a clean, renewable energy source. Solar panels also help reduce our dependency on fossil fuels, which ultimately reduces the emission of toxic gases into the atmosphere.

Greta Thunberg

Greta Thunberg is an environmental activist who has inspired younger people to protest against climate change.

Al Gore

Al Gore is a former US vice president and founder of The Climate Change Reality Project. He won the Nobel peace prize for his work on climate change in 2007.

He said the following about climate change.

1. We have the solutions.
2. It's a moral issue not a political one.
3. We have to act immediately.
4. The impacts are many.
5. We can control the pace of melting ice.

Brain break

What do you think Greta Thunberg meant when she said:

'The climate crisis is both the easiest and the hardest issue we have ever faced.'

The sustainability of management approaches

According to the IPCC report (2018), there are many benefits to keeping the climate change temperature increase at 1.5°C.

- Global sea level would be 10 cm lower compared to a global temperature rise of 2°C.
- Coral reef decline would be around 70–90%, but coral reefs would be virtually gone if the temperature rise was 2°C.

Being sustainable is vital if we are to keep climate change below 2°C, especially as urban areas grow, and the effects of climate change become greater. Reviewing ideas, strategies and policies on a regular basis will help ensure people are thinking about the impact of managing climate change.

Ace your revision

Remember to try using the sliding scale of opinion when you have to justify or evaluate the impact of something

Now try this

1. Evaluate the strategies available to mitigate against the impact of climate change.

3.5.2 Managing threats to our oceans

What are the threats to the biodiversity of our oceans?

Plastic threats to oceans	Climate change	Pollution threats to oceans
Plastic pollution – 80% of marine litter comes from land sources. This affects 100,000 global marine species every year	Sea level rise – by 2050, 800 million people will live in cities where sea levels could rise by more than 0.5 m	Heavy metals can directly affect marine wildlife. Factories and industrial plants discharge sewage directly into rivers and oceans
Eight million pieces of plastic make their way into the ocean every day	The oceans absorb carbon dioxide leading to higher sea temperatures	Oil spills – the Sea Empress disaster off the coast of Pembrokeshire (1996)
Marine animals, from tiny plankton to large whales, can mistake plastic for food. Sea turtles often eat plastic bags because they resemble jellyfish	Rising sea temperatures cause damage to coral reefs, e.g. Australia's Gold Coast	Air pollution – responsible for at least one third of contaminates in global oceans
'Ghost fishing' is threatening marine life. When damaged nets are thrown overboard, they continue to catch marine animals	Ocean acidification – oceans around Australia are acidifying 10 times faster now and more than the last 300 million years	Offshore drilling contributes to climate change and the destruction of marine habitats and coastal communities

Small scale threats to oceans

- **Ocean noise** – from ships and boats causing marine wildlife to move off course because their neurological senses have been affected.
- **Ghost fishing nets** – species becoming trapped in abandoned 'ghost' fishing nets and wires.

Large scale threats to oceans

- **Overfishing** – this led to the collapse of the Canadian fishing industry in the late 1990s.
- **Tectonic** events – can displace sea levels, making them higher.

How can threats be managed?

There are different ways to manage the threats to our oceans at local, national and global scales.

Key terms

- **Acidification:** *a change in pH value to become more acid.*
- **Biodiversity:** *a variety of species.*
- **Carbon capture:** *securing carbon by using wetted upland areas.*
- **Marine:** *saltwater based, e.g. sea, oceans.*
- **Tectonic:** *large scale processes that move the earth's plates, leading to volcanic eruptions, earthquakes and tsunamis.*

Spotlight

The Pacific Ocean has a floating garbage patch the size of Texas containing plastic.

Spotlight

The United Nations Convention on the Law of the Sea (UNCLOS) is a legal framework that manages the world's oceans. Countries only have control over the first 200 nautical miles of their coastline. However, oceans are vast and move between territorial areas, which can lead to concerns over exploitation of resources and ocean pollution. Countries are not necessarily motivated to sustainably manage these vast areas that lie outside their legal boundaries.

	Local scale (e.g. near to where you might live)	National scale (e.g. UK)	Global scale (e.g. world)
Climate change	Alternative energy sources, e.g. solar panels	Carbon capture	United Nations (UN)
	Planting trees	UK government setting carbon zero target by 2050	Kyoto Protocol, 1995
Plastics and pollution	Recycling	Green finance strategy	Paris Agreement, 2015
	Composting food waste	Rewetting upland areas to allow land to capture more CO2	COP (Conference of the Parties)

The sustainability of management approaches

Having a range of strategies to protect and conserve the world's oceans is crucial to maintain the stability of our ecosystems on earth. As it stands, the world's oceans are in grave danger from climate change and human activities.

Australia has a simple approach to tacking plastic waste that involves the 5Rs.

Australia's 5Rs of recycling ▶

Spotlight

The **United Nations** plays a key role in managing the threats around global oceans, for example through UNCLOS.

The **Kyoto Protocol** was an international treaty aimed at combating climate change by getting industrialised countries to reduce their greenhouse gas emissions.

The **Paris Agreement** is a global treaty aimed at addressing climate change and limiting global warming. It was adopted in December 2015 by nearly 200 countries at the United Nations Climate Change Conference (COP21) in Paris, France.

COP is an annual convention of countries that are linked to the United Nations framework on climate change. Key stakeholders come together including charities and climate change experts.

Fun fact

The Plastiki boat is made from 12,000 plastic recycled bottles. It has sailed 7,000 km across the Atlantic Ocean to raise awareness of plastic in our oceans.

▼ *The Interceptor Original, created by The Ocean Cleanup organisation, collects plastic from major rivers, thereby stopping it from entering our oceans*

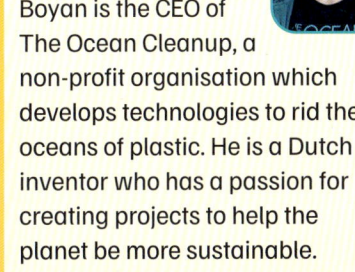

Boyan Slat

Boyan is the CEO of The Ocean Cleanup, a non-profit organisation which develops technologies to rid the oceans of plastic. He is a Dutch inventor who has a passion for creating projects to help the planet be more sustainable.

Unit 3 recap

Inequality
Inequality refers to different standards of living and can be linked to social, economic, environmental or political factors.

Causes and consequences
The causes behind inequality are often interlinked and include access to housing and services, demographic characteristics, industrialisation, location, landscape and resources, transport and communication. The consequences of inequality include regional wealth differences, ethnic segregation and impacts on minority groups.

Indicators
Indicators of social and economic development include GDP, literacy rates and urban population numbers. Countries can be classified by the level of their development.

The development gap
The development gap is the divide between richer and poorer areas. There are several human factors that have led to the development gap including colonialism, urbanisation and industrialisation.

Weather
Weather refers to the day-to-day conditions of the atmosphere, which can frequently change within a 24-hour period. Climate is the average weather conditions experienced in a place over a longer period, e.g. 30 years.

Temperature
Factors that affect Welsh temperature include air masses, altitude, aspect, latitude, ocean currents and winds.

Rainfall
For rainfall to occur there must be warm air rising and condensation. There are three types of rainfall formation: convectional, frontal and relief.

Global atmospheric circulation
The global atmospheric circulation is a global system of winds that move air between areas of high and low pressure. Low pressure at the equator leads to convectional rainfall. Sub-tropical high pressure causes arid conditions. Temperate low pressure leads to depressions moving eastward. Axial tilt impacts global climate.

Low pressure and high pressure
Low pressure systems (depressions) are caused by a large amount of air rising. They have an impact on weather in Wales and the UK. High pressure systems (anticyclones) are caused by a large amount of air sinking. Extreme low pressure events can cause hurricanes. Extreme high pressure events can cause droughts and forest fires.

Climate change
Climate change is influenced by natural factors such as Milankovitch cycles, sunspots, and volcanic eruptions over different time scales. The greenhouse gases are carbon dioxide, nitrous oxide, water vapour and methane. Human activities can increase emissions, causing an enhanced greenhouse effect.

Well-being goals for Wales
These seven goals are important milestones to help Wales achieve a healthy, prosperous nation.

Revision round up

The geography of inequality

1. List the regional inequalities in Wales and the UK for as many factors as you can, e.g. education, etc.
2. Copy and complete this table to show the causes of inequalities in Wales and the UK.

Physical causes	Human causes

3. Complete this spider diagram to show the impacts of these inequalities.

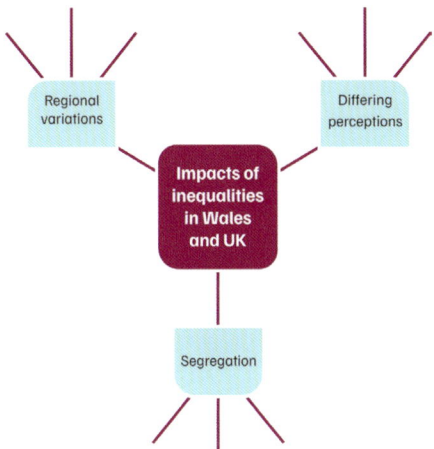

4. Create one fact file for each of the different ways in which the Welsh and UK governments have tried to reduce inequalities. Explain the strategy and link it to impacts.
5. Copy and complete this table to show the causes of the development gap.

Physical causes	Human causes

The highs and lows of our weather

6. Copy and complete this table to describe how the following factors affect temperature.

Factor	Description of how it affects temperature
Air masses	
Altitude	
Aspect	
Latitude	
Ocean currents	
Prevailing winds	

7. Create a flash card to explain the formation of each rainfall type (include a diagram).
8. Draw a diagram of the global atmospheric system to show where high and low pressure is created.

Wild weather

9. For a low pressure and high pressure hazard, create a fact file for each to show causes, impacts and responses to the hazard.

Continual climate change

10. Copy and complete this diagram to explain the causes of climate change:

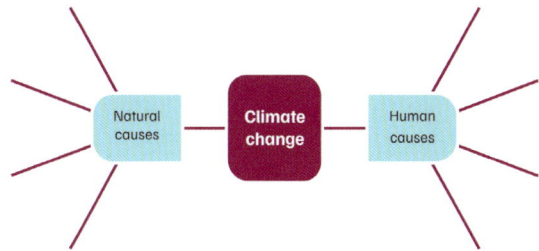

11. Explain how the following can be used as sources of evidence of climate change:
    - ice core data
    - tree rings
    - IPCC/NASA
    - keeling curve
    - retreating glaciers/ice sheets
    - sea level rise.

12. Create a fact file to show the impacts of a changing climate on people and the environment in two contrasting places.

Managing global challenges

13. Suggest three strategies used to manage climate change and assess the sustainability of these strategies.
14. Copy and complete this table in relation to threats to our oceans.

Threat	How is this a threat to ocean biodiversity?	Scale of the threat	Strategies to manage the threat	Sustainability of the management approaches
Climate change				
Plastics and pollution				

135

Unit 4
Sustainable Solutions

The Great Green Wall in Africa aims to restore 100 million hectares of degraded land by 2030.

Introduction

During this unit you will learn that sustainability is something we need to consider across all areas of our lives. You will learn how to consider the validity of sources to enable you to make informed and reasoned decisions.

Did you know! The total annual coffee cup waste in the UK is enough to fill the Albert Hall in London.

The assessment:

This unit is a non-examined assessment and is worth 15% of the qualification. It has a total of 60 marks.

Assessment objectives

The assessment objectives assessed in Unit 4 are:

AO2 Apply knowledge and understanding of geographical terms, skills and concepts to different contexts.

AO3 Analyse, evaluate, or make judgements from a variety of sources, synthesising where appropriate.

AO4 Select, use and apply skills and techniques in practice used by geographers to support geographical enquiry.

Contents

In Unit 4 you will cover the following:

Chapter 4.1: The concept of sustainability..............................138
4.1.1 Developing ideas of sustainability..138
4.1.2 The three pillars of sustainability..139
4.1.3 Sustainability goals..140

Chapter 4.2: Making sustainable decisions............................144
4.2.1 The skills of decision making..144
4.2.2 Using evidence to identify issues...146
4.2.3, 4.2.4 Potential benefits or negative impacts of proposed solutions..147
4.2.5 Sustainability impact assessment..148

In 2024, the ONS said 7.24% of homes in Wales had small-scale renewable energy installations.

By the time we're finished you will...

▸ be able to describe what sustainability means and the three aspects of it
▸ be able to describe the goals of sustainability
▸ be able to analyse evidence to assess its value
▸ be able to make informed and justified decisions.

Chapter 4.1 The concept of sustainability

AO2 AO3 AO4

4.1.1 Developing ideas of sustainability

🔑 **Key terms**

- **Brundtland Report:** *Our Common Future* report that defines sustainable development.

The concept of sustainability

In 1987, the **Brundtland Report** (also known as Our Common Future) was published by the United Nations. The report stated that sustainability is about 'meeting the needs of the present without compromising the ability of future generations to meet their own needs'.

The definition of sustainability

The definition of sustainability is using resources responsibly so that they can support current and future generations.

What types of sustainability do we have?

- **Resources** such as water, food, energy.
- **Environmental** such as ecosystems, biodiversity, hazards and atmosphere.
- **People** including housing.
- **Economy** including jobs, income and cost of living.

The importance of seeking sustainable solutions

Why do we need to make sure we are being sustainable?

- We could fall into a catastrophic decline of our natural systems, which would affect our economy and environment to the point where we cannot recover.

What is the tipping point?

- The tipping point is the critical point in the earth's system that once reached will create irreversible effects.

Gro Harlem Brundtland

Gro is a Norwegian politician in the Labour Party and former Norwegian prime minister.

She chaired the Brundtland Commission which wrote the report on sustainable development.

Sir David Attenborough

Sir David Attenborough is a television broadcaster, natural historian and writer.

He has said the world is very close to the tipping point and once this has been passed, the damage will be catastrophic.

'We are facing a man-made disaster on a global scale. Our greatest threat in thousands of years'

4.1.2 The three pillars of sustainability

The Brundtland report recognised **sustainability** as three **interconnected** pillars or elements: environmental, social and **economic**. The stool of sustainability was a concept model designed to show how the economic, **social** and environmental factors are interconnected and to highlight these as the three challenges facing humanity. If one of the legs is missing, the sustainability stool can't balance, and it wobbles or collapses. All three legs of the stool require attention to ensure balance.

The key factors underpinning the stool of sustainability

Environmental	Social	Economic
Reduce pollution	Community feeling	Employment
Increase renewable energy	Healthcare access	Good infrastructure
Restore forested areas	Good education system	Security

Egan's Wheel is a tool used to evaluate how sustainable an area is. Planners can use the wheel to help design new communities. Geographers can use it to assess how well developed an area is.

Key terms

- **Economic:** *money, finance.*
- **Egan's Wheel:** *a series of factors linked to sustainable environments.*
- **Interconnected:** *linked factors or traits.*
- **Social:** *involving people.*
- **Sustainability:** *to maintain and preserve for future generations.*

▲ *The stool of sustainability*

Ace your revision

Think about discussing **all** three parts of the stool of sustainability to get top marks in a 6- or 8-mark question.

Brain break

True or false? Sustainability solutions involve renewable energy, waste reduction and improved water quality.

Now try this

1. Look at an area you have studied and evaluate how sustainable it is.
   - Make sure you include four well developed points.
   - Use the sliding scale of opinion to show both sides of the discussion.
   - Use named places.
   - Make sure the examiner knows you understand what sustainability is.

Key terms

- **NGO:** *non-government organisation, e.g. charity.*
- **NHS:** *National Health Service.*

4.1.3 Sustainability goals

The 17 United Nation's Sustainable Development Goals (SDGs)

The 17 United Nation's Sustainable Development Goals (SDGs) are at the heart of the 2030 plan for global sustainable development. The goals are a universal set of ideas that focus on economic, environmental and social development. There are many organisations, governments and **NGO**s involved in making sure these goals are followed and checked.

SUSTAINABLE DEVELOPMENT GOALS

  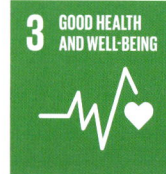   

How do the SDGs link to the well-being goals for Wales?

In 2015, the Welsh Government (the Senedd) decided to put Wales on a path in line with the global SDGs through the passing of the Well-being of Future Generations Act (Wales). As part of the Well-being of Future Generations Act, seven key interconnected goals were determined:

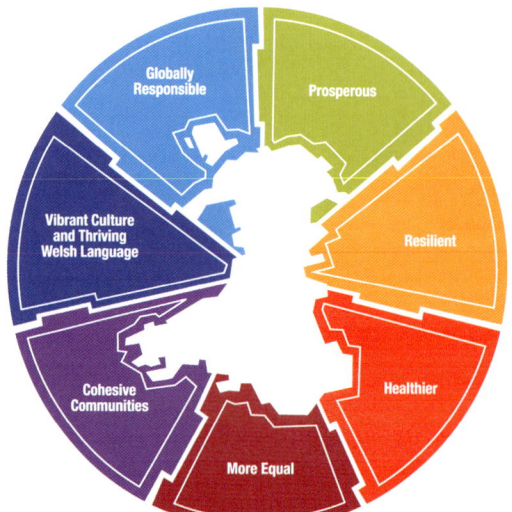

◀ *The seven well-being goals from the Wales Well-being of Future Generations Act, 2015*

Fun fact

The Wales well-being goals are part of a national conversation for the 'Wales We Want 2050' campaign.

National indicators were used by health organisations including the National Health Service (NHS) and local councils to assess quality of life and allow effective target setting.

Wales was the first country to link the SDGs to domestic policies (how the government works and what it focuses on). Wales also used the SDGs to set specific goals linked to age and diversity, so that future generations will have the same quality of life as we have now.

How do the SDGs relate to the three pillars of sustainability?

Grouping each SDG under the stool of sustainability allows us to categorise and look for interconnectivity between the goals and the three pillars (legs) of the stool. For example, protecting nature and respecting the planet's resources can easily come under the pillar of environmental sustainability. If one of the legs of the stool were to wobble or be damaged, the rest of the stool would fall. If we fail to protect the environment, this could lead to climate change issues due to damage from deforestation in the tropical rainforest. The knock-on effect would be more frequent natural hazards such as tropical storms. This would have an economic effect if homes were damaged and needed repair.

Organisations can easily use the goals and the pillars to drive policy changes and improve quality of life using measurable indicators of performance.

If we look at the 5 Ps of sustainable development, People, Prosperity, Peace, Partnership and Planet, they are interconnected as a framework. Meeting all 5 Ps gives the world an equal chance of building a more prosperous world for the future generations. The 5 Ps for sustainable development were developed from the 17 SDGs by the United Nations and have been driven by Emmanuel Ola-Olowoyo from Nigeria.

Emmanuel Ola-Olowoyo

Emmanuel is a co-founder of the Advance Initiative for Innovation and Development in Africa. He played a key part in developing the 5 Ps of sustainable development linked to achieving the Agenda for Sustainable Development by 2030.

▼ *The 5 Ps of sustainable development*

Now try this ▼

1 Complete the table below by placing the national well-being indicators for Wales into the correct well-being goal.

*Tip – there could be more than one indicator in each row.

The seven well-being goals	Well-being indicators
A prosperous Wales	
A resilient Wales	
A healthier Wales	
A more equal Wales	
A Wales of cohesive communities	
A Wales of vibrant culture and thriving Welsh language	
A globally responsible Wales	

National Wales well-being indicators:
- healthy babies
- air quality
- adults with qualifications
- fair pay
- sense of community
- people speaking Welsh every day.

How can the goals contribute to sustainable solutions?

Wales has used the SDGs to link in with the 7 well-being goals and provide a framework for local governments to work with the national government on improving people's quality of life both now and in the future.

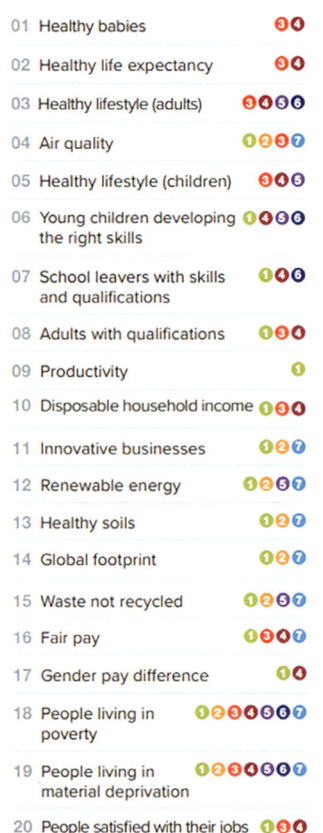

 Put into practice

Try taking each one of the 5 Ps and giving an example of how you would make sure it happened in Wales.

Wales has invested in several key schemes to help drive the well-being goals and SDGs.

Well-being goals: A healthier Wales and prosperous Wales

In order to promote healthier lifestyles, improve air quality and reduce greenhouse gas emissions, Transport for Wales (TfW) and Network Rail have teamed up with the Vale of Glamorgan to deliver the Nextbike scheme outside of Penarth station.

Spotlight

The 17 SDGs link with the 5 Ps of sustainability and to Agenda 2030. Agenda 2030 seeks to end poverty, protect the planet and achieve gender equality amongst other targets.

Well-being goals: Improving access to facilities and services as well as promoting healthy life expectancy

The Stakeholder and Community Engagement team from Transport for Wales, Save a Life Cymru and the Welsh Ambulance service have partnered together to increase public access to defibrillators. A defibrillator delivers a jolt of energy to the heart. Using a defibrillator and cardiopulmonary resuscitation (CPR) within the first three minutes of a cardiac arrest can increase the patient's chance of survival by up to 70%.

Transport for Wales is committed to playing a key role in protecting the environment. They have designed a framework that provides a guide for developing a net zero carbon source business, while demonstrating the role people can play in managing the impact in their day-to-day activities. The logo above shows that TfW has achieved this key milestone.

Now try this

1 Evaluate the effectiveness of attempts to be sustainable using examples you have studied as well as your own subject knowledge.

Chapter 4.2 Making sustainable decisions

AO2 AO3 AO4

🔑 Key terms

- **Bibliography:** *a list of books and resources that have been used whilst producing a piece of work.*
- **Cite:** *to refer to something as reinforcing evidence.*

Put into practice

Use the map to interpret why Pontypridd town centre flooded in December 2024.

'All my stock is ruined, I will lose thousands of pounds and might have to close.' – **shop owner**

'We have had to move out as downstairs is covered in mud.' – **young family**

'We are dealing with a major emergency and are working round the clock to support the community. We are exhausted.' – **emergency response**

4.2.1 The skills of decision making

The assessment for Unit 4 asks you to make sustainable decisions about a given scenario. When interpreting the information, presenting your findings and justifying your decisions, there are several skills that you will be expected to use.

- **Cartographic, graphical, numerical and statistical skills** — You will be expected to read, interpret and identify patterns and trends in maps and graphs, so you can draw information from the data, which will inform your decision making. Look back at chapter 2.3 to remind yourself of the types of maps and graphs geographers use. You may be given data in a table so that you can apply techniques in order to see trends or patterns. Your numerical skills (such as calculating percentages) will enable you to put the data into a format that you can compare and analyse more easily.

Pontypridd floods

▼ *Ordnance Survey map of Pontypridd area*

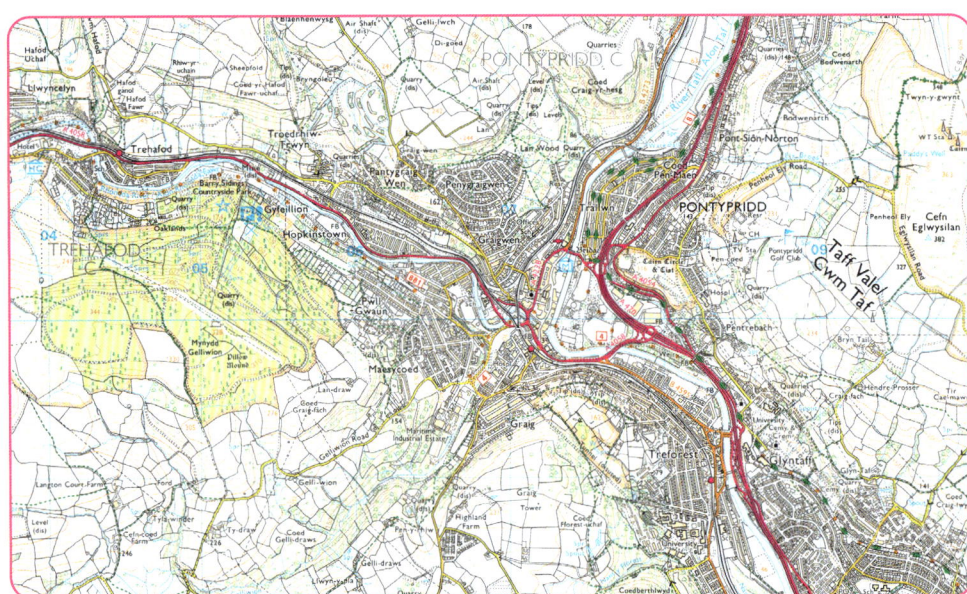

- **Communication skills** – you will need your written communication skills to convey your decisions to the examiner. You will need to justify your decisions. Remember to include your reasoning and evidence to show how you have come to your decisions. You will also need your communication skills to interpret the information provided. Is there bias in the writing that you have been provided with, e.g. a newspaper article?
- **Evaluative skills** – in order to make your decisions you will need your skills of evaluation. Evaluating pieces of evidence to judge their reliability and validity is essential if that evidence is informing your decisions on sustainability. You will also be required to evaluate the possible outcomes for sustainability, providing strengths and weaknesses of each.
- **Interpretative skills** – can you look at data or a report and extract the overall information that it is providing? If so, you are using skills of interpretation. So rather than just summarising or providing extracts from a resource, you must add meaning. What does the resource tell you about the issue that you are researching?
- **Problem-solving skills** – the whole assessment for Unit 4 requires you to problem solve an issue around sustainability. Can you come up with or decide upon the most appropriate sustainable solution? To do this you must evaluate each of the solution options, assess the impacts and make an informed decision.
- **Referencing skills** – part of your assessment requires you to carry out further research on the case study you are given. It is important to include this research as part of your work and you will need **cite** a resource when making reference to it in your report and also create a bibliography. Your **bibliography** should contain the resource's title, author, year of publication, name of publisher, page numbers or website information.

Now try this ▼

Scenario – a new housing development of 200 houses has been proposed on the edge of a small rural village in Powys.

1. What do you think the views of the following people may be and what are the reasons behind those views?
    - A   An elderly resident of the village.
    - B   The local councillor.
    - C   The housing developer.
    - D   The owner of a factory 5 miles away from the village.
    - E   A family of five currently living in a 2-bedroom house.

2. What research would be useful for you to find out about the area?

3. What impact could the development have on the village and surrounding area?

4.2.2 Using evidence to identify issues

Whether it be the sources you are provided with or information that you have researched yourself, evidence will be the foundation of the decisions that you make and their justification. You must be able to use and research evidence to identify geographical issues.

Key terms

- **Synthesise:** the skill of bringing together materials from more than one source to create new material.
- **Vested interest:** an interest in influencing something so that you can benefit from it.

Identifying key information within sources and supporting materials

You will be presented with a range of resources of information. You need to be able to identify the key information within those resources. This might be easier when the information is presented in graphical or map form, but when you have a large passage of writing, this may take a little longer. Use a highlighter pen to identify the key information and read each of the resources more than once. Remember, every item in the resource pack is there for a purpose, so you need to work out what key information it is telling you.

Researching appropriate information

The first part of your assessment involves you spending 3 hours not only examining the information in the given resource but also undertaking your own research to explore the issue further. Knowing the types of resources that might be relevant to a topic would be helpful ahead of the 3-hour period, e.g. house prices if the issue is around housing development.

Spotlight

Town planners use these strategies to help inform their planning decisions as to where new buildings can be built, or extensions made to existing buildings.

Put into practice

Find three sources of information that you could research to find data for each of these sustainability issues:
- air pollution from industrial areas
- river flooding
- household recycling rates.

Synthesising the information to clearly identify the issue

As part of phase one of your assessment you are required to produce two pages of notes which are to be submitted along with the other tasks. You will need to **synthesise** all the information you have so that you know what the key factors are for and against the possible solutions. This will enable you to make an informed decision.

Referencing the researched information

This was mentioned in topic 4.2.1. Accurately referencing researched information is very important when writing your report. Ensure you include all the information needed to enable the reader to find the same source.

Ace your revision

When synthesising information, remember to:
- look at the words, phrases and data that you have highlighted
- think about how you will put together the ideas from all the sources
- reference where each idea came from and put any quotes in quotation marks
- use a balanced amount of information from each resource
- don't give your opinion at this stage, you are summarising the evidence.

You must consider both the benefits and the negative impacts of all proposed options. Marks will be awarded for each so don't focus on benefits or negative impacts, you need both!

Recognising misleading or invalid information, including bias and vested interest

It is important to recognise the validity of the information that you are using to inform your opinions. Is the information misleading in anyway? Some information may contain bias, which means it is written by someone who wants to provide their own point of view. Other work may be produced by someone who has a **vested interest**, e.g. an environmental impact report produced by the company who wants to build a wind farm at a location. If someone has a vested interest, is their information going to be neutral and purely factual?

If you look back at the *Now try this* question 1 on page 145, each person is likely to have a different view, which would be based on their vested interest and may not be objective.

4.2.3, 4.2.4 Potential benefits or negative impacts of proposed solutions

In the second part of your assessment, you are required to present the potential benefits and negative impacts of each of the proposed options. You need to look at these in terms of impact on society, the environment and the economy. The types of factors that you might consider for each are shown in the diagram below.

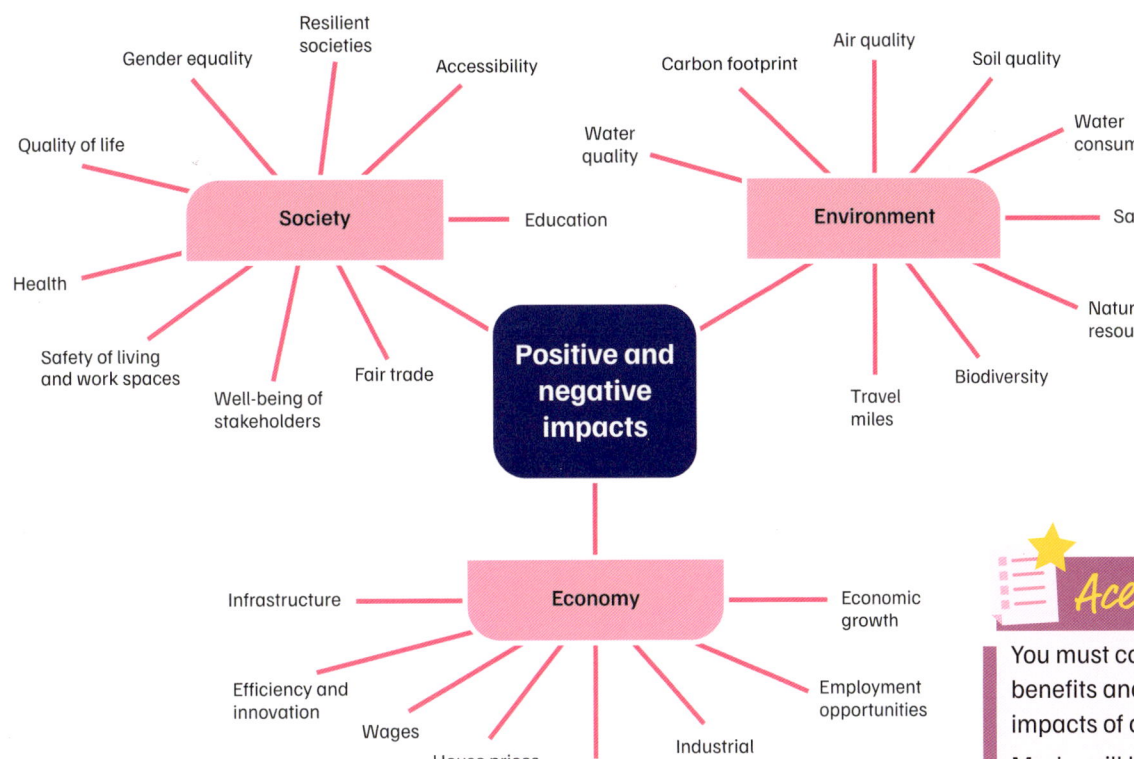

Ace your revision

You must consider both the benefits and the negative impacts of all proposed options.

Marks will be awarded for each so don't focus only on benefits or negative impacts, you need both!

Spotlight

Many large companies, such as Panasonic, carry out sustainability surveys to ensure that they are accountable for their sustainable impact.

Put into practice

Complete the following table for the proposed housing development in Powys (from page 145) showing the benefits and negative impacts of this proposal.

	Benefits	Negative Impacts
Social Impacts		
Economic Impacts		
Environmental Impacts		

Now try this ▼

Consider the impacts on sustainability (both benefits and negative impacts) of the following actions.

1. The construction of a dam in the upper course of a river where small towns and light industry are located. The river often floods in the lower course.

2. The construction of a recycling plant which processes soft plastics. It is to be built on the outskirts of a city where there are high levels of unemployment.

Key terms

- **Sustainability Impact Assessment:** *an assessment that provides in depth analysis of a proposal's impacts on people, the environment and the economy.*

4.2.5 Sustainability impact assessment

To help you work out the effect a proposal will have on sustainability, you can use a tool known as the **Sustainability Impact Assessment** (SIA) which makes comparison easier. An example of a SIA is given below.

▼ *Sustainability impact assessment template*

	Review questions	Assessment of impact Negative = -1 Neutral = 0 Positive = 1 Unknown = ?	Brief description of impact	If negative, how can it be mitigated? If positive, how can it be enhanced?
Impacts on society	e.g. will the proposal impact gender equality?			
Environmental impacts	e.g. will the proposal impact carbon footprint?			
Economic impacts	e.g. will the proposal increase the availability of jobs?			

Simply add in sustainability questions that are relevant to the proposal, make an assessment of the impact using the scale provided, describe what the impact will look like and then suggest actions that would make the factor more sustainable.

Put into practice

1. Your local council is looking at proposing a cycle to school scheme to reduce carbon footprint and improve health and well-being. Complete an SIA for this proposal.
2. Discuss how this SIA could be improved.

 Spotlight

The NHS health boards use SIAs to assess the impact of new practices on their sustainable goals.

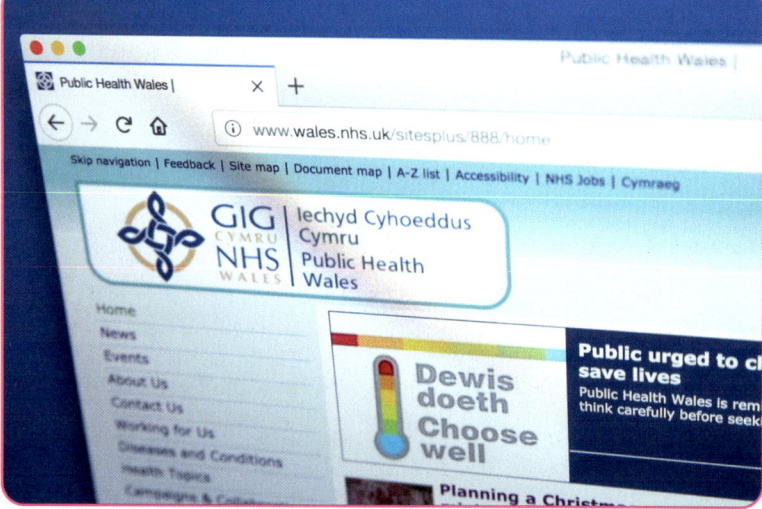

 **Ace your revision**

It is important to consider why some proposals may be rejected. Remember to also consider the proposals against the SDGs and well-being goals (see pages 140 and 142).

Reaching decisions

Once an SIA is completed it is easier to see the whole impact of a proposal. Very often a proposal may have benefits on one aspect of sustainability but drawbacks on another. The SIA removes this confusion. Some options will be rejected due to their negative impact on sustainability. This will enable a decision to be made on the most appropriate option.

SWOT analysis

Strengths	Weaknesses
Opportunities	**Threats**

Did you know

St Lucia is classified as a Small Island Developing State (SIDS). It is ranked 129th out of 192 on the World Climate Risk Index.

It is the 122nd most vulnerable country on the Vulnerability Risk Matrix.

It is highly dependent on FDI and donations.

It experiences extreme weather due to climate change, which affects fisheries, crops, tourism and salt water.

▼ *Vulnerability readiness matrix*

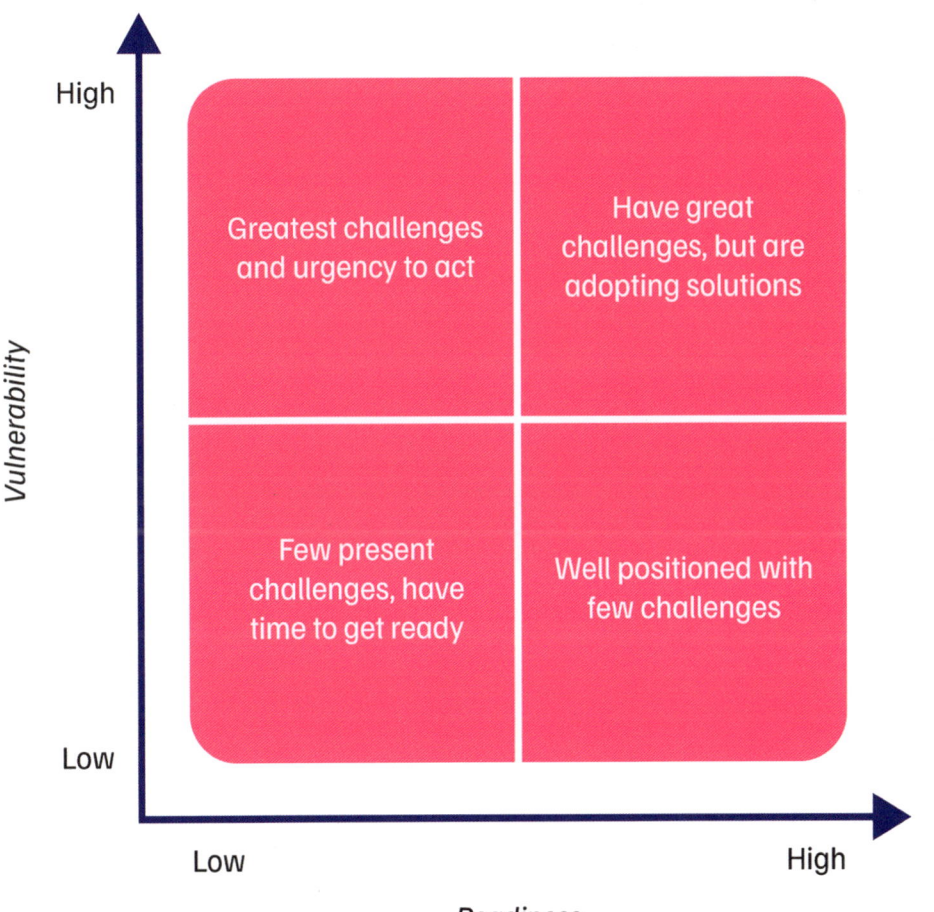

Now try this ▼

1. Prepare a SWOT analysis using the template, the fact file on St Lucia and your own research.

2. You may research up to two sides of A4 notes to support your answer to the following question. The residents of St Lucia are at risk of becoming climate change refugees. How far do you agree with this?

Unit 4 recap

Sustainability
Using resources responsibly so that they can support current and future generations. Sustainability has three pillars: environmental, social and economic.

Decision-making skills
Use cartographic, graphical, numerical, statistical, communication, evaluative, interpretative, problem-solving, and referencing skills for decision making.

Using evidence to identify issues
Use evidence to find geographical issues by identifying key information, researching, synthesising, referencing, and recognising misleading information like bias or vested interest.

Benefits and negative impacts of different options in a decision
Evaluate benefits and negative impacts of proposed options on society, economy, and environment, including human rights and diversity considerations.

Sustainability impact assessment
Assess sustainability impacts, justify rejection of options, and choose based on the sustainable impact assessment.

Stool of sustainability
When one leg wobbles, the concept collapses.

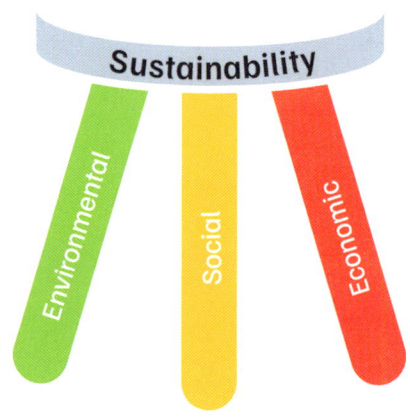

Achieving a sustainable community
Egan's Wheel can help planners decide how sustainable a development is.

Revision round up

Your non-examined assessment for this unit will be a decision making exercise based around a sustainability issue.

The concept of sustainability

1. Give a definition of sustainability.
2. Suggest three reasons why it is important to seek sustainable solutions.
3. Copy and complete the following table to explain the three pillars of sustainability.

Three pillars of sustainability

Economic	Environmental	Social

4. Create a flash card for each of the UN Sustainable Development Goals. On each card state the aim of the goal, which pillar it contributes towards, and provide an example of where people are working towards the goal.

5. Copy the diagram below and add the SDGs to the relevant Well-being Goals to show how they interrelate.

Making sustainable decisions

6. Explain how each of the following skills are important to use when decision making:
   - cartographic skills
   - graphical skills
   - numerical and statistical skills
   - communication skills
   - evaluative skills
   - interpretative skills
   - problem-solving skills
   - referencing skills.

7. Create a research reference file to list various sources of research information for the following sustainability contexts:
   - pollution – split into land, water and air
   - energy
   - urban/industrial development
   - transport
   - tourism.

8. List the sources of information that should be included when referencing researched information.

9. Create a revision card on sustainability impact assessments. Describe what is included and what they are used for.

151

Exam preparation and practice

Assessment objectives

Assessment objectives (AOs) form the basis of how you will be assessed across all four units and guide the examiner on how to mark your response. Therefore, it is really important that you know what the assessment objectives are and how to work out which objective is being asked in a question. In the Geography GCSE there are four assessment objectives.

AO1 Demonstrate knowledge and understanding of places, people, environments and processes at a variety of scales.
Questions based on AO1 are examining your knowledge and understanding of what you have learnt in class. Command words and phrases you might see include:

- Describe how
- Explain why
- Identify
- Give reasons
- What
- State
- Define
- List
- Name
- Complete…

AO2 Apply knowledge and understanding of geographical terms, skills and concepts to different contexts.
Questions based on AO2 are examining how you can apply your knowledge and understanding of the geographical concepts and skills you have been taught to unfamiliar contexts. For example, you might be asked about the potential hazards of a hurricane on a Caribbean island. Command words and phrases you might see include:

- Suggest
- Annotate
- Discuss
- Identify from a source
- Apply/use
- Demonstrate
- Illustrate
- Summarise…

AO3 Analyse, evaluate, or make judgements from a variety of sources, synthesising where appropriate.
Questions based on AO3 require you to look at sources of information provided and analyse, evaluate and synthesise the information to make judgements. Command words and phrases you might see include:

- Analyse
- Compare
- Discuss
- To what extent do you agree
- Distinguish
- Justify
- Assess…

AO4 Select, use and apply skills and techniques in practice used by geographers to support geographical enquiry.
Questions based on AO4 are examining the geographical skills and techniques that you have learnt in relation to your geographical enquiry. Command words and phrases you might see include:

- Calculate
- Complete
- Communicate
- Select
- Use…

Unit 1

Remember, Unit 1 will be assessed by an examination that will contain questions using the following AOs:

AO1 – these questions will test your knowledge and understanding of people, processes and landforms that you have learnt in class. They are recall questions.

AO2 – these questions ask you to apply your knowledge and understanding to contexts that you might be unfamiliar with through a case study you will be given. You will also be tested on geographical skills such as interpreting maps, graphs or data.

AO3 – these questions ask you to use the higher-level skills of evaluating, analysing or making judgements. Chains of reasoning should be used throughout AO3 responses. When answering these questions, you need to understand what the question is asking you to do.

Answers ▼

You can find answers here:
extendeducation.co.uk/answers

Evaluating

If a question asks you to evaluate, you must discuss both sides of the argument and then give a reasoned conclusion showing which side of the argument you agree with. The question might start with the word 'evaluate', or ask 'to what extent do you agree?'.

Analysing

If asked to analyse, you need to examine all the resources provided in the question, looking for trends and patterns to support your answer. You should include a selection of the data to help justify your points.

Making judgements

When making judgements, you need to decide which option you think is most appropriate and provide reasoning as to why you have chosen this option. You should discuss all the options giving the pros and cons of each and then reach a justified conclusion.

Practice questions

1ai) *Define* the term megacity. (AO1)

1aii) *Explain* the difference between a megacity and a global city. (AO1)

1aiii) *Suggest* five sustainability issues that are commonly found in global cities. (AO1)

1bi) Study the photograph below. *Suggest* strategies to increase the sustainability of the issues shown in the global city of Rio de Janeiro. (AO2)

▼ *A housing area in the global city of Rio de Janeiro*

2a) *Draw* a diagram to show the following key features of a drainage basin: watershed, source, tributary and confluence. (AO1)

2b) Study the OS map extract below.

▼ *OS map extract of the River Usk*

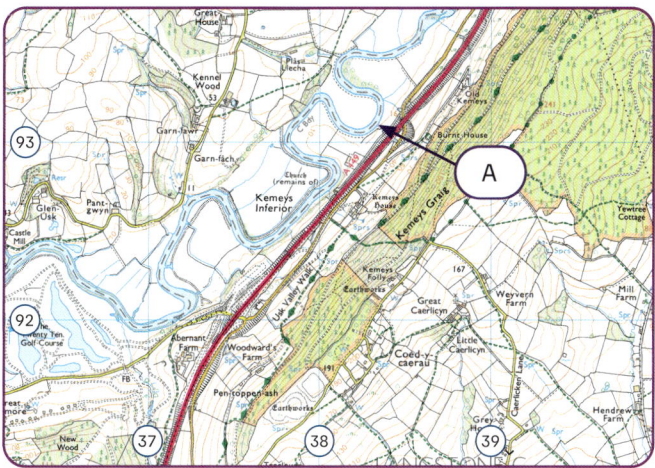

2bi) *Name* the river feature A shown on the map. (AO2)

2bii) *Give* the six-figure grid reference for feature A. (AO2)

2biii) *Suggest* which features of the map indicate that it shows the middle course of the river. (AO2)

2c) *Explain* why building houses on floodplains is often seen as unsustainable. (AO1)

3a) Study the map below.

▼ *Map showing movement of migrants from Nigeria to the UK in 2023*

3ai) *Describe* the pattern shown in the map. (AO2)

3aii) *Suggest* three reasons for this pattern. (AO2)

3aiii) *Describe* the impacts of large-scale migration on the source country. (AO1)

4ai) *What* type of waves lead to deposition at the coastline? (AO1)

4aii) *Draw* an annotated diagram to explain the formation of a spit. (AO1)

4aiii) The three factors below affect the rate of coastal change.

- Settlement
- Industry
- Agriculture

Choose the factor which, in your opinion, has had the greatest impact. *Justify* your choice. (AO3)

Unit 2

Remember, Unit 2 is a non-examination assessment (NEA) that will contain questions using the following AOs:

AO2 – these questions ask you to apply your knowledge and understanding in the context of your geographical investigation (the area that is the focus of your study).

AO3 – these questions ask you to use the higher-level skills of evaluating, analysing or making judgements when responding to the data that you have collected. Chains of reasoning should be used throughout AO3 responses.

AO4 – these questions ask you to use and apply your geographical skills to support your enquiry, e.g. using OS maps, graphical and mapping skills, etc.

NEA style questions

To answer the following questions, choose a context on which to base a geographical investigation in the location area shown in the map below.

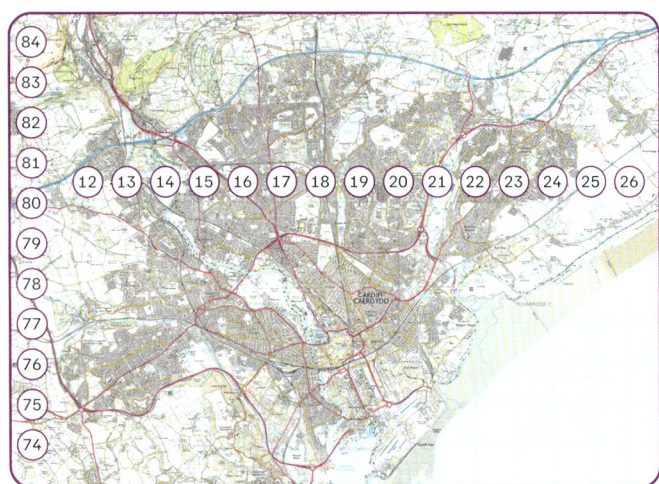

1ai) Suggest a key question/hypothesis for your enquiry. (AO2)

1aii) Explain why you have chosen this question/hypothesis. (AO2)

1bi) Use the map to decide your data collection locations. Give the six-figure grid reference for each. (AO4)

1bii) Suggest reasons why these locations would be appropriate to carry out this investigation. (AO4)

1c) Discuss the potential risks to yourself, the public and the environment when carrying out your data collection. (AO2)

2ai) What sampling approach would you use to collect this data? (AO4)

2aii) Explain your reasons for using this sampling approach. (AO4)

2bi) Describe the data collection techniques that you would use to collect your required data. (AO4)

2bii) What secondary data would you aim to collect to answer your hypothesis? Explain why this data would be important to the successful outcome of your study. (AO4)

3ai) Suggest two numerical or statistical techniques that you could use with the data you are collecting. (AO4)

3aii) Select two appropriate presentation techniques for the data you will be collecting. Explain why they are appropriate. (AO4)

4) Look at the data below. Analyse the patterns/trends shown by the data. (AO3)

Site	Distance from source (km)	Velocity (m/s)	Width (m)	Average depth (cm)
1	0.3	0.19	1.4	5
2	1	0.41	3.0	14
3	1.4	0.30	4.4	25
4	1.8	0.50	5.5	29
5	2.6	0.29	4.6	23
6	3.2	0.47	6.3	41
7	4	0.55	7	53
8	5	0.56	10.5	46
9	7	0.62	10.6	61
10	8.5	1.12	14.2	68

5) Using the table, calculate the:
- range of velocity.
- mean width of the river. (AO4)

6) For the enquiry hypothesis 'the river's channel increases in size from source to mouth', use the table above to draw reasoned conclusions. (AO3)

7) Evaluate the enquiry planning that you completed for question 1. (AO3)

Unit 3

Remember, Unit 3 will be assessed by an examination that will contain questions using the following AOs:

AO1 – these questions will test your knowledge and understanding of people, processes and landforms that you have learnt in class. They are recall questions.

AO2 – these questions ask you to apply your knowledge and understanding to contexts that you might be unfamiliar with by providing a case study. You will also be tested on geographical skills such as interpreting maps, graphs or data.

AO3 – these questions ask you to use the higher-level skills of evaluating, analysing or making judgements. Chains of reasoning should be used throughout AO3 responses. When answering these questions, remember to evaluate, analyse and make judgements.

Practice questions

1a) Study the graph below.

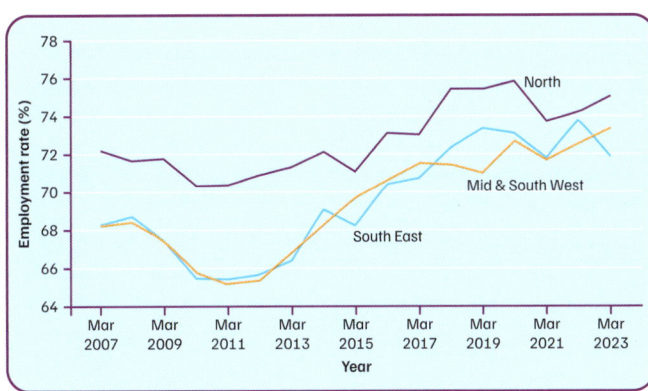

▼ *Welsh region employment rates*

1ai) Describe the overall trend in employment rates across Wales. (AO2)

1aii) Suggest reasons for the differences seen between the regions. (AO2)

1aiii) Name two other factors, other than employment, where regional variations can be seen. (AO1)

1aiv) Describe the physical causes that may cause inequalities in Wales. (AO1)

1bi) 'The development gap seen between countries is mainly caused by human factors.' To what extent do you agree with this statement? (AO3)

2 ai) What is meant by the term climate? (AO1)

2aii) Describe two factors that affect temperature in the UK. (AO1)

2aiii) Explain why low pressure forms at the equator. (AO1)

2aiv) Describe the differences between summer and winter anticyclones. (AO1)

2b) Study the information below.

Storm Darragh – December 2024
- A severe storm that caused a rare red weather warning in England and Wales.
- Led to the cancellation of many flights.
- Caused 44 flood warnings and over 200 flood alerts in England and Wales.
- 2.3 million people were without electricity.
- Many roads were blocked by falling trees.

2bi) Evaluate the importance of emergency responses to storms such as Darragh as opposed to future mitigation strategies. (AO3)

3ai) Draw a diagram to explain the greenhouse effect. (AO1)

3aii) Suggest two different ways in which human activity enhances the greenhouse effect. (AO1)

3aiii) Compare the impacts of climate change for two contrasting places that you have studied. (AO3)

3aiv) Describe how people manage the physical impacts of climate change at a global level. (AO1)

3av) Describe how climate change management strategies can be sustainable. (AO1)

Unit 4

Remember, Unit 4 will be assessed by an NEA which will contain questions using the following AOs:

AO2 – these questions ask you to apply your knowledge and understanding in the context of the sustainability issue in the resource materials.

AO3 – these questions ask you to use the higher-level skills of evaluating, analysing or making judgements when responding to the data in the resource and from your own research. Chains of reasoning should be used throughout AO3 responses.

AO4 – these questions ask you to use and apply your geographical skills to understand and support your answer, e.g. using OS maps, graphical and mapping skills etc.

Example of sustainability resource

The sustainability issue – Should the M4 relief road be built?
- The M4 relief road was a proposed motorway to bypass the city of Newport in South Wales and avoid the congestion created by the motorway reducing to two lanes through the Brynglas tunnels.
- The proposed relief road would run to the south of Newport whereas the current motorway runs to the north of the city.

155

Resource 1 – Extract from the Welsh Government's Sustainable Development report

3.2 Existing situation

3.2.1 The M4 in South Wales forms part of the Trans-European Transport Network (TEN-T), and plays a key strategic role in connecting South Wales with the rest of Europe. It is a key east-west route, being the main gateway in South Wales and one of the most heavily used roads in Wales. The M4 is critical to the Welsh economy as it facilitates the transport of goods, links people to jobs and employment sites and serves the Welsh tourism industry.

3.2.2 The existing M4 between Junctions 28 and 24 was originally designed as the 'Newport Bypass' with further design amendments in the 1960s to include the first motorway tunnels to be built in the UK. This stretch of the existing M4 does not meet modern motorway design standards and has many lane drops and lane gains, resulting in some two lane sections, an intermittent hard shoulder and frequent junctions. It is often congested, especially during weekday peak periods, resulting in slow and unreliable journey times and stop-start conditions with incidents frequently causing delays.

3.2.3 Existing problems relate to capacity, resilience safety and sustainable development. Traffic forecasts show that existing problems are predicted to worsen in future. Some of the problems related to sustainable development, as set out in the 'M4 Corridor around Newport – WelTAG Stage 1 (Strategy Level) Appraisal Report (Welsh Government, 2013a), include:

"There is a lack of adequate sustainable integrated transport alternatives for existing road users.

Traffic noise from the motorway and air quality is a problem for local residents in certain areas.

The existing transport network acts as a constraint to economic growth and adversely impacts the current economy."

Resource 2 – Map showing proposed route of M4 relief road

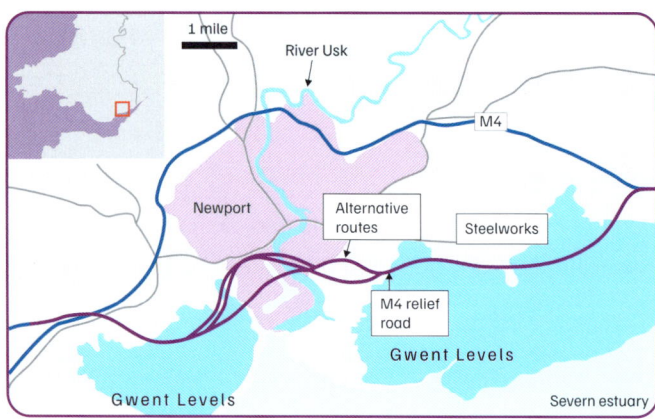

Resource 3 – Extract from a news article

Plans to build the M4 relief road have been abandoned, saving the Welsh Government £1.6bn

Mark Drakeford, First Minister of the Welsh Government, decided against the building of the M4 relief road after reconsidering the staggering costs and impacts on the environment.

The scheme was originally coined in an attempt to reduce traffic around Newport by building a 14-mile motorway as an alternative route into South Wales.

Ministers decided to abolish the project due to the extraordinary cost of £1.6bn. After Brexit, the financial position of the Welsh Government remains uncertain, making such an expense too big a risk. However Mark Drakeford was more concerned about the effects the project would have on the Gwent Levels, and declared he would not have proceeded with the plans, even if the project was affordable.

Opinions were divided on the decision against the construction of the M4 relief road. While Friends of the Earth said it was 'great news for Wales and the planet', Welsh Secretary Alun Cairns was disappointed at the outcome.

Resource 4 – The Gwent Levels

- The Gwent Levels are a wetland habitat of international significance to the south of Newport.
- They are home to many rare aquatic invertebrates and protected species such as the dormouse, grass snake, otter, great crested newt, water vole and some bat species.
- They are a site of special scientific interest (SSSI).

There are three proposed options.

Option 1 Go ahead with the proposed M4 relief road.

Option 2 Do not go ahead with the proposed M4 relief road.

Option 3 Improve public transport to reduce the number of vehicles on the M4.

NEA style questions

1. Look at the resources above and **summarise** the geographical issue that they present. (AO2)
2. Carry out your own research into this geographical issue and **present** your findings. (AO4)
3. **Describe** the potential benefits of each option on society, the economy and the environment. (AO4)
4. **Describe** the potential drawbacks of each option on society, the economy and the environment. (AO4)
5. **Analyse** the information provided and your own research to decide which would be your preferred option. **Justify** your choice. (AO3)
6. **Explain** why you have rejected the other options. (AO2)
7. **Describe** how your chosen option links to specific sustainability goals. (AO2)

Index

A
Abrasion/corrasion, 8
Accessibility, 60
Acidification, 132
Aeolian factor, 26, 27
Agglomeration, 43
Agriculture, 26
Aid, 98
Air masses, 102
Air pressure, 109, 110
Alluvium, 14
Altitude, 102
Anticyclones. *see* High pressure weather systems
ArcGIS, 77
Arches, 24, 25
Arctic air mass, 102
Arid, 106
Asylum seekers, 30, 32, 36
Attrition, 8
Axial tilt, 107

B
Beach, formation of, 25
Bibliography, 75, 144, 145
Bilateral aid, 98
Biodiversity, 17, 18, 132
Biological weathering, 8, 20
Bi-polar survey, 66
Brain drain, 34

C
Carbon capture, 130
Carbon dioxide, 121, 122
Caves, 24
Central business district (CBD), 42
Chemical weathering, 8, 20
Choropleth maps, 74
Cite, 75, 144, 145
Climate graphs, 100
Climate change, 89, 134
    consequences of, 125–129
    evidence, 123–124
    greenhouse effect, 121–122
    managing, 130–131
    natural causes of, 118–120
    threats to our oceans, 132–133
Closed system, 6
Cloud cover, 109, 110
Coastal management, 26
Cold front, 108
Collecting evidence, 54
    data collection locations, 62–65
    primary data, collection, 66–69
    representative and inclusive samples, 63
    sample size, 65
    sampling, process of, 63
    secondary data, collection, 70–71
Colonialism, 96, 97
Communication skills, 89, 145
Community, 34, 46
Compass diagram, 68
Concordant coastlines, 25
Condensation, 104
Conference of the Parties (COP) 21, 27, 130, 133
Conflict, 32
Confluence, 9
Constraint considerations, 60
Constructive waves, 22
Continental air mass, 102
Continuous data, 73, 74
Convectional rainfall, 104
Culture, spread of, 35

D
Data, 54, 76
    collection, 82
    presentation, 82
    processing and presenting, 54
Debt relief, 98
Deforestation, 122
Deindustrialisation, 86
Demographic
    characteristics, 96
    inequalities, 89
Dendrochronology, 123
Deposition, 9
Depositional landforms
    human factors, 28
    physical factors, 29
Depressions. *see* Low pressure weather systems
Development continuum, 94, 95
Development gap, 96, 134
    human factors, 96
    physical factors, 97
    reducing, 98–99
Differential erosion, 13
Discordant coastlines, 25
Discrete data, 73, 74
Diversity, 60

E
Economic factors
    migration, 32
    sustainability, 139
Economic migration, 31, 32
Economy, 46
Elliptical, 118
Employment
    inequalities, 87, 89
    sectors, 94
Enquiry
    process, 54
    question, 56
Environmental factors
    migration, 32
    sustainability, 139
Equipment, availability of, 60
Erosion, 8
Ethical considerations, 60
Evaluating techniques, 82
Evaporation, 7
Evapotranspiration, 7
Evidence, analysing and applying
    enquiry question, selecting relevant data, 76
    interpreting trends and patterns, 77
Evidence, processing and presenting
    graphical techniques, 73
    mapping techniques, 74
    qualitative data, 74
    quantitative and qualitative techniques, 72
    referencing, 75

F
Famine, 96
Ferrel cell, 106
Fetch, 23
Field sketch, 74
Fieldwork enquiries, 78–79, 82
    geographical topics, 79
Fieldwork investigation, 54
5Rs of recycling, 133
Floodplains, 9, 14, 17
Flow line map, 74
Forced migration, 30
Fossil fuels, 122
Freeze-thaw weathering, 8, 20
Fringe settlement, 42
Frontal rainfall, 104
Fuel combustion, 122

G
Geographical information systems (GIS) data, 58
Geographical location, 89
Geographical theory, 78
Geographical topics, 55
Geology, 10–11, 29
Glacial period, 120
Global atmospheric circulation, 106–107, 134
Global cities, 40, 44–45
Global economy, 87
Global hydrological cycle, 6
Globalisation, 96
Global urbanisation, 46–49
GOAD maps, 68
Gorges, 13
Gradient, 11
Gravity, 25
Greenfield land, 17, 18
Greenhouse effect 121, 122
Greenhouse gases, 121
Gross Domestic Product (GDP), 94
Groundwater flow, 7

H
Hadley cell, 106
Hard river engineering, 19
High income countries (HICs), 40, 94, 95
High pressure (sub-tropical high), 106
High pressure hazards, 116–118
    human causes, 116
    impacts of, 117
    physical causes, 116
    responses to, 117
High pressure weather systems, 110–111
Host country, 31, 32
Hotspot analysis, 77
Housing, access to, 89
Humanitarian aid, 98
Human rights, 30, 60
Hydraulic action, 8
Hydro-electric power (HEP), 18
Hypothesis, 56

I
Ice core data, 123
Immigration, 37
Income, 89, 94
Industrialisation, 89, 96, 122
Industrial zones, 42
Inequality, 134
    Black, Asian and minority groups, 91
    consequences, 89–90
    development gap, 96–97
    factors leading to, 87
    features of, 87
    human causes, 89
    physical causes, 88–89
    reducing, development gap, 98–99
    regional inequalities, 86–93
Infiltration, 7
Informal settlements, 43
Infrastructure, 46
Infrastructure project (HS2), 92–93
Inner city areas, 43
Inputs, 6
Integration, 34, 35
Interception, 7
Interconnected, 139
Interglacial period, 120
International migration, 30, 31, 37–38
Interpretative skills, 145
Investigation, 80
Investment, lack of, 96
Irregular migration, 30, 37

L
Landfills, 122
Landlocked, 89
Landscapes, 89
Landslide, 21
Land use zones, 42
Lateral erosion, 15
Latitude, 103
Leeward side, 104
Literacy rate, 94
Load, 8
Longitudinal profile, 10
Longshore drift, 20, 21
Long-term evidence, 123
Lower course, 10
Low income countries (LICs), 40, 89, 95
Low pressure 106

Low pressure hazards, 112–115
    human causes, 112
    impacts of, 112
    management cycle, 114
    physical causes, 112
    responses to, 114–115
Low pressure weather systems, 108–109

M

Marine, 132
Maritime air mass, 102
Maritime climate, 101
Mass movement, 21
Mean, 72
Meanders, 14
Mechanical/physical weathering, 8
Median, 72
Mega cities, 44
Methane, 121, 122
Middle course, 10
Middle income country (MIC), 94, 95
Migrants, 36, 37, 39
Migration
    definition of, 30
    ethical considerations, 39
    impacts of, 34–36
    managing, 37–39
    public perception, 39
    pull factors, 33
    push factors, 32–33
    reasons for, 30–31
Milankovitch cycles, 118
Misconceptions, 44
Mitigation, 114
Mode, 72
Monoculture, 18
Mud slide, 21
Multiculturalism, 35
Multilateral aid, 98
Multinational company (MNC), 98, 99

N

National migration, 30
Natural disasters, 89
Natural resources, lack of access, 89
Net zero, 91
Nitrous oxide, 121, 122
Non-government organisations (NGOs), 140
Non-sustainable resources, 18
North Atlantic drift, 103
Northern lights, 119

O

Obliquity, 118
Ocean currents, 103
Open system, 6
Opportunistic sampling, 65
Orbital precession, 118
Ordnance Survey (OS) maps, 57
Outward migration, 96
Overfishing, 132
Overland flow, 7
Oxbow lakes, 15

P

Paris Agreement, 133
Park response model, 114
Pay inequalities, 87, 89
Percentages, 72
Percolation, 7
Permanent migration, 30
Physical factors, migration, 31, 32
Plunge pools, 12–13
Points based migration, 38
Polar air mass, 102
Polar cell, 106
Political factors, migration, 32
Political systems, 96
Population, 63
Precipitation, 100, 111
    frequency, 109
    intensity, 109
Predicted outcomes, 56
Prevailing wind, 103

Primary data, 66–69
    collection sheets, 66
    environmental quality survey (EQS), 66
    fieldwork equipment, accurate and reliable results, 67
    quantitative data collection techniques, 68–69
Problem-solving skills, 145
Productivity, 86, 90
Proportional flow lines, 77
Proportional symbols map, 74
Purchasing power parity (PPP), 94

Q

Qualitative data, 68–69
Quantitative data, 68
Quaternary Period, 120

R

Rainfall, 134
Rain shadow, 104
Random sampling, 64
Range, 72
Referencing skills, 145
Refugees, 30, 31, 32, 36
Regional inequalities, 86–95
Regular migration, 30
Reliability, 71
Relief rainfall, 105
Remittances, 34
Reradiated, 121
Response, 114
Retreating glaciers, 124
RICEPOTS, 68
Risk 59
Risk matrix, 114, 115
River velocity
Rock fall, 21

S

Saltation, 22
Sample size, 65, 82
Sampling, 64
Sand dunes, 27
Scale, 72
Seabed dredging, 29
Sea level rise, 124
Seasonally, 6, 7
Secondary data, 70–71
    advantages and disadvantages, 71
    availability of, 60
    find, select and use, 70
    good, 70
    reliability, 71
    validity, 71
Sediment, 26, 27
Segregation, 35, 89
Settlement change
    characteristics, urban places, 41
    global urbanisation, 46–49
    land use patterns, urban, 41–43
    urbanisation, 40
Short-term evidence, 123–124
Six-stage enquiry process, 54, 82
    constraint considerations, 60
    posing, enquiry questions, 56
    risk considerations, 59
    selecting a topic, 55
Slip-off slope, 15
Slumping, 21
Soft engineering, 28, 29
    river, 19
Solar panels, 131
Solution/corrosion, 8
Source country, 31, 32
Spit formation, 26, 27, 27, 28
Stack, 24
Stakeholders, 75
Statistical techniques, 72
Stores and flows, hydrological system, 6
Strategies, 98
Stump, 24
Suburbs, 42, 43
Summer
    anticyclones, 110–111
    waves, 23

Sunspots, 119
Suspension, 22
Sustainability impact assessment (SIA), 148–149, 150
Sustainability/Sustainable, 46
    climate management approaches, 131
    communities, 139
    concept of, 138–143
    definition of, 138
    goals, 140–143
    stool of, 47, 117, 150
    three pillars of, 139
Sustainable Development Goals (SDGs), 140–142
SWOT analysis, 149
Sympathetic geographers, 60
Synoptic chart, 108
Systematic sampling, 64

T

Tally count, 76
Target population, 62
Tectonic events, 132
Temperature, 109, 111
Temporary migration, 30
Thermal expansion, 124
Topography, 102
Tourism, 18, 99
Traction, 22
Trade blocs, 96
Trade winds, 106
Transnational companies (TNCs), 89, 98, 99
Transport for Wales (TfW), 142, 143
Tributary, 9
Tropical air mass, 102
Tropopause, 106

U

United Nations (UN), 40, 133
United Nations Convention on the Law of the Sea (UNCLOS), 132, 133
United Nations Programme on HIV/AIDS (UNAIDS), 87
Upper course, 10
Urbanisation, 96

V

Velocity, 26, 27
Vertical erosion, 12
Visa free travel, 38
Volcanic eruptions, 120
Voluntary aid, 98
Voluntary migration, 30–31
V-shaped valleys, 12

W

Wales
    climate of, 101
    regional inequalities, 86–95
    restore national peatlands, 130
    SDGs, 142
    temperature and precipitation, 100
    topography of, 102
    well-being goals, 91, 134, 142
Warm front, 108
Waterfalls, 12–13
Watershed, 9
Water vapour, 121
Wave cut platform, 24
Weather
    global atmospheric circulation, 106–107
    high pressure weather systems, 110–111
    low pressure weather systems, 108–109
    rainfall, factors affecting, 104–105
    temperature, factors affecting, 102–103
Weathering, 8
Well-being goals, 142–143
Westerlies, 106
Wind speeds, 109, 111
Winter
    anticyclones, 110–111
    waves, 23
Word clouds, 74
Workforce, 35